CW00348322

THE MOUNTAINS OF GREECE
A WALKER'S GUIDE

ABOUT THE AUTHORS

Tim Salmon

Tim first visited Greece as a schoolboy in 1958. Since then he has lived and worked in the country, visited countless times, written and translated books and articles about it, and made a documentary about shepherd life for Greek TV.

Michael Cullen

Michael was born in Greece and spent his childhood there, returning in 1990 to set up his own trekking business. He has spent most of the last 15 years researching and leading hikes throughout the country, as well as compiling walking guidebooks and accommodation websites.

THE MOUNTAINS OF GREECE
A WALKER'S GUIDE

by
Tim Salmon
with
Michael Cullen

2 POLICE SQUARE, MILNTHORPE, CUMBRIA LA7 7PY
www.cicerone.co.uk

© Tim Salmon 2006

Second edition 2006
ISBN-10: 1 85284 440 X
ISBN-13: 978 1 85284 440 0

First edition 1986
ISBN 1 85284 108 7
Reprinted 1993

British Library Cataloguing-in-Publication Data
A catalogue record for this book is available from the British Library.

Photographs by Tim Salmon, unless otherwise attributed.

Dedication

For Fulla and John Chapple, my base camp for half a lifetime,
and
in memory of Kate, my long-time writing partner.

Notice to Readers

Readers are advised that while every effort is taken by the authors to ensure the accuracy of this guidebook, changes can occur which may affect the contents. It is advisable to check locally on transport, accommodation, shops and so on, but even rights of way can be altered. The publisher would welcome notes of any such changes.

Front cover: Vardhoúsia: looking west over the valley of the Kariótiko stream

CONTENTS

MAP LIST

Map Key

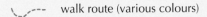   walk route (various colours)

road

dirt road or track

footpath

(🚶)   start of walking route

E4   path numbers

habitation

▲   summit

dam

sea/lake

river

◯ ◉   city/town/village

⛪ ⛪   church/monastery

▢   house/building

🌉   bridge

↗   pointer to places off map

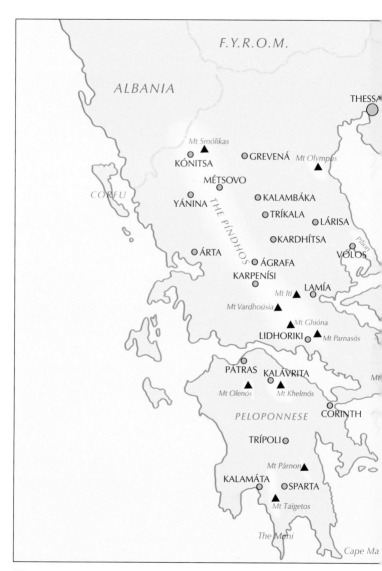

BULGARIA

TURKEY

▲Athos

Dhirfis

Mt Ókhi▲

ⁿNS

N

THE GREEK MOUNTAINS

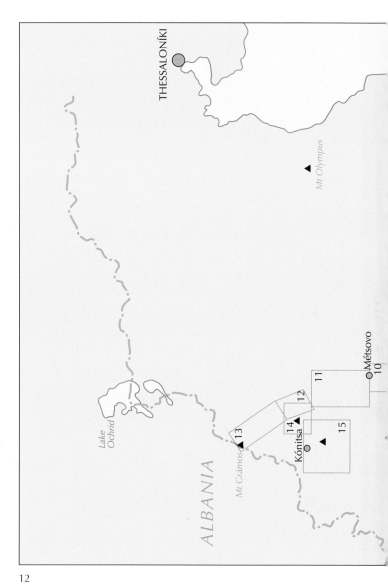

THESSALONÍKI

Mt Olympus

Lake
Ochrid

ALBANIA

Mt Grámos

Métsovo
10

Kónitsa

11

12

13

14

15

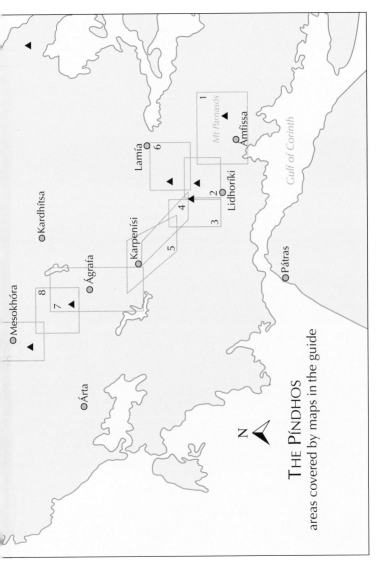

THE PÍNDHOS
areas covered by maps in the guide

Mesokhóra

Árta

Kardhítsa

Ágrafa

Karpenísi

Lamía

Mt Parnasós

Amfissa

Lidhoríki

Pátras

Gulf of Corinth

N

1
2
3
4
5
6
7
8

13

Going up to Refuge A – Mítikas on the skyline (Chapter 8, Mt Olympus)

PART 1 – INTRODUCTION

Mountains cover most of Greece; many are over 2000m in altitude. Most are limestone, the massifs cut by a complex and apparently illogical geometry of deep ravines. To people who know only the summertime seaside the mountains are surprisingly green, forested and well watered. In their more southerly reaches the Greek fir, *abies cephallonica*, is the characteristic tree cover from 800–1800m. Further north the black pine takes over, with extensive beech woods on the colder faces. Springs abound, and rivers run all year round. Snow cover lasts from November to April. But the mountains' special beauty lies in the fact that they have remained unfortunately not untouched, but largely bypassed by modernity.

They are hillwalkers' rather than climbers' mountains, but you do need to be in good physical shape ro explore them. Routes – though not technical – are physically demanding because of the variations in altitude, the distances involved and the absence both of organised facilities for the walker and of restorative creature comforts. Meals and supplies – when available – are basic. There are a number of fairly active local branches of EOS, the Greek mountaineering club (known in Greek as *eleeneekós oreevatikós seendhesmós*, and in English as the HAC or Hellenic Alpine Club), but they are not really of any use to the visiting walker and their huts are, with only two or three exceptions, unstaffed and locked.

Since the early editions of this guide modern life has impinged on the mountains, mainly in the form of roads and bulldozed tracks. This has made navigation more difficult, both because road construction has damaged paths and – more importantly – made them redundant. Peope travel by vehicle, and the paths are no longer maintained.

On the plus side, there is a growing awareness among Greeks – formerly not at all interested in outdoor pursuits – that their own back country is worth exploring and that walking, climbing, canyoning and mountain biking are worthwhile ways of doing it. There are also signs that even the local rural authorities have woken up to the fact that there may be some commercial advantage in encouraging such pursuits. It is not always consistent, but there are several areas where there have been attempts to clear and waymark paths. Guesthouses are springing up in the remotest villages. Most importantly, from the walker's point of view, the mapmaking publisher Anávasi has appeared on the scene with a growing series of detailed and accurate maps designed for walkers.

Armed with map, compass and guide, you should not encounter too many problems. Indeed, our guess is that you will come to see the relatively virgin, uncommercial and primitive nature of these mountains as an essential part of their charm.

TRADITIONAL MOUNTAIN LIFE

You can still get a sense of how traditional mountain life must once have been, although much has changed over the last 30 years since this book was first researched. The

Goats and their masters at Ftéri (Chapter 2, Agrafa)
(photo Michael Cullen)

Soúfles peaks (Chapter 1, Vardhoúsia)

biggest change has been the end of all economic – essentially agricultural – activity in the mountains. Already in the 1970s the population had been drastically reduced by emigration, but those who remained were still able to maintain a bit of farming activity. Now they are too old and too few. There is no longer any cultivation. There are no young children, no schools anywhere. The only economic activity is the arrival of the shepherds in May, bringing their flocks to the mountain pastures for the summer, and the seasonal return from the cities of now retired émigrés, sometimes with their children and grandchildren in the school holidays. Many villages are almost completely deserted in the winter.

There is a certain melancholy in the overgrown fields and crumbling terraces, the ancient footpaths washed off the mountainside or impenetrably overgrown. Yet, paradoxically, there is more life and investment than there has been for years. The children of those who emigrated have become prosperous enough to rebuild family homes for holiday times. Village squares are freshly paved. Churches are restored. There is at last a sense that there was something valuable about the life that has been lost, and people have begun to take a pride in saving what they can.

A LITTLE HISTORY

In the north and west of Greece you still find descendants of the shepherd clans, the Sarakatsani and the Vlachs, who have preserved a separate and distinctive identity to this day. The Vlachs in particular are interesting because their language, in contrast to all the other Balkan tongues south of Romania, is Latin-based. No one quite knows who they are or how they come to

Path to the Akhelöös (Chapter 2, Northern Agrafa)

speak Latin. Traditionally semi-nomadic, with no written language, they have left no records. They call themselves *arumani* – Romans. While they are obviously not that, the language they speak is probably not much different from that heard round shepherds' campfires 2000 years ago.

There are villages throughout the mountains, and you wonder why places so rugged and inaccessible should ever have been populated. But it is this very inaccessibility which provides the answer. People sought refuge in these natural fastnesses, especially from the Turks, who overran and controlled the lowlands from their capture

18

of Constantinople in 1453 until, in the case of northern Greece, World War I. The outlawed sheep-rustlers and brigands – *klephts* – made their lairs in the mountains and formed what we would now call the liberation army that finally drove the Turks out and instituted the beginnings of the modern Greek state in the 1820s.

During World War II many Greeks again took to their mountains to form one of Europe's biggest Resistance movements. With the outbreak of Civil War in 1946 – for which many Greeks blame the British – a new generation of outlaws made the mountains their base. This time they were Communist guerrillas, mostly veterans of the Resistance, who felt that Anglo-American domination, restoration of the monarchy and the return of the old politicians from their safe wartime haven in Egypt, was not what they had fought for. It was this war which occasioned the promulgation of the Truman Doctrine and America's first attempt to halt the feared domino effect:

the obsessive notion that if one state fell under Communist influence, then others would follow.

The mountain communities endured 10 years of war in the 1940s, more than their fragile economy could stand. Populations were evacuated to the lowlands to prevent them supporting the guerrillas. Children went to school, adults found jobs. By the time peace came in the 1950s village fields had reverted to nature and there was no other work. Many families never returned to their mountain homes.

FLOWERS AND WILDLIFE

You see surprisingly little wildlife for such wild and remote terrain. The occasional fox or hare, perhaps a deer, an adder, salamander, or tortoise, the odd eagle or griffon vulture, and smaller species like chough, partridge, wheatear, accentor, perhaps a wallcreeper. If you are lucky you might see mountain goats or a wild boar in the

Scorpion on Kióna (Route 41)

19

The monastery at Doliana (Chapter 4)

northwest. Bear and wolf exist – the latter, apparently, in increasing numbers – but you would be extremely lucky (or unlucky) to meet either.

Flowers, on the other hand, abound. The best season for seeing them depends on altitude and latitude. Take Mt Parnasós, for instance, in the southern part of central Greece. In the first half of May you will find fritillaries, orchids, ophrys, violets, aubretia, iris, anemones and *daphne oloeides* up to 1200m or so. As you approach the melting snow patches, around 1600–1800m, there are crocuses, squills, *corydalis solida*, saxifrages and many others. Further south spring comes earlier; further north, later. Tulips, gentians, narcissus, campanulas, geraniums, aquilegias,

lilies – all sorts of glorious species are to be found, over 600 of them endemic.

MAPS AND WHERE TO FIND THEM

The problem of finding reliable maps has been largely resolved by the appearance on the scene of Anávasi, specialist mapmakers and publishers. Their maps, varying in scale from 1:25 000 to 1:50 000 and 1:100 000, cover the majority of the most interesting walking areas of the country. You could do worse than confine your activities to these areas. No other maps are remotely as good.

The Greek army's (HAGS) 1:50 000 sheets, still treated as classified material, are interesting historically, for they mark all the old and now mostly vanished mule paths, but are out of date and extremely difficult to get hold of. Those produced by the National Statistical Survey of Greece (NSSG) exist only at 1:200 000 and are also out of date. Road Editions (1:50 000 for selected areas) are useful, but more for the motorist than walker.

An additional advantage of the Anávasi maps is that many include a verbal description of the routes and also incorporate the new metric grid Greek Geodetic Reference System (GGRS 87), which can be added to a GPS as follows:

Adding the Greek Geodetic Reference System to your GPS

User Grid
Longitude of origin	+24.00000E
Scale factor	0.9996
False easting	+500000
False northing	+0.0

User Map Datum
Dx	–200
Dy	74
Dz	246
Da	0
Df	0

Maps can be obtained from:
UK
Edward Stanford, 12 Long Acre, London WC2E 9LP (tel: 020 7836 1915; www.stanfords.co.uk)
The Map Shop, Upton-on-Severn; freephone 0800 085 40 80; tel: 01684 593146; www.themapshop.co.uk; email: themapshop@btinternet.com

Athens
Anávasi, 6A Stoá Arsakeíou, towards the Omónia Square end of Panepistemíou Street – on the left if you are coming from the central Síntagma Square: tel/fax: +30 210 3218104; www.mountains.gr and www.anavasi.gr

SLEEPING AND EATING

Country towns almost always have at least one reasonable hotel, and increasing numbers of mountain villages offer informal rooms or guesthouses – the latter at around 25–35 euros per room. They do not, however, very often have any shops. What they do have is a coffee-shop-cum-general-store, the *maghazeé*. This is the place to make for on arrival, for information about a place to sleep or eat or where to get supplies. Very often the *maghazeé* will be the only place able to supply you, and they will always fix you something to eat if there is no regular taverna. The menu will be basic – eggs, macaroni, potatoes, tomatoes, beans – costing (with a beer) around 7–10 euros.

Food for the road can be a problem. Special backpacking products do not exist. In general you have to make do with local fare: bread, cheese and olives, supplemented by endless tins of sardines or spam, which is all that is available in remote places.

The rule has to be: whenever you hit a place with a restaurant and shops, have a blow out and stock up. Avoid things that leak and squash in rucksacks or are dry and salty – they are horrible when you are hot and thirsty. Be careful with cheeses, especially the ubiquitous *féta*. The dry variety is often salty, and the more edible wet

Looking down Goudouváka ravine towards Anthokhóri (Chapter 4, Mt Peristéri)

one leaks. I go for the hard *gruyère* type of cheese, *graviéra*, when I can get it. Taste cheeses before committing yourself. Whole salamis are good, and though they sweat they keep. Halva (*khalvá*) is a good sugary energy-giver. Nuts, sultanas and dried fruit are readily available in the towns. I am a muesli addict; it is light, unmessy and quite palatable when mixed only with spring water, but unobtainable outside Athens supermarkets. Greeks eat no breakfast, so you need to bring something with you if you do not like the idea of cheese and olives first thing.

The refuge huts are really of little use to the visitor. With the exception of those

on Olympus, Gamíla and Smólikas, they are unstaffed and locked. The palaver involved in getting and returning the keys far outweighs any benefits – in summer.

Monasteries are a better bet, if you are a man. You can always ask for food and shelter there, but you have to be modestly dressed, which means no shorts. Women are not usually allowed in.

Camping, on the other hand, is possible anywhere in the mountains and no one will object. As the land belongs to no one, there is no question of trespassing. You do not need a tent in summer; a bivvy bag is quite sufficient. Just be careful of sheepdogs.

CAVE CANEM!

This is a serious warning. The sheepdogs – guard dogs, not collies – are the greatest danger you are likely to encounter in the mountains. It is not the little mongrels that guard some flocks that you have to worry about, but the Molossi. They are wolf-sized, half-starved, unused to strangers and very fierce and, like the arrows of outrageous fortune, never come one at a time but in gangs. They will never let you pass without attacking. If at all possible, give them a very wide berth. Always carry poles or a stout stick and be aggressive. Keep them at pole's length and throw rocks at them with the intention of hurting them. If you don't, they will hurt you.

GETTING ON WITH PEOPLE

Mountain people are extremely friendly and hospitable. It is, however, up to you, the stranger, to break the social ice by saying hello first. The simplest greetings are *kaleeméra*, good day, or *yásoo*, good health to you (*yásas*, if there is more than one person). That immediately dispels what can appear to be hostility, but is in reality merely polite reserve.

Do not forget that mountain people are still rather old-fashioned in their attitudes. Women, in particular, should be careful how they dress and act.

WEATHER AND WHEN TO GO

There is snow on the mountains from November to April. Quite extensive patches sometimes persist until mid-June, and later on the higher and more northerly ones. The weather begins to settle in May, and to break again at the beginning of October.

June–September is the most settled period. It is also the hottest, but once you get into a big range like the Píndhos, and high up, the heat is not too bothersome. Above 2000m the temperature rarely rises above 25° even in July and August, and at night drops to 10° or 12°. I have found my water frozen in the morning at 2000m near the Albanian border in September.

Certainly, the weather can be beautiful, but you should not be lulled into a false sense of security. Greek mountains behave like other mountains. Even in midsummer violent storms can blow up with little warning. Nights are cool, especially in contrast to daytime temperatures; you definitely need a fleece.

WHAT TO TAKE

In summer conditions, you need a combination of light and warm clothing. Shorts are essential and I would recommend a hat and shirts with collar and sleeves, if you are at all susceptible to sunburn. Take some protective cream if you have a vulnerable Anglo-Saxon nose, and for the backs of the knees. Warm clothing (including your sleeping bag) does not need to be heavy, just enough to protect you in bad weather and against the chill of tiredness and night. Take a windproof and waterproof cagoule. A good pair of lightweight Vibram-soled boots is sufficient in the way of footwear. Take a survival/bivvy bag and basic first aid kit, including some mosquito repellent for use in the lowlands.

If you are packing a stove petrol is the most widely available fuel, but camping gas and equivalents are also available. If you are travelling by air, remember that fuel bottles need to be scrubbed clean enough to pass for water bottles.

EMERGENCY SERVICES

In effect, there are none, so do not have an accident. You would be wise to have an insurance policy that will get you home if you need any serious treatment.

GETTING TO THE MOUNTAINS

For most destinations in this book, buses are the best means of transport. All major country towns have daily connections with Athens. Buses for the Peloponnese and parts of central Greece west of the Píndhos mountains (Yánina, for instance) leave from the terminus at 100 Kifisoú Street; to get there, take bus 051 from the corner of Vilará and Menándrou Streets near Omónia Square. Buses for Delphi, Ámfisa and parts east of the Píndhos leave from 260 Liosíon Street, near Áyios Nikólaos metro stop. The only way to be absolutely certain about departure times is to go to the appropriate terminus.

Onward journeys from provincial centres into the mountains are more problematic. Most villages still have bus connections, usually leaving the village for the centre at crack of dawn and returning in early afternoon, but the service is much less frequent than formerly and the only way to find out times is generally on the spot. There is always the chance of a lift – easiest to arrange from village to town, when you can ask in the *maghazeé* if anyone is going. Alternatively, just step into the road and flag someone down. That is what the locals do. Vehicles are rare birds in out-of-the-way places, and

you cannot afford not to make your intentions absolutely plain.

Taxis are not expensive by general European standards. You are not likely to be using a lot of them. If there are any problems with other means of transport, take a taxi – but fix the price before you get in.

USING THIS BOOK

The original inspiration for writing this book was reading the account of Lord Hunt's 1963 Anglo-Greek traverse of the Píndhos mountains in the journal of the RGS (vol 130, part 3, September 1964). And just as the Píndhos chain forms the backbone (in all senses) of the Greek mountain experience – in spite of the changes outlined earlier in this introduction – I have thought it important to keep a Píndhos traverse as the backbone of this edition too.

The routes described in the guide are arranged in three groups: the Píndhos Range, Athens and the East Coast, and the Peloponnese. The Píndhos Range, which comprises six chapters, accounts for the vast majority of them. They can be put together to form continuous multi-day hikes – including going the whole hog from Delphi to Albania – or treated as a straightforward ascent of a single peak. Similarly, the routes described under the other two groups can be used as day walks or as building blocks for something longer.

The art of rendering Greek words in English letters is in a state of utter chaos, and no doubt some people will think my system is crazy too. I have given place names in a spelling not too different from what you are most likely to encounter on

Daybreak over the Aegean (Chapter 13)

bilingual road signs. Where it seems important to get the pronunciation right I have a given a guide in brackets (see Appendix 1).

The estimates of walking times exclude halts, and are records of our own times. I was occasionally accused of walking too fast in earlier editions. Youth is well behind me now, so the times should be more generous.

L(eft) and R(ight) directions are given in relation to the walker's line of march. This applies also to the flanks of valleys and gullies. The only exception is actual stream or river banks, when L and R are indicated in relation to the direction of the current. We have also given compass

bearings and GPS positions (using GGRS87) when we have used a GPS device.

Walks are graded on a scale of 1 to 3. You will find that nearly all are graded 3, not because they require a high degree of technical expertise or involve any serious danger – with rare exceptions they do not. But they do demand a considerable degree of commitment because of their remoteness and inaccessibility, and the absence of organised facilities. Routes are often long, with nowhere to stop between start and finish. The terrain is unremittingly difficult and navigation often far from easy. Most of them are definitely not for the fainthearted or inexperienced.

PART 2 – THE PÍNDHOS RANGE

Yidhovoúni from the E4 (Chapter 1, Vardhoúsia)

The Píndhos range forms the backbone of the northern half of mainland Greece, its axis running northwest–southeast from the Albanian frontier to the Gulf of Corinth. It is in effect the dying southward extension of the Alps and Dinaric Alps. Strictly speaking the name refers only to that stretch of mountains immediately north and south of the town of Métsovo, but we use the name for the complete range.

Until about 30 years ago it was possible to walk the entire range using only the footpaths and mule trails that had, since time immemorial, served as lines of communication between the villages of the Píndhos.

In the 1980s some Greeks marked out the E4 (intended to form part of a trans-European network of hiking routes), which was – in its southern part – almost identical to my original route. Both have been spoilt by modern road building, and there has been no attempt to re-route the E4. Most of it now follows roads, including considerable stretches of tarmac. The remaining footpath sections are so broken up and badly waymarked it is hardly worth trying to find it. Where it is worth the effort we have indicated it in this guidebook.

It is, however, still possible – though a bit more demanding – to link up our routes to form an almost complete traverse that does not involve spending too much time either on roads or having to make your own way cross-country.

Vromerí ridge: a reluctant mount (Chapter 3, Northern Agrafa)

You would need to link the following routes to complete a full traverse, starting from Velítsa on the eastern flanks of Mt Parnasós:

• Velítsa to Delphi over Mt Parnasós (Route 1, including E4 link to Mt Ghióna).

• Mt Ghióna traverse via the Reká ravine to Sikiá and on to Áno Mousounítsa on the eastern flank of Mt Vardhoúsia (Route 2, Route 4 in reverse, Route 5).

• Áno Mousounítsa to Karpenísi either via the E4 (mostly road work; Routes 6 and 10) or following the ridge via Mt Sarándena to Rákhes Timfristoú (Route 9), with bus on to Karpenísi.

• Karpenísi to Kréndi either by bus or by the E4 (mostly road work; Route 10) and on to Monastiráki and Epinianá; or Karpenísi to Dhitikí Franghísta by bus and on to Epinianá and Mt Delidhími by Route 12 (Stages 1 and 2) and Route 13 (Stages 1 and 2).

• Mt Delidhími to Mesokhóra via Spiliá monastery, Kalí Kómi and Mt Khadzí (Route 15, with the possibility of using Route 16 as an easier alternative at the end).

• Mesokhóra to Métsovo via Khodja's ridge (Route 17) or via Mt Peristéri (Route 17 with Route 18 in reverse for the last section).

• Métsovo to Mt Grámos via Vália Kálda, Vovoúsa and Samarína (Route 19), with the option of joining up with Routes 23 and 20 in a long loop westward over Mts Gamíla and Mt Smólikas.

CHAPTER 1

SOUTH CENTRAL:
PARNASÓS, GHIÓNA, VARDHOÚSIA, ÍTI

These four adjacent massifs form a distinctive block of mountains at the very accessible southern end of the range, almost on the shore of the Gulf of Corinth. Separated only by a river valley or, in one case, a high pass, they can easily be linked into a continuous circuit.

A: MT PARNASÓS

Mt Parnasós from the south

Mt Parnasós (2455m), rising directly above the great classical site of Delphi, is a conveniently accessible mountain if you do not have time for longer expeditions. It is also temptingly close to the pretty seaside village of Galaxídhi (*ghalakseédhee*).

There are, however, some drawbacks. Mt Parnasós has become a popular ski resort in recent years. Tarmac roads lead into the heart of the mountain, and there is a lot of ongoing chalet construction. On the Delphi side, the classic hike from the EOS Sarandári refuge to the Liákoura summit is rather dull.

If you want to bag the summit, do it from Áno Tithoréa (or Velítsa, as the village is still usually called) on the east side of the mountain. It is an arduous but spectacularly beautiful route. If you have to start from the Delphi side, I would recommend two possibilities: either a complete traverse from Delphi to Velítsa via the EOS refuge and summit (14hrs), or just the Delphi to the refuge stage (about 6hrs).

Location:	On the north shore of the Gulf of Corinth above the town of Delphi, about 4hrs drive northwest of Athens.
Maps:	Anávasi Topo 25 Central Parnasos 1:25 000.
Bases:	Delphi and Arákhova on the south side are large touristy villages with numerous hotels, restaurants and shops. Káto Tithoréa to the east has some shops, and accommodation only at Café Ziákas on the square.
Information:	National Tourist Office in Delphi.
Access:	Daily buses from Athens to Delphi and Arákhova. Káto Tithoréa best reached by train.

Route 1
Parnasós Traverse: Velítsa to Delphi

Stage 1 – *Áno Tithoréa/Velítsa (450m) – Tsáres spring (1360m) – Liákoura (2455m)*

Walking time:	6hrs
Distance:	11km
Waymarks:	Red squares
Height gain:	2000m
Height loss:	0m
Difficulty:	3

When you get off the train at **Káto Tithoréa** you will be about 7km from the start of the walk at Áno Tithoréa. The route follows a long straight stretch of tarmac, without interest, except for the view of the mountain rising abruptly out of the plain. Best to get a taxi; ask in the village square.

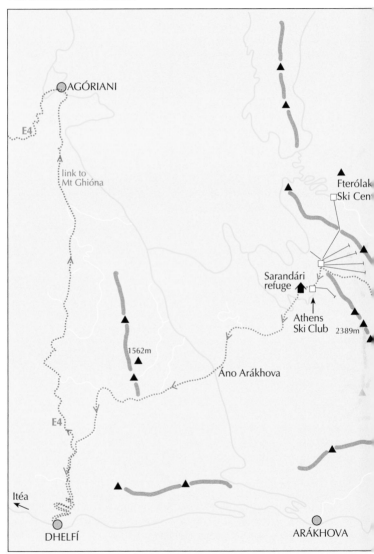

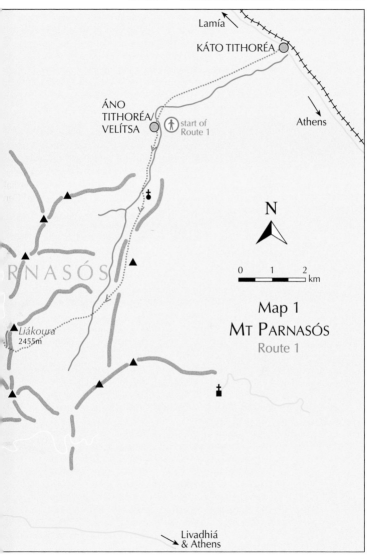

Map 1
MT PARNASÓS
Route 1

At the entrance to the village of **ÁnoTithoréa/Velítsa** the road crosses a deep gully before winding up through the picturesque streets to a plane-shaded square with a taverna. Pass the taverna and continue up to the R. The road soon ends by a spring at the foot of a plane tree. Bear L and continue up to another spring and plane tree on the very edge of the precipitous Velítsa ravine: the highest point of the village. Above you stretches a wall of red cliffs riddled with caves, in the furthest of which – some 30mins walk away – Odhiséas Andhroútsos, hero of the the early 19th-century wars against the Turks, made his lair.

From the highest point of the village go straight ahead on a paved path which shortly turns into a dirt path traversing high above the ravine L. The waymarks are red squares. Keep a close eye on them, for various smaller paths lead higher up the slope. Gradually wind down L into the streambed (**25mins**) below an old watermill, cross over and begin the steep climb up the other side, emerging on the far rim of the gully at **40mins**, with a long view L back over the plain. In front of you is an open water conduit – which you can drink from – and, just the other side, a rough grassy track. Turn up to the R towards the track and the beginning of the fir trees higher up.

Keep an eye on the waymarks. At **55mins** leave the track and turn up to the L. About 3mins later turn R on a higher track which leads in a few more minutes to a picnic kiosk and the chapel of Áyios Yiánnis. There is a tap for drinking water by the kiosk and a grassy open space on the edge of the ravine where you can camp.

Continue upwards, crossing a track at **1hr 15mins** and again a few minutes later. The ascent begins to steepen and the forest of firs closes around you. The path is clear and well signed, though there is the occasional fallen tree to negotiate. Gaps in the trees permitting, there are tremendous views R of the crags leading to the summits.

At **2hrs 5mins** emerge from the trees to climb across an open stony shoulder. About 20mins later you come out on a ridge which drops sheer away on the further side, with long views over the Boeotian plain. As you climb, the ridge becomes broader and flatter and more open until, at **2hrs 50mins**, the path begins to descend gently towards the R along the L flank of the Velítsa ravine. The trees open out and at **3hrs 15mins** you descend to the copious Tsáres spring (E0382034, N4265960; *last water before the summit*).

Bear R at the spring and down to the stream below it. (About 100m downstream on the true L bank of the stream is a prominent rock overhang, a perfect shelter in bad weather. There is a grassy campsite just beyond.) Cross over and zigzag steeply up the stony slope opposite through the last scattered firs. After about 25mins of climbing pass some sheep pens. A further 45mins bring you to a stone hut in the mouth of the hanging valley (**4hrs 25mins**). Thereafter, just keep up the valley floor to the head (about 1hr 10mins; **5hrs 35mins**), where you scramble up a steep rocky couloir – frequent waymarks – to a gap in the ridge above (E0379411/N4265204). ▶

For Liákoura (at 2445m the summit of Mt Parnasós), turn R at the top of the couloir and climb north up the clear ridge-line path, marked with red diamonds and paint splodges (30mins; **6hrs 5mins**). Aside from the wonderful views, you also get a clear view of the onward route: aim for the highest gantries of the ski lifts, visible at about 276° below the further-most corner of the bare Yerondóvrakhos peak, to the front and left as you look west.

The best campsite below Liákoura is occupied by a sheep-fold. If it is tenanted, there is another flat grassy spot about 15mins to the north below a long zigzag in the Fterólaka track. There is no reliable water in either case.

For a bad-weather escape route, from the gap turn sharp R over rocks on to the end of a rough track, leading north and west for 7.5km (downhill) to the ski resort at **Fterólaka**.

Reaching the Liákoura summit

If you have come up to Liákoura by car – it needs to be a robust vehicle – the grassy spot below the Fterólaka track would make a good base for walks on the surounding peaks (Yerondóvrakhos, Tsárkos, Sidheróporta on the route marked with a white 22 set in red diamonds).

Stage 2 – *Liákoura (2445m)* – *EOS Sarandári refuge (1800m)*

Walking time:	2hrs 30mins
Distance:	7km
Waymarks:	Red squares
Height gain:	50m
Height loss:	845m
Difficulty:	2

This is a slightly dull section without shade or water, and marred by the lift network of the Fterólaka ski resort.

From the track at the foot of the Liákoura ridge, head north down a shallow gully into the grassy hollow below the sheepfold, leaving the track above you on the R. In the hollow bear L or west across the grass and up the rocky enclosing slope to a small saddle (**20mins**).

Following the red squares, continue west past a big boulder and sheepfold, then, bearing northwest, up and over the spur of Kotronórakhi with the long ridge of Yerondóvrakhos over your left shoulder. Losing height gradually, bear westward across the line of the ski lifts to meet the 22/red diamond path coming down off the northwest ridge of Yerondóvrakhos.

Shortly after the junction, at a ridgetop signpost, double back L or south and descend in fairly steep zigzags towards the lifts and buildings of the small Athens Ski Club nestling in a bare hollow beneath the northwest slopes of Yerondóvrakhos. Past a lone juniper tree, the path brings you out on bare bulldozed ground by the fourth pylon – a double one – above the buildings (**2hrs 15mins**). There are various waymarks around but, if in doubt when coming up, aim for this fourth pylon. There is a big water cistern for sheep down towards the buildings, normally with a bucket handy. The water is not very appetising, but there is no other sure source before Áno Arákhova.

For Sarandári (15mins; **2hrs 30mins**), the location of the EOS refuge, either follow the tarmac for a few minutes or take

Sarandári refuge

the path that heads up the slope behind the ski terminal (red squares, 22/red diamonds, yellow squares and a red arrow).

Stage 3 – *Sarandári refuge (1800m) – Áno Arákhova (1120m)*

Walking time:	1hr 15mins
Distance:	4.9km
Waymarks:	Red squares
Height gain:	0m
Height loss:	680m
Difficulty:	2

From the refuge, walk on to the road and turn R for 20m. Turn off the road to the L and head downhill to the R across grassy and stony ground towards some old stone huts. Your general direction for this stage is about 215°, passing between two obvious wooded hills.

Once past the huts turn L down to the road. Cross over and descend into a hollow sinkhole. Keep to the R edge in open firs, then up R through firs and down across a second hollow. Bear L and down to the road again. Cross over and continue down through trees, bearing L along the foot of the first of the two wooded hills.

A pleasant downhill section mostly in open fir forest, about half on old paths and half on modern, albeit rough, tracks.

35

At **15mins** cross a rough track and continue down over open ground, keeping close to or occasionally on the track. In 5mins more reach the bottom of the open ground and turn L on the track for about 50m. Separate red and yellow squares guide you all the way. The yellow squares continue along the track. Turn off R following the red squares towards the defile that separates the two wooded hills. Across an expanse of open meadow (Láka Pasá) towards the mouth of the defile, you hit another track (**25mins**; E0375279/N4265551) and turn R.

The track follows the contour along the R flank of the defile for about 15mins (**40mins**) to an open grassy saddle, where a faded framed map and a bench stand just below the track L. Turn L off the track, heading towards a ruined circular stone hut on the saddle. Áno Arákhova and the surrounding plateau, slowly filling with new construction, are clearly visible through the opening of the defile L, and there is a red-and-white telephone mast on the opposite flank. Turn L by the hut and zigzag down, first L, then R, through the firs (plenty of waymarks) and on to an open grassy slope below an outcrop of craggy rocks R. The route bears R – passing a spring that may be no more than a seepage late in the year (**just under 1hr**) – and descends along a red gritty gully clear of the trees and mostly on its L flank until you encounter a fence round a property. Follow the fence down, keeping it on your R. (*Coming up, keep to the L of the main stream gully*.) Cross the main stream on a concrete culvert by a very ugly house and turn R down the concrete lane to the main road from Arákhova to Agóriani (**1hr 10mins**).

Stage 4 – Áno Arákhova (1120m) – Delphi (620m)

Walking time:	3hrs
Distance:	12km
Waymarks:	Red squares and black-and-yellow flashes
Height gain:	50m
Height loss:	500m
Difficulty:	2

The first half of this stage is on dirt roads. If the start is obstructed by construction, aim for the southern tip of the obvious wooded ridge ahead to the west. The best bit of the route is the final descent to Delphi on the well-preserved old *kaldereémee* with wonderful views over the huge olive groves of Itéa, the Gulf of Corinth, and the Peloponnesian mountains of Zíria and Khelmós on the further shore.

At the main road, turn L for 20m and then R on a track heading slightly south of west, first between new houses and then across the open ground that once was fields. Aim for the southern tip of the obvious wooded ridge ahead, where a dirt road passes through the gap between this ridge and a lower hill to the L. Meet the dirt road after about **25mins** and turn L. The waymarked route runs slightly R of the road but joins up with it again before you reach the chapel of Paliopanayiá (**55mins**; *spring*). Here a path heads up the end of the spur above you on the R to the Corycean cave, renowned in ancient times for its association with the god Pan and the nymphs, but of little interest today.

When people mention Delphi in Greek you will hear them say *dheltoós*. This is because the accusative case is used when talking about going to and from a place.

Áyios Kosmás, looking west to Chióna

Just over 10mins beyond the chapel a minor track turns down L into thick fir forest (red squares). After about 300m, branch off L on to an old forest track (waymarks) that follows the L flank of a stream gully pretty much the whole way to the spring and cattle troughs at the locality known as Króki (**1hr 50mins**).

Here the path turns L and south down a dry gully beside the water conduit that carries Delphi's water supply (E4 markers/black-and-yellow paint flashes). This is also the line of the E4 as it heads north to Agóriani, a village some 6hrs march away. Another 20mins (**2hrs 10mins**) brings you to the beginning of the *kaldereémee* zigzagging down the slope above the archaeological site of Delphi. You come out by the upper corner of the ancient site, follow the fence down through almond trees past the house/museum that once belonged to Ángelos Sikelianós, one of Greece's best-known poets, and into the upper reaches of the village (**3hrs**).

E4 link to Mt Ghióna

The E4 runs north from Delphi, much of the time on dirt tracks, to Agóriani (*hotels, tavernas, bus, taxi*) in about 6hrs. From there it continues in a northwesterly direction to the pass between Ámfissa and Graviá known as Km51 on the main Ámfissa–Lamía road in another 7hrs approximately.

For Agóriani, make your way back to the Króki spring, close to a lone juniper tree (**1hr**). There is a shepherds' shack on the track just above it. The E4 starts uphill from the bend in the track below the shack, following the (mostly) underground water pipe on a bearing of 320°. After 15mins pass the first of several concrete junction boxes in the water pipeline and the path levels out through open fir woods. Another 10 mins brings you to a ridge above a gentle grassy spur with scattered juniper trees, where the path veers L at 280° and contours along the reverse slope to join a good dirt road at **2hrs**.

Continue almost due north, or just east of north, without much variation in height with just occasional stretches of footpath for nearly 3hrs to the Láka Aréndi, where you begin to descend down a rough track to cross a well-used mining road at E0368508/N4270270 (1275m). Cross straight over the road and down what is now a concrete track (with a signpost to some new chalet developments and an E4 sign a little way down) to a spring at Áyia Triádha, cutting off the corners where you can. The path may be further disturbed by new construction. You reach the Agóriani 'ring road' just before the road down into the village.

For the continuation to Km51, turn L. Follow the ring road past the turning into the village. At E0368163/N4272390 (861m) – just after this turning – a black-and-yellow arrow on a wall indicates the start of the path. Turn L up a rough track, which bends R past a spring and then immediately L at a fork (signed). The path heads south, then west up the steep slope, crossing a transverse track serving the village water supply, enters the fir forest and reaches the mining track again on the ridge top above at E0366894/N4271187 (1343m). Here turn R and follow a series of tracks for about 10km with occasional E4 signs. Past a beautiful stretch of ridgetop meadow round the chapel of Áyios Kosmás you come to a fork just below a well-established sheepfold (*water*). Take the rougher LH branch, which contours round above a deep valley with the village of Dhrosokhóri lying below L (see Anávasi map), until you finally head off R on a path which, judging by the first hour from the Km51 end, is findable but not at all clear. From Km51 the E4 is tarmac as far as Kaloskopí.

To reach the start of the Ghióna ascent via the Reká ravine, turn L on the main road at Km 51 by the headquarters for the bauxite mines that scar the landscape round about. Turn R a short distance later on to a secondary road that leads down to the village of Víniani in the little plain below in about 4km.

Viola gracilis

B: MT GHIÓNA

Although only a few kilometres west of Delphi and Mt Parnasós, Ghióna (2507m) remains much less accessible and much less frequented. Of all the peaks within comparatively easy reach of Athens it is the most dramatic. Though scarred by recent road building, the classic traverse up the Reká ravine and over to the village of Sikiá remains unspoilt. The main ridge, culminating in the 2507m Piramídha peak, is a long limestone blade, steep on the east and with 1000m cliffs on the west, providing some of the longest climbs in Greece, while Reká ranks among the most imposing of Greek gorges.

Mt Ghióna: Piramídha summit in spring

Location:	On the north shore of the Gulf of Corinth, west of Delphi, about 200km by road from Athens.
Maps:	Anávasi Topo 50 Central Greece, Giona Oeta Vardousia 1:50 000 and the older edition Mt Giona 1:40 000 with handbook and route maps at 1:25 000.
Bases:	Ámfissa, a small town on the south side not far from the sea, has banks, shops and hotel. Lidhoriki in the Mórnos valley to the west also has banks, shops and accommodation. Rooms in Kaloskopí and Mavrolithári.
Refuge:	At Láka Karvoúni.
Access:	Daily buses from Athens to Ámfissa via Delphi, and onward to Lidhoriki (60km). For Kaloskopí (west of Brálos at km175 on the Thebes–Lamía road) take a train to Amfíklea or Káto Tithoréa on the Athens–Lamía line and then a taxi.

Route 2
Ascent of Piramídha (2507m) from Víniani (500m) via Reká ravine

Walking time:	7hrs 30mins
Distance:	16km
Waymarks:	None
Height gain:	2007m
Height loss:	0m
Difficulty:	3

This is the classic ascent route and the first part of the traverse. It is very much neglected nowadays – wrongly, in my view, for it is a wonderful route – in favour of the more accessible and shorter northern approaches. Immediate access is from Víniani. The Reká ravine begins barely 1km from the village. On foot it can be reached either by the E4 link from Parnasós via Km51 (see end of Route 1) or, following the road, from Ámfissa via the village of Prosílio. The most convenient approach is by taxi from Ámfissa.

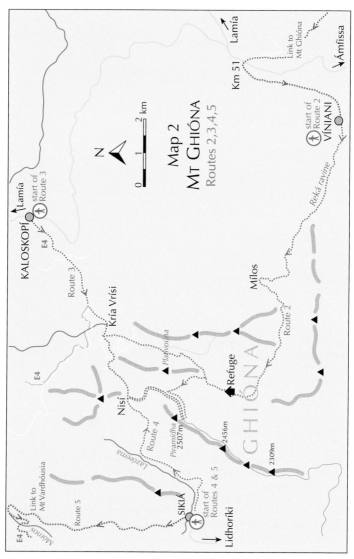

Map 2
Mt GHIÓNA
Routes 2, 3, 4, 5

N

0   1   2 km

Lamía

Km 51

Link to
Mt Ghióna

Ámfissa

start of
Route 2
VÍNIANI

Reká ravine

Lamía

start of
Route 3

KALOSKOPÍ

E4

Route 3

Kría Vrísi

Platwouna

Mílos

Route 2

Refuge

GHIÓNA

E4

Nisí

Route 4

Piramidha
2507m

2456m

2309m

Lazórema

Link to
Mt Vardhoúsia

Route 5

Mórnos

E4

SIKIÁ

start of
Routes 4 & 5

Lidhoríki

Head out of Víniani along the road in a northwesterly direction. Where the riverside meadow ends the ravine begins (**20mins**); you cannot mistake it. The gravelly, dry bed of the river fills it from side to side. Occasional red paint marks show the way, although there is no real need as the ravine guides you for the next 4hr. Soon you are enclosed within a narrow trench some 300–400m deep. Trees and shrubs lean out precariously from the nearly sheer walls. It is hard going, with the loose gravel shifting under your feet. The ravine twists and turns, climbing all the time. You realise how quickly you have been gaining height by the presence of firs right down at the edge of the riverbed.

After about 2hrs (**2hrs 20mins**), and just after a series of bends, the ravine opens out a little, with a terrace of flat firm ground on the R for the first time, with fir trees growing along it. Some 20mins later you come to a wide bowl-shaped opening in the ravine, with a narrow wooded defile ahead and a steep tributary gully running down off the heights R (*campsite*). The main riverbed swings sharply L. There are the remains of a watermill; this is **Mílos** – the mill. A spring about 100m to the R above the path feeds a rusty metal pipe visible in the ravine. There is a large red tap symbol painted on a cement block, but it cannot quite be seen from the path.

The path is clear here, running along the top of a low retaining wall. Follow it into the defile ahead, keeping to the R bank. At the further end (**2hrs 45mins**), cross to the L side of the gully and zigzag steeply up an open stony slope. At the top it levels out and you find yourself once more trudging along the gravelly riverbed under the firs. About 50mins later (**3hrs 35mins**) there is a great red cliff L, dripping with water and verdant with hanging plants. Clamber up the scree to its base and you will find plenty of water (at least until early summer).

About 20mins beyond the red cliff (**4hrs**) emerge from the shade of the firs into a wide sunny place where the sides of the ravine at last recede. Here is the first glimpse of the summit ridge of Ghióna, a long grey wall of rock towering ahead, jagged with numerous peaks over 2300m. To the L (south) of this line of peaks – and standing somewhat apart – is the tower-like peak of Profítis Ilías (2298m). The riverbed here describes a substantial curve to the L. On the R of this bend is a hard flat terrace, where a stream debouches from a narrow wooded gully. Do not continue up the main river. The path for the

The only reliable source of water before the refuge is the spring at Mílos about 2hrs into the ravine.

43

The Karvoúni refuge and Skasmádha col

Ghióna refuge climbs up the spine of the wooded spur dividing the course of the main river from the new tributary gully,
pretty well bisecting the angle of junction (1535m).

The path strays a bit L and R of the spine of the spur. A
20min climb (**4hrs 20mins**) brings you out above the treeline
in a patch of meadow, where a clear path bears R (north), keeping close to the treeline all along the base of the summit ridge.
The pink-roofed refuge is in view all the way, reached in about
an hour (**5hrs 20mins**; 1750m). There is a separate hut next to
it where you can shelter, and water in the gully just above the
refuge. The area is known as Láka Karvoúni.

Above the refuge, the summit ridge rises to its highest
point in the Piramídha peak (2507m), before dropping to the
north into the col of Skasmádha (*to dheeyáselo tees skasmád-
has*), then curving round to terminate in the lower peak of
Plativoúna. These two peaks and the col together enfold the
corrie or *láka* which lies directly behind the refuge.

From the refuge, head north up the streambed and then
up the grassy lower slopes of **Plativoúna** towards the crags at
its RH edge (**5hrs 55mins**). There you pick up a path which
takes you up L across the screes below the crags past tall jagged
outcrops to the Skasmádha col (**6hrs 35mins**; 2180m).

Another path climbs just east of north to the col below the east flank of Plativoúna
in 45mins and thence down through the sheepfold at Kritharólaka. It cuts across
the track to Kaloskopí, touching it again at its easternmost loop and joining up with
the path described under Route 3 below close to the spring of Kría Vrísi (**1hr 40mins**).

From Skasmádha bear quite sharply L or west, then southwest,
climbing steadily up a rocky slope to hit the ridgeline just south
of the summit (**7hrs 30mins**; 2507m). The view is superb, with
Mt Íti to the north, the distinctive conical shape of Mt Veloúkhi
far off to the northwest and the heights of Ágrafa beyond, the
merest fudge of blue at this distance. To the west you look
sheer down into the deep valley of the Mórnos river with the
long craggy ridge of the Vardhoúsia massif opposite.

To continue from Skasmádha towards Sikiá or down towards
Kaloskopí, reverse Routes 3 and 4 below.

Route 3
Ascent of Piramídha (2507m)
from Kaloskopí (1100m)

Walking time:	5hrs 20mins
Distance:	12km
Waymarks:	Red squares and diamonds
Height gain:	1407m
Height loss:	0m
Difficulty:	3
Map:	See Route 2

An all-weather track runs along the north flank of the mountain between 1300–1400m: the route of the E4 from Kaloskopí to Strómi. The first kilometres on the road are unavoidable if you are on foot. If you have a vehicle the best thing is to leave it at the big spring and cattle trough of **Kría Vrísi** (1350m; 6.6km from Kaloskopí). The shepherds drive on to the end of the secondary track at Kárkanos at 1580m, but it is rough.

The main tarmac road passes just above the village of Kaloskopí. A dirt track branches off to the southwest signposted Mnímata. There is a four-way crossroads at Mnímata (**45mins**). Keep straight ahead, then L at the next two junctions (leaving the E4 at the second) to reach **Kría Vrísi** R of the track in a clearing in the fir forest (**1hr 30mins**). About 5mins later take the track climbing steeply L. At the first RH hairpin a red arrow and pole (E0350227/N4280938; 1400m) mark the start of a path climbing steeply to the southwest up the R flank of a gully. Hit the track again after a short distance at the next RH hairpin (E0350155/N4280875) and continue up again, still following the R flank of the gully. The way is fairly well marked with red squares. Bear R and up the slope of a grassy spur.

Continue to bear R diagonally across the flat of the spur to join the rough Kritharólaka track. Turn R, and follow the track downhill for about 300m. Ignore the junction with the Kría Vrísi track coming up from the R and carry on (double-headed red arrow) to the end of the track at Kárkanos right in front of you (**2hrs 20mins**; E0349337/N4280794; 1580m). This is where the shepherds leave their vehicles.

The well-trodden and well-signed path (red squares and diamonds and paint) starts directly above the end of the track, climbing steeply up the L side of a gully beneath crags and clear of the trees. After about 30mins (**2hrs 50mins**) the gradient eases and the path traverses more gently along grassy slopes, above and L of the stream, which eventually it meets near the junction of two gullies (**3hrs 20mins**). Above the slope of the RH gully is the plateau of Spanáki, where the friendly Yiórgos Siópatos has his sheepfold. On the lower slopes of the LH gully an abundant spring (E0348554/N4279876; 1820m) gushes from a length of pipe.

For Piramídha, continue up the L flank of this gully to the top of the grassy ridge overlooking Vathiá Láka, a grassy hollow at the foot of Piramídha's north face where the Goúvalis family from Panouryiá make their summer sheepfold (spring). The path circles L round the *láka* and up to the col of Skasmádha (2180m) in about 50mins (**4hrs 20mins**). Allow another hour for the summit (**5hrs 20mins**).

Climb from the spring at E0348554/N4279876 southwest up the R flank of the gully in front, and on to the spur dividing it from the next gully to the R, to find the abandoned sheepfold of **Nisí**; the half-ruined enclosure makes the best dog-free campsite in the area (E0348270/N4279801). It is also the crucial landmark for finding the head of the route to Lazórema and Sikiá (see Route 4 below).

Nisí sheepfold

Route 4
Ascent of Piramídha (2507m)
from Sikiá (700m)

Walking time:	5hrs 45mins
Distance:	8.75km
Waymarks:	Sporadic red paint
Height gain:	1800m
Height loss:	0m
Difficulty:	3
Map:	See Route 2

Sikiá is a tiny village about 18km up the road that runs up the Mórnos river valley north from the little town of Lidhoríki (walkable, but tarmac all the way; better to get a taxi).

The village lies in a dramatic setting at the lower limit of the fir tree zone, with the cliffs of Ghióna at its back and the jagged heights of Vardhoúsia in front. The Lazórema stream cuts a deep gully between the two halves of the village, its further bank riddled with caves used for storage and livestock. The friendly Békos *maghazeé* opposite the church will fix you a meal and find accommodation.

Coming into Sikiá from Lidhoríki, continue downhill past the church and *maghazeé* into the bottom of the Lazórema gully. There is a basketball pitch and, on the R, a spring. Two red blobs of paint on a boulder mark the start of the path.

Turn R up the plane-lined stream gully, sticking to the L side, for about 500m. Cross to the R bank (**25mins**) and bear uphill towards two tall plane trees. Cross the old water conduit (full of water) and bear L on a good path winding eastward up towards a big dry gully splitting the cliffs ahead (red paint). Zigzag steeply up the L flank of this gully, all the while bearing L or north towards the mouth of the Lazórema ravine, which you pass above and come to a distinct saddle (**1hr 10mins**; E0346084/N42784290). From here you look ahead into the Lázou valley, enclosed by fir-clad ridges, where once the villagers of Sikiá cultivated fields. Above you rises the 1000m west wall of Ghióna.

Resting above Lázou

The path descends slightly over grassy slopes before levelling out below open forest. At just under **1hr 30mins** you pass through a sloping grassy clearing with the remains of terracing and come, about 10mins later, to a second clearing, with a sheepfold under the firs beside the stream (E0346513/N4279757; 1192m). There is a spring in the side of the gully 50m upstream from the shepherds' hut. It is a perfect campsite.

About 200m north of this clearing there is a second sheepfold under the trees and right across the path. The dogs here have a reputation for being ferocious, so be careful. Beyond it an increasingly faint path continues, still on the true L bank and just above the stream, bearing gradually R-wards and uphill. There are remains of old terrace walls, long since overgrown by the forest. Very soon you come to a junction of stream gullies.

A tributary comes down from the R (east) to join the Lazórema stream at almost 90°. Bear sharply uphill to the R, following the R bank (true L) of this tributary. There is no longer a proper path. Climb steeply up through the trees, keeping reasonably close to the stream. Past the junction with another stream coming steeply down from the L (north), bear gradually R away from your gully towards the light now visible through the trees above. Come out on the spine of the steep spur you have been ascending. An open grassy clearing cut by avalanches runs down the middle. There is no obvious path: head up the centre of the clearing until the rock wall at the top comes in sight and you can make out the emplacement of a cave-like overhang. As you reach the end of the more or less open ground, bear L into the dry stony gully (the upper reaches of the gully you left lower down), where a fairly clear path appears (E0347795/N4279669; 1670m), and cross to the L side (**2hrs 45mins**).

A steep bare slope rises above you, a mix of scree and tufted grass. Zigzag up it towards the cave overhang directly above. When you reach it (**3hrs 5mins**; E0347880/N4279593; 1799m) traverse sharply L on a level stony sheep path below a sharp conical peak to the mouth of the hanging valley. Contour along the R flank of this valley to reach the **Nisí** sheepfold in about 30mins (**4hrs**; see Route 3 above). Allow another 1hr 45mins for **Piramídha** (**5hrs 45mins**).

Descent from the Nisí sheepfold to Lázou

Contour northwest, then west along the L flank of the grassy gully that opens beneath the rocky height overlooking the sheepfold. At the mouth of the gully where the stream – probably dry – tips over into a very steep descent there is a scattered stand of fir trees. Do not go down into the gully. Maintain your level and bear sharply L and south round the end of the rocky height. Follow the sheep path along the contour until your reach the cave overhang (about **50mins** from Nisí).

From the cave make your way down the R flank of the gully beneath and cross over (**1hr 5mins**) to the L flank. Descend down the middle of the grassy clearing between the trees. Approaching the bottom end of the clearing, make your way to the R and down towards the bank of the stream gully below R, and follow that down. After roughly 30mins come to the remains of terrace walls under the trees, and 5mins later to the junction with the Lazórema stream. Follow the L bank of the united streams down to the campsite clearing described above (**1hr 50mins**). It is 1hr 10mins back to Sikiá, reversing the route described above.

Route 5
Link to Mt Vardhoúsia
Sikiá (700m) – Athanásios Dhiákos/
Áno Mousounítsa (1000m)

Walking time:	4–4hrs 30mins
Distance:	17km
Waymarks:	None
Height gain:	300m
Height loss:	100m
Difficulty:	2

Áno (Upper) Mousounítsa (*áno moosooneétsa*), which lies on the east side of the Mórnos valley a little to the north of (and not visible from) Sikiá, is the most accessible base for walks and climbs on Mt Vardhoúsia. Although it is now officially called Athanásios Dhiákos after a nationalist hero of the Greek war of independence (and appears on the map under this name) local people continue to use Áno Mousounítsa.

The simplest way to get to it is by road: a 4hr slog on the tarmac. Turn L at the crossroads 1hr 30mins north of Sikiá (signposted 8km). About 20mins descent brings you to the Daoút bridge over the Mórnos. There follows an hour's steep climb to Káto (Lower) Mousounítsa, where you bear R, and a further hour takes you over a thickly wooded ridge and down to Áno Mousounítsa.

Via the E4 from Daoút bridge
Alternatively, there is a footpath section of the E4 which cuts off about 4km of tarmac. It is fairly well signed with plastic E4 markers as well as black-and-yellow paint blazes, although there is no particularly clear path. It rejoins the road between Káto and Áno Mousounítsa in about 1hr 30mins.

A few metres past the bridge a ramshackle shed sits on the slope R of the road. A grassy track, supported by a concrete wall, leads R below the buildings. There is no indication that this is a footpath, and the start of it is fenced off. Squeeze round the wire and go up the track. It very soon comes to an end past a rotting car and below a ramshackle hut in the trees. A sheet of corrugated iron serves as a gate; step over and continue across the rather steep friable slope in front of you. There is not much of a path to start with.

Very soon you contour along the upper edge of some old fields with the tree-filled course of the river running parallel just below R. Come to the end of the 'field' about 200m past the corrugated iron gate. Turn sharply up L, then L again by an E4 signpost so that you are now heading back in the direction from which you have come, parallel to the river but higher up. The path runs clear between scrubby bushes and stunted oak, crossing the nose of the spur you are going to be climbing all the way to the road. After a few minutes make a sharp R turn and climb a good path through scrub and oak along the R flank of a considerable gully.

Mt Ghióna: view from the west

In about 15mins (**20–25mins**) emerge in the bottom corner of a patch of sloping meadow, known as Kostínga. Bear up the slope at 330°. Towards the top R corner there are signposts and E4 markers (E0344267/N4283966; 768m). Here the gradient increases; climb steeply up the nose of a gritty spur among scattered trees. The path – though it hardly deserves the name – follows various rain gullies. Keep your eyes skinned for the markers. The trees thicken as you gain height, sometimes barring your way with fallen trunks. The direction is between 250° and 270°. Emerge onto more open ground where someone has tried to build some log steps up the slope and then, after 25–30mins the gradient eases and you reach a clearing with a signpost (E0343830/N4283954; 920m).

Climbing quite steeply again (E4 diamonds on trees and black-and-yellow paint) come out on the spine of the spur. Keep along the upper R edge of a biggish sloping clearing with a signpost (**1hr 10mins**) and, sticking to the spine of the ridge among the firs, come to the road in about 10mins. Turn R and follow the road into Áno Mousounítsa (**2hrs 10mins**). ▶

For a general idea of what is at stake, stand on the edge of the tiny square by the church in Sikiá and look out northwest across the Mórnos valley. On the far side of the valley – just upstream from the confluence with the Lazórema stream flowing down the broad gully in front of you – there is a very obvious narrow spur whose rocky spine sticks clear of the scrub on its slopes. Above it and in line with its axis, some 1200m from the river at an altitude of around 900m, is a track. If you can get to the track, all you have to do is follow it into Káto Mousounítsa (about **3hrs 30mins**). I think the best way to reach it is by following the R or north flank of the spur. To get to the base of this spur, there is a track from just north of Sikiá which brings you out on the Mórnos river bank.

You can go on to Áno Mousounítsa by road, but an attractive path starts from the track just above the village at E0342450/N4283475. In **20mins** you come to a stream in a glade of juniper and planes and 10mins later reach the top of the ridge, still in the forest (**4hrs**), with a fine view back to Ghióna. Another 15mins brings you out on the tarmac. Turn L; the houses of Áno Mousounítsa are visible R. The advance buttresses and screes of Kórakas (2495m), Vardhoúsia's highest peak, rise above you. In 5mins you enter the village (**4hrs 20mins**).

Cross-country to Káto Mousounítsa
I have not done this route for many years and there is no path at all for much of the way, but I think it could be worth the attempt – if some rash reader would care to try it for me!

C: MT VARDHOÚSIA

Vardhoúsia: Yidhovoúni from the E4

The Vardhoúsia (*vardhoósya*) massif is one of the most interesting areas for both walker and climber. More than 40 peaks over 2000m are arranged in three groups round a beautiful central area of sloping pastures. Unusually rocky and precipitous, they are a favourite stamping ground for Greek climbers. Kórakas, the highest peak at 2495m, overlooks the village of Áno Mousounítsa. There is a wonderful but arduous ridge walk from Kórakas south to the village of Kouniákos, which we have not done (but would be interested in hearing about). One of the best sections of the E4 crosses the area.

Áno Mousounítsa/Athanásios Dhiákos, on the east flank of the mountain, is the most convenient base. A pretty village, full of planes and sweet chestnuts, it is an oasis of broad-leaved green amid the surrounding firs. The road brings you to the square/*plateéya* with the Ravánis *maghazeé* and a bust of Athanásios Dhiákos, the village's illustrious son, who was roasted alive by the Turks for refusing to renounce his Christian faith.

Location:	Immediately west of Mt Ghióna, and separated from it by the River Mórnos.
Maps:	Anávasi Topo 50 Central Greece, Giona Oeta Vardóusia 1:50 000 and the older edition Vardhoúsia 1:40 000 with handbook.
Bases:	Áno Mousounítsa (Ravánis taverna and rooms, tel: 2265 063214); Artotína (taverna, rooms).
Access:	Daily buses to Lidhoríki from Ámfissa, then taxi to Áno Mousounítsa. Buses to Artotína from Náfpaktos.

Route 6
E4 Traverse: Áno Mousounítsa (1000m)
to Artotína (1200m)

Walking time:	6hrs 15mins
Distance:	20km
Waymarks:	E4 and black-and-yellow flashes (sporadic)
Height gain:	1020m
Height loss:	820m
Difficulty:	3

The route follows the old pre-vehicle 'road' to Artotína. The first objective is the col of Stavrós, the obvious gap in the ridge directly above **Áno Mousounítsa**. The path, marked with standard E4 black-and-yellow signs, begins in a tree-lined gully on the L of the road as you approach from Káto Mousounítsa just before the turning into the *plateéya*. The tarmac ends here, but the continuation of the road also leads to Stavrós. This is the track the shepherds now use; getting a lift should not be difficult.

The path winds up through open firs to meet the shepherds' track just past the remains of old fields at Yiatákia (**40mins**). Turn L on the track and follow it to the first sharp RH bend. Here the path branches off L and zigzags steeply up above a deep stream gully to a grassy level clearing by a small stone shrine (*eekóneesma*) dedicated to Profítis Ilías (**1hr 15mins**: *good campsite*; 1380m). There is a spring in the clearing; should it be dry, there is more water higher up.

Emerging above the treeline, continue on the track for a few metres before heading off L up a grassy spur to rejoin the track on an eastward loop after 30mins. Thereafter stay on the track. Ignore a first L turn (path south up to the refuges) and a short distance later you come to a second: this is **Stavrós** (**2hrs 15mins**). From here, the ground slopes away west and north, reaching its lowest point in the pasture known as Skasméni. There the Kariótiko stream, which rises in these pastures and later becomes the River Evinós or Fídharis (Snake river), plunges into a ravine which leads out of the northwest corner of the massif. This is the route of the E4, contouring round the northern

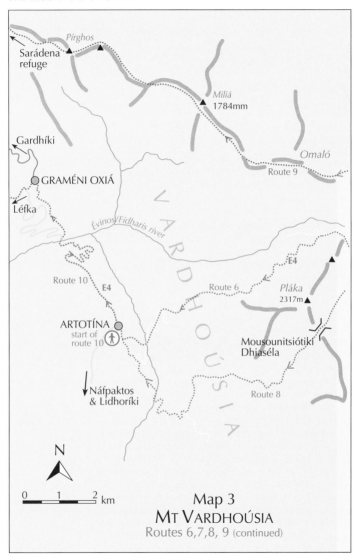

Map 3
Mt VARDHOÚSIA
Routes 6,7,8, 9 (continued)

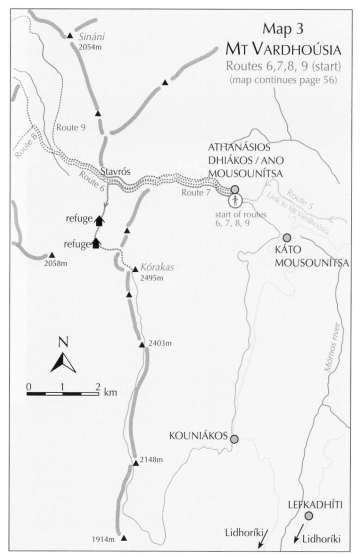

Map 3
MT VARDHOÚSIA
Routes 6,7,8, 9 (start)
(map continues page 56)

Sináni
2054m

Route 9

Route 8

Route 6

Stavrós

refuge

refuge

2058m

Kórakas
2495m

2403m

N

0   1   2 km

2148m

1914m

ATHANÁSIOS
DHIÁKOS / ANO
MOUSOUNÍTSA

Route 7

Route 5

Link to Mt Vardhoúsia

start of routes
6, 7, 8, 9

KÁTO
MOUSOUNÍTSA

Mórnos river

KOUNIÁKOS

LEFKADHÍTI

Lidhoríki   Lidhoríki

*Mt Vardhoúsia:
Kórakas and the
Pittimáliko meadows*

slopes of the Yidhovoúni peak. Facing you to the west across the valley of the infant Evinós is a wall of high peaks, in the middle of which is a very distinctive gap, the col known as the **Mousounitsiótiki Dhiaséla**, an alternative way out to Artotína (see Route 8 below).

From Stavrós, follow the track downhill for about 35mins to the second L fork (E4 sign), where you turn down and cross the river and continue north–northwest on the further slope to the Skasméni sheepfold (**3hrs 10mins**). Stay on the track, gradually losing height, and continue, first north, then bearing west, round the base of the reddish-looking Yidhovoúni peak (Goat Mountain) until, almost directly under the peak itself (E0334750/N4287600), the E4 bears off L in a southwesterly direction on the old footpath (**3hrs 40mins**). Keep bearing southwest (230–240°) along the foot of the crags, in the upper edge of the fir woods and pretty much on the contour, for nearly 1hr until you meet a path bearing diagonally R on a long wooded spur running out west. There is a blue sign at the edge of the clearing as you bear on to this spur (E0331918/N4285775). It indicates Páno Stavrós and a spring further up the ridge L. Bear R at 268°, keeping slightly R of the ridgeline down to the shrine on another col of Stavrós (E0331530/N4286086; 1340m; **4hrs 50mins**).

At the shrine turn down L bearing diagonally R or west along the south-facing flank of the spur. Another 20mins brings you to a clearing where the path climbs again for a short distance, before descending once more and emerging on to open ground. Make for the grassy ridge ahead just below the firs (**5hrs 15mins**). Cross the ridge – Artotína is now in view on the opposite slope of the valley – and bear L, then R down across old grass fields to the track below. Cross over and down to the track again. About 100m R is a primitive old house and sheepfold, permanently inhabited (*water*).

Turn L on the track for a few metres, then down R on a more primitive section, to rejoin the main track on a LH hairpin. Around 200m later, just round the first RH hairpin, double back to the L and down once more to the track. Turn R for 100m and cross one stream (**5hrs 40mins**), then a second. Shortly after turn R on a path climbing a steep bank above the track and make your way up to the village of **Artotína** through abandoned terraces in about 30mins (**6hrs 15mins**).

Route 7
Áno Mousounítsa (1000m) to Kórakas summit (2495m)

Walking time:	4hrs 40mins
Distance:	9.5km
Waymarks:	E4 and black-and-yellow flashes; red paint on latter part of route
Height gain:	1495m
Height loss:	0m
Difficulty:	3
Map:	See Route 6

Follow Route 6 as far as the first col of Stavrós. If you want to follow the track up to the refuges, turn up L here (**2hrs 10mins**). If you prefer to stick to the grass, turn up L at the junction before Stavrós and walk up the rounded spur which leads nearly due south to the refuges. There is a strong spring in the

stream gully just below the first refuge (1960m; **2hrs 35mins**) and another signed just past the second (2000m; **2hrs 45mins**). Both refuges stand right on the crown of the spur dominated by the west flank of Kórakas.

The clearest route to the summit starts from the upper refuge. At the edge of the track below the south end of the building there is a rock with a blob of red paint (E0337308/N4283296; ignore the prominent red arrow which points to a nearby spring).

There does not appear to be any obvious way from here over the rather forbidding rocky ridge above. The crossing point lies at 82° from this rock, not the gap further R. Head up the steepening scree slope at 110° for about 200m, then at 50° towards a rain-scoured channel with big red arrows marked on some rocks. The scree gives way to more solid rock. In the last few minutes step L-wards over a rib of rock and finish the climb in a steepish rocky couloir. It is a very mild scramble with plenty of red paint marks and solid footholds. Emerge after about an hour (**3hrs 45mins**) at the top on the rim of a wide grassy hollow, Méghas Kámbos. The summit is to your R. Cross the intervening hollow on to the ridge and across a narrow rocky bridge to the summit in about 45mins (**4hrs 40mins**), with fantastic views all round and towards the sea to the south.

It takes about 1hr 15mins to return to the refuge.

60

Route 8
Áno Mousounítsa (1000m)
to Mousounitsiótiki Dhiaséla (200m)
to Artotína (1200m)

Walking time:	8hrs
Distance:	23km
Waymarks:	E4 and black-and-yellow flashes as far as Skasméni
Height gain:	1370m
Height loss:	1170m
Difficulty:	3
Map:	See Route 6

Follow Route 6 as far as the sheepfold at Skasméni Stroúnga (**3hrs 10mins**). From here, head southwest up the grassy boulder-dotted slope to the obvious col, the **Mousounitsiótiki Dhiaséla**, between the Pláka peak (R) and the Aloghórakhi peak (L). There is no particular path, but it is a beautiful climb early on a summer's morning with the sun on your back. The turf is springy and soft and full of flowers: pinks, geraniums, *edraianthus*, marsh orchids. In the meadows below flocks of sheep move down to their pens for the morning milking, their bells chiming harmoniously.

From the col (**4hrs 40mins**) you look west down into an enormous cirque which has a flattish grassy floor with a shepherds' hut in the middle. The most impressive of the peaks enclosing the cirque are the four Soúfles off L, honed by the weather into sharp-pointed teeth. The only exit from the ring of peaks is down the narrow ravine of the Vardhousiótiko stream, which flows due west to Artotína.

From the col, bear down L across steep screes, aiming for the shepherds' hut. At the bottom cross two streams and climb a low bank on to the meadows round the sheepfold (**5hrs 40mins**). From the sheepfold a path leads across the meadows into the corner formed by the Vardhousiótiko ravine and the Kostarítsa peak, which closes the western side of the cirque, where it now joins up with a track that descends into the Artotína valley. Although I have not been this way myself for many years, the track, used by shepherds and marked on the Anávasi map, should not present any difficulty. Be careful to turn R on to a more substantial track at around 1400m altitude before dropping down to the river (**7hrs**). It is about an hour from here to Artotína (**8hrs**).

Route 9
Áno Mousounítsa (1000m) to Karpenísi (Rákhes Timfristoú, 1200m): ridge walk via Sarádena refuge (1740m)

This is a tough but superb two- to three-day walk, far from villages. From **Stavrós** (see Route 6) you swing north and west along rocky tops as far as the **Sarádena refuge** (close to the col on the dirt road to Gardhíki above the village of Graméni Oxiá). From there the route heads northwest along grassy rounded tops – more like what the French call *montagnes à vaches* – to the main Lamía–Karpenísi road.

Bad weather has twice prevented me from doing anything more than 2 or 3hrs at the northern/Karpenísi end. The route stays between the 1600 and 2000m contours, pretty much on the watershed. There are some markers – occasional red paint and stone cairns – although there is no real path. Friends say the southern part is trickier, with some navigation problems to avoid precipitous sections, including a bit of a detour at the north end to get on to the col below the Sarádena refuge. It is perhaps not a route for the fainthearted, but there is no doubt that it is much the most satisfying way of getting to Karpenísi, avoiding all the road work now entailed by following the E4.

Some waypoints in WGS84

1	Stavrós	E22° 07.964'/N38° 42.043'
2	Cheesemaker	E22° 07.475'/N38° 42.212'
3	Track	E22° 07.033'/N38° 43.569'
4	Col	E22° 06.298'/N38° 44.371'
5	Col	E22° 04.331'/N38° 44.632'
6	Summit 1614m	E22° 01.695'/N38° 46.07'
7	Summit 1730m	E22° 01.076'/N38° 45.996'

8 Summit 1713m	E21° 59.808′/N38° 46.380′
9 Gardhíki – Graméni	
Oxiá road col	E21° 59.158′/N38° 46.325′
10 Sarádena refuge	E21° 58.872′/N38° 46.245′
11 Sarádena 1923m	E21° 56.786′/N38° 46.991′
12 Track	E21° 56.737′/N38° 47.419′
13 Track junction	E21° 56.373′/N38° 48.348′
14 Track	E21° 54.929′/N38° 49.770′
15 Col	E21° 53.973′/N38° 50.306′
16 Trig point 1664m	E21° 53.356′/N38° 51.372′
17 On to track	E21° 52.905′/N38° 51.593′
18 Junction with road	E21° 52.267′/N38° 51.998′
19 Rákhes Timfristoú	E21° 52.884′/N38° 53.301′

One possibility – easier than doing the entire ridge from Stavrós – is to follow Routes 8 or 9 to Artotína. Continue on the E4 (see below) to Graméni Oxiá, and then climb the dirt road (6km) to the col. The refuge (*locked*) is 500m up the track that climbs L from the col. At the upper limit of wonderful beech forest, it makes a great campsite, with spectacular views of the Vardhoúsia massif. If its spring is not running, the nearest water source is a roadside spring 300–400m on the east/Gardhíki side of the col. ▷

Gardhíki is 20km away, so getting out this way is difficult. There is some traffic in summer, so a lift is possible.

Sarádena refuge to Rákhes Timfristoú road

Walking time:	8hrs
Distance:	20km
Waymarks:	Occasional cairns
Height gain:	556m
Height loss:	625m
Difficulty:	3

From the refuge the route heads west to **Sarádena** peak, the highest point, veers north to **Aloghovoún**i, then keeps steadily northwest. On a clear day you can see it unfolding far ahead. For much of the way there are shepherds' tracks below to the west.

When you reach the **Kokália** peak (E0316822/N4301585; 1715m) towards the northern end, bear 300° down across

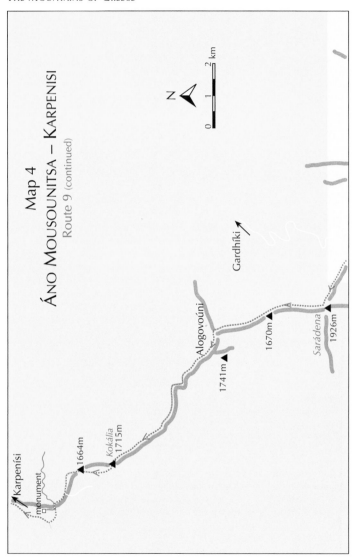

Map 4
ÁNO MOUSOUNITSA – KARPENISI
Route 9 (continued)

Karpenísi

monument

1664m

Kokália
1715m

1741m

Alogovoúni

1670m

Sarádena
1926m

Gardhíki

N

0 1 2 km

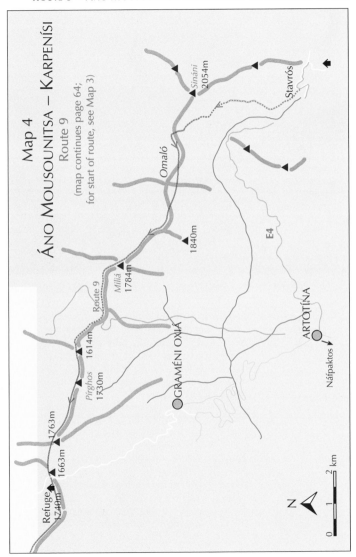

Map 4
ÁNO MOUSOUNÍTSA – KARPENÍSI
Route 9

(map continues page 64; for start of route, see Map 3)

Mt Vardhoúsia, seen from Oxiá ridge

grassy meadows to a mast, then 320° to a rounded peak with a stone cairn (E0316698/N4302657; 1663m; 20mins). The conical peak of Mt Veloúkhi above the town of Karpenísi is right ahead to the northwest. Cut straight down the grassy slope (faint vehicle tracks) in front at 330°, passing various stone shelters built by shepherds. Cross a bulldozed track and keep on down to meet it again.

The track veers L; keep straight on down, following the faint vehicle tracks, and bear L at 220° to join a lower track. Turn L down to a low grassy col (E0316025/N4303177; 1464m) 30mins from the last peak. There is a stone shepherds' hut to the L. Bear up R on a broad grassy ridge to a wooden drinking trough and spring. Bear 295° over open grass on a faint track among juniper and young firs to reach a concrete cattle trough (8mins). Here the track bears 350° through firs and L down to a spring and stone pillar commemorating a victory over Celtic invaders in 278BC (5mins).

Route 10
E4 link: Artotína to
Karpenísi and Ágrafa

Maps:	Anávasi Topo 50 Central Greece, Giona Oeta Vardousia 1:50 000 covers Artotína to Graméni Oxiá, and Topo 100 Evritanía 1:100 000 Mandhriní to Karpenísi.

The greater part of this journey used to be along footpath or, at worst, little-used dirt road. Now much of it is tarmac, and very little footpath. It still traverses, however, very remote and beautiful country, so some may feel it is still worth walking. The remaining sections of footpath are waymarked in characteristically capricious style and marked on the Anávasi map. They should be passable, although very likely rather overgrown. I have not walked some of them for many years, so cannot vouch for the state of the paths.

Here is a summary of what to expect:

Artotína (1200m) – Graméni Oxiá (1100m) 10.5km, 3hrs
Tarmac and path.
Tarmac to the Fídharis river bridge (**1hr 50mins**). Path on the other side to Graméni Oxiá (*food and accommodation in summer*).

Graméni Oxiá (1100m) – Léfka (1000m) 6.5km, 1hr 30mins
Tarmac.

Léfka (1000m) – Mandhriní (1000m) 6km, 1hr 15mins
Tarmac ends in Léfka, dirt road thereafter.

Mandhriní (1000m) – Ámbliani (1150m) 6km, 2hrs 15mins
Dirt road and path.

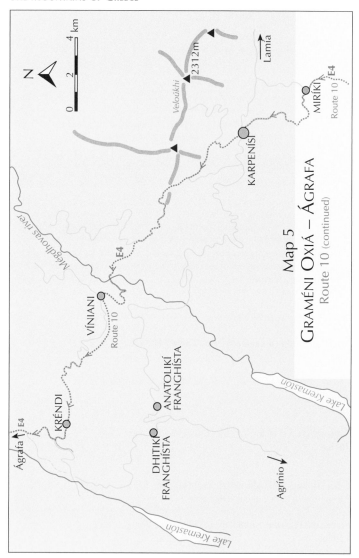

Map 5
GRAMÉNI OXIÁ – ÁGRAFA
Route 10 (continued)

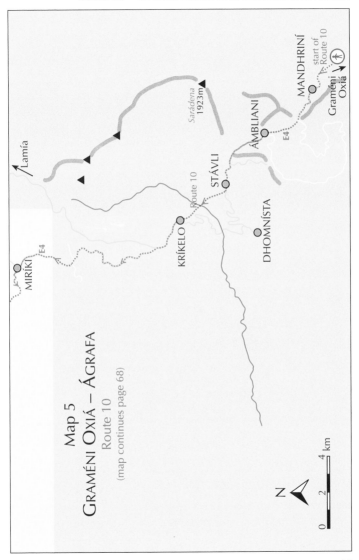

Map 5
GRAMÉNI OXIÁ – ÁGRAFA
Route 10
(map continues page 68)

MANDHRINÍ

start of
Route 10

Graméni
Oxiá

ÁMBLIANI

E4

Sarádena
1923m

STÁVLI

Route 10

DHOMNÍSTA

KRÍKELO

Lamía

MIRÍKI

E4

N

0   2   4 km

Beyond Mandhriní the road is suitable only for high-wheel-based vehicles. Follow it down to the Kapsalórema river (800m). Just after the river crossing – where the track enters a tunnel of greenery and crosses a tributary stream – an E4 sign (**45mins**) in the bank marks the start of a path climbing R (north–north-west) up the flank of a spur. This passes the chapel of Áyios Yiánnis in a clump of fir trees at the top of the spur at **1hr 40mins** and runs on to Ámbliani (*food and accommodation in summer*).

Ámbliani (1150m) – Stávli (1200m) 7km, 2hrs 30mins
Tarmac and path.
A section of E4 path cuts over the Paliókhano ridge northwest of Ámbliani to rejoin the main road about 3km short of Stávli. Used to be well signposted (*summertime accommodation in Stávli*).

Stávli (1200m) – Kríkelo (1100) 5km, 2hrs
Path and track.
From a corner of the Ámbliani road a path cuts down to the Krikelopótamos river and continues over the other side on a combination of track and path to Kríkelo village (*tavernas, shops, accommodation; buses to Karpenísi*).

Kríkelo (1100m) – Karpenísi (1000m) 18km, 6hrs 30mins
Tarmac, dirt road, E4 path.
Tarmac to the Sigrélo turning (on top of the ridge **50mins** along the Karpenísi road). Branch L on a dirt road, then R at **1hr 25mins** up to the col west of Pírghos (E0310794/N4302279, 1325m; **3hrs 30mins**; 10km from the tarmac, mostly contouring through fir forest), where a black-and-yellow arrow on a derelict tin shrine by a derelict tin hut marks the start of the path down to Miríki, visible below on the opposite side of the valley (**5hrs**). Head downhill at 350°. There are E4 signs but you need to keep your eyes open; the path is not very clear.

After 15mins (E0311091/N4303015, 1195m), the path disappears; bear R and cross a stream, then turn sharp L and downhill again 15m up the opposite bank. At E0311221/N4303213 (25mins), cross another stream by a big plane tree intertwined with a fir. At E0311129/N4303625, hit a dirt track and follow it to the R for 150m before turning off it to the L (E4 signs) and

Graméni Oxiá

descending to a big sloping meadow (40mins), with Miríki straight ahead. Keep along the upper (LH) edge of the meadow, cross a further track and bear L down the RH edge of open grass to the bridge in the bottom. From Miríki, follow the dirt road via Kallithéa all the way to Karpenísi (*hotels, shops, banks*).

Karpenísi – Kerasokhóri/Ágrafa 25km, approx 7hrs 30mins

Three sections of footpath survive (see Anávasi map Evritanía) accounting for perhaps a little over half the distance. The rest is roadwalking.

D: MT ÍTI

Mt Íti (2150m) forms the northern apex of a triangle of massifs with its neighbours Ghióna and Vardhoúsia. Its south-facing slopes are rounded and rise quite gently from the valleys that separate the three. On the north side, by contrast, it drops dramatically into the fertile valley of the River Sperkhiós. In ancient times the route from northern Greece squeezed between the sea and the foot of the mountains here via the pass of Thermopylae, made famous by the last stand of Leonidas. In 480BC, with 300 Spartans, Leonidas fought to the death to keep the Persians from penetrating any further into Greece.

The upper reaches of the mountain consist of two extensive forest-ringed grassy plateaux at Katavóthra and Lïvadhiés, which support a mass of crocuses in May, so dense you cannot avoid treading on them. The classic hike is the complete traverse from Pávliani in the southeast to Ipáti in the northwest. The advantage of this route is that you ascend by the gentler gradients and descend by the steepest. The disadvantage is that much of the south-side route now follows dirt tracks and ends with a section in thick forest where the path has almost completely disappeared. This is the route I have described and it can be linked up with a traverse of neighbouring Ghióna or Vardhoúsia, at the expense of, nowadays, pounding road or track for a few kilometres.

The best link with Ghióna and Vardhoúsia used to be through the village of Pirá on the south side of Íti, but I can no longer find the path. A possible compromise could be the rough forest track that climbs up to the Katavóthra plateau. It is not marked on the 2002 edition of the Anávasi map, but begins just to the east of Pirá village at E0349492/N4289774 and joins the track ringing the south side of the summit at E0349723/N4292102 at around 1620m (about 3hrs on foot).

The route from Ipáti on the north side is dramatic and much easier to find. If you are not wedded to the idea of a traverse, it makes sense to go up and down this way.

Location:	200km northwest of Athens, overlooking the valley of the River Sperkhiós and the town of Lamía.
Maps:	Anávasi Topo 50 Central Greece, Giona Oeta Vardousia 1:50,000.
Bases:	Lamía is a sizeable town with all amenities. The villages of Ipáti, Pávliani, Kaloskopí and Mavrolithári have accommodation and restaurants.

| **Refuge:** | At Trápeza (1750m) below the Grevenó peak. |
| **Access:** | Regular bus and train service from Athens to Lamía. Frequent buses from Lamía to Ipáti on the north side. The south-side villages of Pávliani and Kaloskopí are served only infrequently. Best to take a train to Amfíklea, Káto Tithoréa or Livadhiá, and then a taxi. |

By train from Athens

The train journey from Athens is worth making for the dramatic descent from the plain of Viotía to Lamía. The narrow-gauge line, built originally by British engineers, threads its way through some amazing defiles and gorges before emerging above the Sperkhiós valley on a precarious ledge of rock. On the way you cross the Gorghopótamos viaduct which was blown up in November 1942 by a combined force of British saboteurs and Greek Resistance fighters. The purpose of the sabotage was to disrupt German supplies to Rommel's Afrika Corps in North Africa, which came down that little track.

The village of Brálos, which overlooks the beginning of the gorges, was the scene of a brief stand by British and Commonwealth troops against the rapidly advancing Germans in 1941. They were quickly overwhelmed, an event recalled by the older inhabitants of the village. There is a British and Commonwealth military cemetery.

Route 11
Íti Traverse: Pávliani to Ipáti

Stage 1 – Pávliani (900m) – Katavóthra (1500m) – Pírghos summit (2150m)

Walking time:	5–6hrs
Distance:	12km
Waymarks:	Sporadic red paint
Height gain:	1250m
Height loss:	0m
Difficulty:	3

Map 6
MT ÍTI
Route 11

The route starts with a fairly gentle climb up through the trees on the south side of the mountain and out on to the extensive meadows of the Katavóthra plateau where local farmers run their cows and sheep in summer. The waymarking is amateurish but adequate, and the route is not used much any more. A track leads across the plateau without any real need for waymarking, but where you meet the trees on the northwestern rim you run into serious navigation problems. The path has more or less vanished through neglect, and you have to be on constant lookout for the next plastic ribbon hanging in the trees. It is do-able, but requires determination. A pity, because it was a fine route.

Take the rough track heading north (R) from the upper edge of **Pávliani** village for about 1km to the junction with a secondary track at E0355373/N4290147 (**15mins**) that cuts sharply back L and uphill. Red paint marks the start of the path (not very clear) as it turns up L above this junction and into the firs. Make your way up through old terraces with walnut trees on to the secondary track, and turn R until you come to a cattle trough (*poteéstra*) on the L. There is a red paint mark on the concrete side of the trough.

Leave the track and bear up L into the trees, with the track below R. Rejoin the track (**25mins**) and continue uphill for 10mins. Leave the track and head up L by red paint on a rock. In 10mins hit the track again, coming up from your R (**45mins**). A red arrow on a tree opposite points L. Go L up the track, here enclosed by firs.

About 5mins later leave the track and turn R across an open grassy space (red paint on a rock in the grass; E0354616/N4291110). At the top of the knoll ahead keep straight on and up (paint marks; E0354347/N4291306) until you hit the track again (coming from your L now; **1hr 10mins**). Cross over and continue (stone cairns) over open grassy ground, passing a shepherds' hut L, until you rejoin the track. Follow it, heading west, for about 10mins, until it takes a 90° turn to the R (E0353785/N4291389).

On the crown of this bend (red paint), leave the track and go straight up the bank ahead (west: the same direction in which you have been travelling). The stony line of the old path is visible. You are on open ground: the trees of the forest are to your L. The path winds up bearing gradually R towards more trees, then L up to the open skyline and a slight saddle. Bear

Mt Iti: Pírghos summit from Katavóthra

L down into a gully and R up the other side to a second small col. A couple of minutes later, past a lone juniper tree, come to a third col with two or three obvious heaps of stones. Ahead is a marked depression. Pass along its RH edge and up to the further rim about 40m L of a prominent rock outcrop (**1hr 40mins**), with a view west across a wide plateau with the Pírghos peak in the distance at 300°.

Bear L on to the start of a faint vehicle track in the grass; follow it until you get your first glimpse of the main track below R. Cut down the shallow gully leading to it and join it by a concrete culvert with a red paint mark (E0352503/N4291281; **1hr 50mins**). Turn R on the track and stay on it for about 400m to a fork. Take the L branch and cross the plateau in a north-westerly direction, climbing slightly, then descending slightly. The R fork passes the **Katavóthra** sinkhole (which gives its name to the plateau) after 1km, continues to the Livadhiés plateau and spring in 12km, and on to the refuge in another 1.5km.

After about 45mins (**2hrs 40mins**) cross the Riniórema stream and take the R fork to the north–northwest (where the main track loops sharply L or south and continues eventually to the village of Mavrolithári). Head up this beautiful level grassy valley bottom close to the stream for about 500m until stream and road divide (E0350119/N4293438). There is a red mark on a tree by the stream. Take the L fork and follow the track across open grass, keeping close to the small stream on your R, for about 200m to where the track enters the first fir trees (**3hrs 30mins**).

From the point where the trees begin, leave the faint track (which continues bearing L-wards) and follow the true R bank of the little stream on your R upstream for about 100m. Cross the stream, heading diagonally R through fairly open trees to a faint stony track and then, almost immediately, to an indistinct grassy track. Turn L, and after 50m or so you should see the first waymarks (E0349727/N4293758), which here are ribbon-like strips of faded red-and-white plastic tied to the branches of trees.

The route (now only sporadically what you could call a path) heads northwest, up an overgrown slope on to a spur, bears R up the spur, then L and subsequently R along the L flank of a further spur with a stream gully below L.

The path bears west across the head of the stream gully at approximately E0349450/N4294500 and 1800m altitude. A further 30mins brings you clear of the trees, with another 30min climb over open ground to the summit of **Pírghos** (**5hrs 15mins**).

Stage 2 – *Pírghos (2150m) – Trápeza refuge (1750m)*

Walking time:	1hr 40mins
Distance:	6km
Waymarks:	None
Height gain:	0m
Height loss:	400m
Difficulty:	2

Northeast of Pírghos – and some way off across the intervening meadows – lies the Grevenó peak (2116m) with the Trápeza refuge below its northwest corner, reached through a narrow defile on the far side of the furthest expanse of meadow. The route lies along the track on the far side of the valley ahead, through the dark belt of trees in the middle distance and across the meadow beyond.

From the top of **Pírghos** aim north straight for the track, keeping along the ridge or slightly R of it, reaching it in about about 30mins (E0348489/N4296793; 1929m). There is a cairn and a shrine built in the form of a church. Turn R and follow the rough winding track through scattered firs for about 35mins (**1hr 5mins**) to a crossroads with a signpost erected by the monastery of Agathónos, which lies on the northwest flank of the mountain. About 100m to the R is a copious spring, *ee vreésee too kalóyeroo* (the monk's spring), overlooking the head of a deep valley running out east. A few minutes further along the main track there is another junction with a clump of firs on a slight rise L, a picnic area and another copious spring in a stone shelter. This is Livadhiés, a favourite campsite, with wide grassy meadows all around and the Grevenó peak in front. The R branch of the track leads back to Katavóthra, the L to the refuge.

Turn L and follow the track north through the defile beside the stream that rises at Livadhiés. As you emerge from the defile the refuge comes into view ahead on the flat top of a rocky shoulder, where the stream swings R and plunges into a ravine below Grevenó. A short side track cuts back R and down to the **Trápeza refuge** at **1hr 40mins**.

It is a beautiful spot and there is plenty of room to camp on the grassy ground round about. There are two springs in the gully behind the refuge. Facing the near end of the building, turn sharply back L and down the side of the gully. You will see the path. The first spring dries up, but there is a second permanent one 50m further on in the trees.

Stage 3 – *Trápeza refuge (1750m) – Ipáti (450m)*

Walking time:	3hrs 5mins
Distance:	8km
Waymarks:	Red paint (inconsistent)
Height gain:	0m
Height loss:	1300m
Difficulty:	3

From the refuge climb back to the track and follow it down to the R for 600–700m where it enters a series of zigzags. The old path, marked with red paint, cuts off the corners. It doesn't matter if you miss the first section, but try not to miss the second. The path cuts down L just past the second RH hairpin (E0349593/N4299784), heading northwest to rejoin the track at E0349326/N4300160 (**25mins**).

Either cross straight over, bearing L and down again, to join a secondary track just above the Perdhikóvrisi spring (*perdheekóvreesee* – partridge spring), or turn L on the main track for a few paces to reach the beginning of the secondary track, which doubles back R and downhill for 200m to the same spot (E0349264/N4300258). Here there is a National Park sign, with a red arrow pointing L and a red diamond on the opposite bank of the track for those coming up. (Carrying straight on along the main track will bring you eventually to the village of Kastaniá.)

Bear L off the track. The Perdhikóvrisi spring is 10m down on the L. The path leads down an open grassy gully among scattered trees. In less than 5mins, at a tree marked with a red square, bear R along the R flank of the gully (regular splashes of red paint). Another 10mins bring you to the edge of a patch of open boggy ground, where the path becomes unclear. Keep along the RH edge of the boggy patch, then follow red paint marks bearing R through young firs down along a black PVC pipe into and across a stream gully. Continue up the opposite bank to the edge of the wide tree-circled meadow of Amaliólaka (*amalyólaka;* **1hr**), named after the first queen of modern Greece – another beautiful campsite. There is water a few minutes further down the path at the *amalyóvreesee* spring. The path keeps along the L edge of the meadow before turning down the R flank of a deepening gully into the trees to the beautiful walled and shady spring.

A further 5mins below the spring the path emerges on to an open slope where you can see ahead for the first time to the mouth of the ravine developing on your L and the flat land in the bottom of the Sperkhiós river valley beyond. Descend across an open shaly spur (E0348572/N4301107; **1hr 25mins**) and re-enter the woods.

Thereafter it is plain sailing, down through the trees with the ravine L till you emerge into a small ridgeline clearing (E0347570/N4301739; **2hrs 10mins**). Bear diagonally R for

This is by far the most dramatic and beautiful hiking route on the mountain, and all but the first 30mins is unspoilt by the intrusion of roads.

40m, then turn R between two prickly oak bushes adorned with blue plastic ribbons. Head straight downhill for 80–100m, ignoring further blue ribbons in the trees L, until you hit a faint and disused track (red paint on a stone; spring 50m up the track R under a lone fir tree). Turn L on the track and down to a sharp LH bend with a hut L and an old rotting green car (E0347415/N4301833). Leave the track here and turn down R at 284° (red paint on a boulder). After 20 paces bear R at 344° down a grassy slope to a big conspicuous plane tree standing on the bank of a stream (**2hrs 25mins**).

Cross the stream by the plane tree and bear down across the sloping grass, first at 280°, then 263°, to the edge of a steeper section of old terraced walnut grove. Bear down across these terraces at 330° and into the fir trees at the bottom corner on a well-worn, groove-like path, bearing R-handed. The path skirts briefly along the edge of grassy ground just clear of the trees. Another 10mins brings you to the end of the groove-like section of path and you emerge on to a rocky shoulder overlooking the plain below (**2hrs 40mins**). The ravine you have been following debouches into the plain in a grey gravelly riverbed below L. To the R you look down on the castle hill or *kástro* of Ipáti.

The way winds down through slabby rocks, then traverses R on a broad path to the base of the *kástro* (**2hrs 50mins**). There are overgrown fields L and a line of small plane trees. A water pipe runs beside the path. Around 5mins later you reach the end of a concrete lane at the upper limit of the village and turn down L by a ramshackle animal shed. Keep L at the first fork and down into the street called Elénis Roúska. Follow the tarmac (red paint blobs) and turn L at the phone booth with a straight run downhill to the village square in **Ipáti** (**3hrs 5mins**).

From Ipáti to Trapeza refuge Take the street leading directly up towards the *kástro* from the square. At the top turn R and keep R. Do not turn up to the L between the houses after 15m; this route is also marked with red paint. You must pass to the R of the castle hill. Going up it takes about **4hrs 30mins** to reach the refuge.

Links to Ghióna and Vardhoúsia

Linking Íti to Ghióna and Vardhoúsia involves a fair mileage of roadwalking. The most direct way would be through the

Descent towards Ipáti

villages of Pirá and Strómi. You will see from the Anávasi map that two paths head south from Strómi to join up with shepherds' tracks leading to Ghióna, and just to the west of Strómi you can pick up a section of the E4 which leads to Vardhoúsia.

CHAPTER 2

ÁGRAFA

Ágrafa is a region in the southern Píndhos so rugged and remote that in Turkish times – and probably earlier – it did not feature on the tax collectors' registers; hence the name, meaning 'the unwritten places'. Over the centuries its inaccessible villages have provided a haven for many thousands of Greeks fleeing the persecution of the more controllable plains, evolving an important culture and economy of their own. Vrangianá, for example, was home to one of modern Greece's first 'universities,' while in 1800 Ágrafa produced almost as much sheep's wool as the Peloponnese, a region 10 times its size, as well as silk, gold, silver, swords and gunpowder.

Now, of course, the plains are safe again and the Ágrafa has lost its *raison d'être*. As in so much of mountain Greece, villages number only a handful of elderly residents. Ironically, as depopulation has intensified, the region has become less and less 'unwritten'; dirt roads link the villages, maps have appeared, and there is even a small hydroelectric plant outside Monastiráki.

Yet however uncertain the area's cultural future may be, its peaks and gorges remain as unassailable and beautiful as ever. Any trip through the region will reward you with a rare sense of wilderness and simplicity, not to mention special human encounters. But it will need careful planning; there is neither public transport nor metalled roads, no shops beyond the occasional *maghazeé*, and of the three mobile phone networks only Cosmote offers a patchy signal.

I have outlined three ways of tackling the Ágrafa. The most comfortable – if you have your own vehicle – is to base yourself in Epininá and/or Ágrafa and make day hikes out of there. Another possibility is to drive to either village and do a two- or three-day circular walk, camping en route. But the most authentic approach – which also lends itself to the use of public transport – is a six- to eight-day traverse of the whole region, starting from Lake Kremastón in the southwest and finishing at Lake Plastíras in the northeast.

Location:	The mountainous area between Karpenísi in the south and the latitude of the Thessalian town of Kardhítsa in the north.
Maps:	Anávasi Topo 50 Agrafa Mts 1:50 000 and Topo 50 Northern Agrafa Plastira Lake 1:50 000.
Bases:	Karpenísi (all amenities); Dhitikí Franghísta, Kréndis, Monastiráki, Epininá (rooms, tavernas); Ágrafa (hotels, tavernas, post office); Vrangianá (basic *maghazeé*); Lake Plastíras (several hotels).

Access:	Daily buses from Athens to Karpenísi. Onward connections to Kréndis or Franghísta. Also daily service from Agrínio to Karpenísi via Dhitikí Franghísta. Departure at end of route by local bus from Moúkha or Belokomíti to Kardhítsa.

Route 12
Lake-to-Lake Traverse: Kremastón to Plastíras (5–8 days)

This route takes in the region's most impressive gorges, some of its finest mule paths and a wonderful 2000m peak. It is a varied and satisfying way of crossing one of Greece's remotest regions on foot.

Stage 1 – *Lake Kremastón (300m) – Monastiráki (650m)*

Walking time:	5hrs
Distance:	19km
Waymarks:	None
Height gain:	900m
Height loss:	550m
Difficulty:	2

This is a gentle, unspectacular 19km hike along minor dirt roads – a good way to break yourself in. If you want to lose a day, this is the one to drop: take transport (hitch or pay a man with a van) along the main valley road to the point 1km after the junction below Monastiráki, where you pick up the 'dirt-road route' at the start of Stage 2 (1hr point).

From Kréndis/Dhitikí Franghísta, take a taxi or hitch the 6km/11km west to the Krionéri bridge across the Agrafiótis river, at the northwesternmost end of Lake Kremastón. Just after the bridge

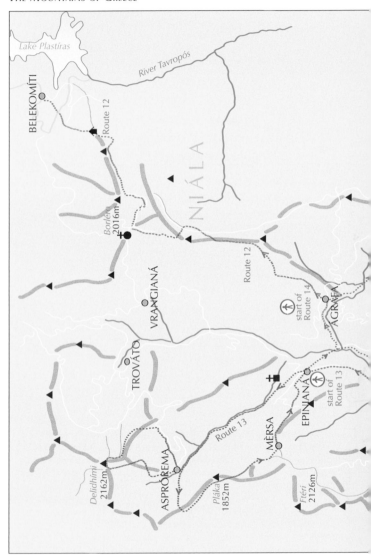

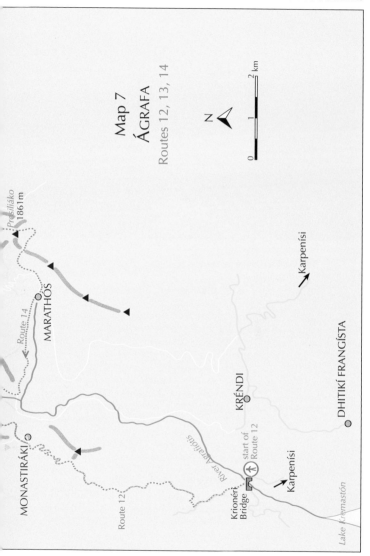

Map 7
ÁGRAFA
Routes 12, 13, 14

N

0 1 2 km

Profíliáko
1861m

MARATHÓS

Route 14

Karpenísi

MONASTIRÁKI

River Agraliótis

Route 12

KRÉNDI

start of
Route 12

DHITIKÍ FRANGÍSTA

Karpenísi

Krionéri
Bridge

Lake Kremastón

Lake Kremastón

(but before the petrol station) take a small track up to the R, signed Ayía Kiriakí and Metókhi.

After 1km (**15mins**), by the huts of Stronghiló, keep L (not towards Áyia Kiriakí and Metókhi). Approaching Áyios Prokópios village you may be able to cut up R and rejoin the track by a shrine. Otherwise, continue into the village (**30mins**) and turn R towards Paliokátouna. Just after the shrine fork L (not along the well-worn road to the empty monastery of Áyios Ioánni) and follow the track uphill, keeping R among the sparse stone ruins of Paliokátouna (**1hr 40mins**). At the ridge (**2hrs 10mins**) ignore the R turn down to Kefalóvriso (Síkhniko), but take the next R, zigzagging up past a fork (keep R) to cross the 1150m saddle (**3hrs 10mins**) west of Piramídha summit, locally called Neroútsiko. It is a stiff but rewarding 30min climb up to the 1305m trig point, keeping along and then R of the spine on small goat trails. From the top you can see much of the 2000m horseshoe ridge surrounding the Agrafiótis valley, as well as Lake Kremastón glinting to the southwest. ◀

Not far from here is the cave used as a hideout by Katsantónis, hero of the Greek war of independence against the Turks.

From the saddle (**4hrs**, including summit ascent), the track – currently impassable for vehicles – zigzags down towards the now-visible hamlet of Monastiráki. At a RH hairpin ignore a new track branching L (west) to the pastures of Áyios Nikólaos. After an hour cross a steep-sided gully on a narrow bridge

(**5hrs**), then contour round to cross a second stream on a new bridge. A 3min walk above this are the astonishingly vigorous springs which power the small hydroelectric plant further down the valley. A final climb brings you into **Monastiráki** proper (**5 hrs 15mins**), with the tin hut *maghazeé* of Khrístos Bakoyiánnis on the L by a plane tree.

The Bakoyiánnises may be able to accommodate three or four guests (tel: 22370 95221), and Khrístos can usually take bags on to Epinianá.

Stage 2 – *Monastiráki (650m) – Apátito gorge (600m) – Epinianá (950m)*

Walking time:	5–6hrs via dirt-road route; add about 1hr for Likórakhi variant, plus 1–2hrs for Apátito gorge excursion
Distance:	11km road route (without gorge)
Waymarks:	Sporadic red dots (first section over Likórakhi only)
Height gain:	500m (road route)
Height loss:	200m (road route)
Difficulty:	3

A tough day, with small paths in the morning, the breathtaking Apátito gorge in the middle of the day, and a hot but panoramic ascent thereafter. The first section, from Monastiráki to the *mandrí* (goat pens) of Makrí Kámbi, can be done either along a dirt road (shorter and safer) or along a little-used path over Likórakhi ridge (prettier but longer and perhaps impassable). If in doubt take the dirt road to ensure you have time and energy for the Apátito gorge.

Follow the dirt road down southeast from Monastiráki to where it joins the main Agrafiótis dirt road (2.5km) and keep L (north) at the junction. Almost exactly 1km after this junction turn sharp L up a dirt track, which bends R and climbs, offering views over Karvasarás hamlet and bridge. After 1.8km you come to the massive animal pen of Makrí Kámbi (**1hr 30mins**).

Variant: the Likórakhi route
From the Bakoyiánnis *maghazeé* in Monastiráki, follow the paved path passing above the hut, climbing gently east. Pass

to the L of the church of the Panayía (Virgin Mary) and continue north up a steepening cobbled path, covered with debris from the crumbling houses. After **15mins**, at a circular stone wall below the red-roofed chapel of Profítis Ilías, turn R across terraces to intercept the jeep track to Vlakhopoúla (Ftéri). Follow this to the R (downhill) for 150m, then fork L up to a makeshift tin goat pen. Go round to the L of this and from behind it cut across kermes oaks to intercept a path climbing east. It is steep and loose-stoned, but it should be passable (sporadic red paint blobs). After 15mins it bears L and passes a rocky outcrop on the R – do not be tempted R, but fork L and uphill, climbing scree-covered slopes with your back to the outcrop.

At **45mins** crest a grassy saddle with Kalóyeros peak looming ahead. Continue straight down (patch of rusting fence R) into the woods, descending steadily north (red dots). Cross a dry gully and climb through a gap between tooth-shaped rocks, before resuming a steady easterly (then northerly) descent through prickly oak woods. Approaching the larger, boulder-choked gully of Koufalórema (*water until July*), the path may need careful negotiation. It resumes on the far bank from a huge plane tree, accompanied by a water hose.

At the terraced fields (**1hr 35mins**), drop one level and contour L. Provided you have chosen the right level, at the end of the fields a small path (fading dots) leads L into a second, dry gully, then climbs steeply. Keep L (uphill) and within 15mins you should crest the ridge by two derelict houses (**2hrs**). From here paths and goat trails continue, initially down the spur, then bearing L, to deposit you at the overgrazed terraces and makeshift pens of Makrí Kámbi (**2hrs 20mins**).

From Makrí Kámbi pass below the lowest pen and, where the track peters out, continue along a descending path. Cross a gully and climb to traverse a huge *sára* (scree slope: liable to washouts). After negotiating some more gullies, curl L-wards around a blue metal shrine and descend. Just before reaching river level (**45mins** from Makrí Kámbi), keep R (downhill) to meet a disused jeep track (see Apátito gorge variant below). The path opposite continues to a lovely arched stone bridge across the Ftéris stream, by its junction with the Agrafiótis. Above and opposite are the abandoned houses of Anifóra (locally called Tsórtia), a scattered settlement once large enough to warrant a primary school.

Variant: Apátito gorge (1–2hrs)

Turn L along the ex-jeep track and, where it hits the river, head upstream. The route crosses the river numerous times. The track turns into a path up the east (true L) bank. After just over 1km (**30mins**), at a L bend in the river with a seasonal trickle joining R, the main stream ahead seems to emerge from a cave, in fact the exit of a gorge so narrow that it appears completely dark and closed overhead.

Only possible June–October. You have to swim; it is also best to wear boots or shoes you can wade in.

It is possible, with care, to swim and wade upstream through this *apátito* (untrodden) gorge. The water is extremely cold. After the initial cavernous pool there are a few small waterfalls up which you have to scramble (good foot- and handholds) before it levels out. After 15–30mins the gorge opens out into a secret valley, with possible bathing spots and patchy sunlight until early afternoon. I have never been much further upstream, as it is slow and overgrown, but it may be possible to continue as far as a disused concrete bridge on the extremely overgrown trail which used to link Anifóra with Plataniás, the lowest settlement of Vlakhopoúla (Ftéri). Return the same way.

To continue to Epinianá follow the path north over the arched stone bridge (500m; **2hrs 20mins**, assuming dirt-road route and no Apátito trip). You may need to negotiate some anti-goat fencing. The path ascends just R of a spur, then crosses to the LH side, passing above a recently abandoned house (Tsamboúria). Just beyond this a tiny path leads down (L) to a spring. Continue uphill, and just after passing below two stone huts on the R turn sharp R (straight on continues to the northernmost houses of Anifóra).

Snake dining on trout in the Apátito gorge (photo Michael Cullen)

Climb steadily through dappled oak shade on a clear, well-graded path. At a broad, open patch the path veers R (the support wall stands out against the rust-coloured stone shards), then L again a few minutes later. At **3hrs 15mins** pass crumbling walls on the LH side and the path bends L. A few minutes later hop up L to a ruined house with threshing floors and great views – a good rest spot after an hour of climbing. Looking northwest you can see firs breaking the skyline like propped-up matchsticks – this is the saddle between Koroúna (rounded hump L) and Sfendámi (knobbly peak R) which is crossed on the Asprórema circuit (see Route 13).

Continuing along the path, bear L after 2mins up to the crest. Ahead lies a steep, rocky spur which you need to climb, passing some defunct telephone poles, before veering R at its top. There is an old path but it is covered in loose rocks and not always clear. It starts just R of the spurline, zigzags once, then clambers up the stony slope before bearing L of the spurline. Some collapsed stone walls make the going uncomfortable. It then switches back and forth up the spur – look out for old sections of supporting wall – before finally bearing R to pass just above the ruined stone hut once known as Élatos (fir) or Agnándi (viewpoint) (**4hrs**). Enjoy the fabulous views over the Apátito gorge – if you didn't make the detour you'll wish you had.

A couple of minutes later pass through a crude gate (1050m) and the ascent is over. The path descends gently northeast, with a steep drop R straight down to the Agrafiótis narrows known as the Trípa, then climbs gently to reach a dirt track. This leads north, offering easy walking past terraced fields and a powerful walled spring L. Ágrafa village comes into view R, with flat-topped Karnópi (1970m) behind. At **4hrs 40mins** ignore the small track forking L up to the chapel of Áyii Anáryiri. The track curves L, then R to reach **Epinianá** about **5hrs 10mins** from Monastiráki.

Epinianá is a strange but functional place, with a lifeless central square and incongruous new summer houses dotted about, all set against the serrated backdrop of Mt Delidhími's outliers. There is one pension-cum-taverna, the Panórama (Kóstas Gatzóudhis, tel: 22370 93212/22370 94122; mobile: 6972 330058).

Stage 3 – Epinianá (950m) –
Ágrafa (800m) via the Trípa gorge (550m)

Walking time:	3hrs 30mins
Distance:	9km (including Trípa gorge)
Waymarks:	None
Height gain:	250m
Height loss:	400m
Difficulty:	2

This is a short and somewhat retrograde stage from the point of view of the complete traverse. Moreover, the initial descent is via a tricky little path, and the final ascent a slightly tedious dirt road. But it does allow you to bathe in the Agrafiótis river at the delightful narrows of the Trípa ('hole'), where water cascades down moss-covered rock faces into the turquoise current. Note that wading is unavoidable if you explore the Tripa gorge. You could continue further downriver to the junction with the Ftéris stream; if you are staying in Epinianá this allows you to create a circular day hike, using Stage 2 (from the 2hrs 20min point) to return.

From the Panórama pension head down (east), passing to the L of the house below it and following a rough jeep track which curls R, then L. You can see the Agrafiótis riverbed way down R. Take the smaller track down to a new stone-faced church, follow it L, R, then slightly L. Pass a stone's throw beneath two large chestnut trees. At the gully turn R along a tiny, brambly path on the same side of the gully. It curls R – ignore small paths descending L – and drops through encroaching tunnels of kermes oak and hornbeam. From here onwards beware fallen telephone wires.

Around **25mins** out of Epinianá the path bends R round a slabby spur, then descends past collapsed stone revetments. At the dry streambed continue a little lower down the far bank and along a fir-shaded stretch. Curling R, re-enter scrub-oak country and pass above old fields. The path curves R across a very tricky washout of loose gravel and earth. At the fork keep L (downhill) and at the RH bend (**1hr**) keep R and wiggle down towards the junction of the main Agrafiótis and the tributary gorge from Ágrafa village. After crossing another tricky gully, enter plane groves and traverse down bouldery terrain. At the

Before leaving Epinianá, devote a day or more to exploring the Asprórema valley (see Route 13). One possibility is a day hike to where the path reaches the river on Stage 1.

dirt road, turn L to the river. There is a wooden footbridge or, at your own risk, a rusting *karoúli*, a sort of primitive cable car on a pulley which enabled people to pull themselves across. Don't try to operate it singlehanded or you may get stuck halfway.

Crossing the Agrafiótis below Trídhendro (photo Michael Cullen)

Cross over and take the track past charcoal-burning mounds up to join the main Agrafiótis dirt road by a black metal shrine (**1hr 20mins**), and follow this R (south). After 500m cross the stream draining the Ágrafa village area, and after another 400m the road bends L.

Variant: detour to the Trípa gorge

The narrow walls of the gorge are visible downstream. Just after this LH bend, and 200m before the T-junction, look out for a path descending the steep bank on your R. The path crosses a stream and contours along the L bank of the Agrafiótis about 50m above the bed. There are some washed-out sections but it should remain passable. On the far bank, below the huts of Samári, an impressively humped re-entrant forces the river to make a sharp bend.

After 15mins (**1hr 50mins**) descend to a plane-shaded meadow and follow jeep tracks to the river banks. By a buttress on the L, either start wading downstream or locate a small path threading over the rock and down again 50m further, from where you will inevitably need to wade. The narrows of the Trípa are visible a stone's throw ahead, with water cascading down the mossy cliffs R. It is a magical spot, and well worth exploring further downstream if you have time and energy. Return the same way to the dirt road (**2hrs 25mins**), not forgetting to bear R at the plane-shaded meadow.

At the dirt road turn R and at the T-junction (**2hrs 30mins**) turn L towards Ágrafa. The road climbs, then bears R through the gorge draining the Ágrafa village area. Cross to the true L bank by a watermill, now converted to a café and trout farm. After 3.2km keep L at the junction and follow the road up a series of zigzags into **Ágrafa**. Pass the *dheemarkheéyo* (regional government offices) in the old school on your L to arrive at the central plane tree and *plateéya* (**3hrs 30mins**).

There are a handful of places to eat, and two or three places to stay: Gatís (tel: 22370 93220) and Kítsios (tel: 22370 24082) on the *plateéya* and – most characterful – the home of Níki and Kóstas Komboyánnis at the top of the hill (tel: 22370 93209).

The central and largest of the 20 or so 'unwritten' villages, **Ágrafa** is set on a small plateau at 800m, ringed by mountains. The population has dwindled from over 1000 to around 300 souls, but this is still twice the size of any other settlement in the region and likely to remain that way with the recent creation of a *Dhímos Agráfon* (municipality of the Ágrafa), whose offices now occupy the once-crowded secondary school. It is truly isolated: 3hrs of bumpy dirt road to either Karpenísi or, when the snows have melted, Kardhítsa. There are several chapels, notably the parish church of Áyios Dhimítrios on the edge of the plateau and, higher up, the chapel of the Panayía, which fills with music and feasting on the eve of 15 August. Alongside the simple stone houses are a few incongruous mansions with 'Disneyfied' fortifications, built by those who have escaped to Karpenísi or Athens and made it rich.

Stage 4 – Ágrafa (800m) – Niála ridge (1750m) – Lake Plastíras (Tavropoú, 780m)

Walking time:	8hrs (excluding detours and peaks)
Distance:	19km
Waymarks:	Sporadic and badly placed signposts to Ag Nicolaos and Zigogianeika
Height gain:	1075m
Height loss:	1125m
Difficulty:	3

This exhilarating hike over the northeastern ridge of the Ágrafa horseshoe can be completed in one long summer's day, or broken into two shorter days with a stopover on the ridge (camping) or in the village of Vrangi-aná. There is now a jeep track along the ridge, but it is the most breathtaking of jeep tracks to walk along.

The two-day option would allow you to tackle one or more of the impressive peaks dominating the Niála ridge. Staying in Vrangianá entails losing – and subsequently regaining – around 700m in altitude, but the views back up to Katarakhiás peak are a suitably impressive reward for having climbed it.

Beware the sheepdogs on the Niála ridge!

From the tall plane tree and post office on the village *plateéya*, follow the small lane north (away from the church) and, after the steps, turn R up a steep concrete lane. At the top turn sharp L up a stepped path, past the first sign to Ag Nicolaos and Zigogianeika. The paved path zigzags up to the chapel of the Panayía, behind which a rough track climbs the spur. At the junction of tracks (**20mins**) fork R (sign to Ag Nicolaos).

Pass a shrine on the L astride the old water channel and the new waterworks. Follow the track uphill and at the top turn L (Ag Nicolaos) up a stone-covered path with a fence on your RH side. An easily missed L/R zigzag breaks the gradient, followed by another one before the scree slope. After the scree comes a lovely stone-built section; then you round a spur to see a gendarme of Koukouroúdzos breaking the skyline. After a good 30mins of steady, largely stony ascent, you reach the spring of Granitsióti (**1hr 25mins**, 1350m), also known as the *peeyeé ton kleftón* – the brigands' spring – after the rebel Katsantónis clan (*klephts*) who used to hide out here.

The path continues rather circuitously round the eastern-most spurs of Fourkoúla, Koukouroúdzos' neighbouring summit, before reaching the saddle (*spring, jeep track, twin shrines*) known as Patímata (**2hrs**; 1450m). For an ascent of Fourkoúla/Koukouroúdzos (1hr round trip), turn L (west) here along the spur towards Fourkoúla. You may prefer to climb straight up Fourkoúla and follow the summitline to Koukouroúdzos. The views belie the modest 1720m elevation, especially the serrated western ridge, softened only by the verdant terraces of Trídhendro.

To continue to Niála, head north from the shrine, up the L side of the ridge descending from Toúrla summit. Between two firs, cross to the R side, then, before a scree field, bear L again, past a tentacle-rooted fir, to regain the spur-line at a sandy patch (**2hrs 15mins**). About 5mins later you pass a randomly placed signpost on a saddle and can see the onward path snaking up the western flanks of the Graméni ridge of Niála. It is easier than it looks – a well-graded climb, still used by the Sarakatsan shepherds. Half an hour later you reach the main watershed (1740m) and turn L along the ridgetop track, which you will follow for about an hour.

This whole grassy, theatrical ridge bears the Sarakatsan name of Niála. It is also the name of the largest of three hamlets visible halfway down the eastern slopes (marked as Neraïdha on some maps). The two smaller hamlets (Khaliás and Paliolóka) are now deserted and Neraïdha only has a couple of families in summer. ▶

Every 20 June Sarakatsani shepherds gather here for a ceremony to mark the start of summer grazing.

After 5mins (**3hrs**), by a small side track, you may spot a plaque commemorating a Civil War battle of 12 April 1947. The inscription gives the ridge its name – *graméni* – meaning 'written'. The *emfílios*, as this conflict is called in Greek, still evokes strong passions and the plaque is regularly vandalised by partisan Greek visitors.

About 20mins later pass a L bend with a metal shrine on the R. This is the best starting point for an ascent of Katarakhiás (1hr round trip)**:** follow the shoulder up to the west.

Variant for Vrangianá (2hrs+)

This is also the point to leave the track for the descent to Vrangianá. Climb northwest – no path – to cross the main ridge between Katarakhiás and the next peak to the north. Descend the gully ahead (northwest) to a boulderfield and skirt down its RH edge until a path materialises, dropping northwards to a jeep track (1520m). Turn L along the track to the hut at its southern end (Goúva), just before which you can strike R (northwest), picking the best way down the steep, fir-covered hillside. Around 1300m altitude, bear slightly R and intersect another jeep track, which you follow R, keeping straight (gently downhill) at the two junctions, until you reach the first houses of **Vrangianá**. Here, turn L for the southern hamlet and the Hellenic Museum of Ágrafa (see below); turn R for the upper houses, including Tákis Khrístou's simple *maghazeé*. From the highest houses, a dirt road – different from the one you came in on – climbs eastwards, allowing you to walk back up to rejoin the main route without retracing your steps at all at the col (1600m) and chapel of Áyios Nikólaos, where you take the middle/RH track past the sheepfolds.

For basic food and accommodation in Vrangianá, the old school building is available by prior arrangement with Tákis Khrístou.

In spite of a stunning location, there is something sad about Vrangianá, with its hundreds of decaying houses reminding you of former glories. In the 17th century, Evyénios the Aetolian founded a school-cum-cultural centre here, which expanded to include a formidable library of Greek, Latin and German texts as well as advanced courses in medicine, rhetoric, languages, geometry and maths. It earned the title of first Hellenic University. Its remains are now called the Ellinomouseío Agráfon, though there is not much to see besides the church of Áyios Kosmás, which is usually locked.

To continue from Niála to Lake Plastíras, keep following the high-level jeep track as it climbs and curls R (northeast, then east). Around **4hrs** from Ágrafa, you reach the high point of the route, the 1800m col between Pláka (L) and Flidzáni (R), whose daunting 2000m peaks are cut off from you by a steep wall of loose rock. Continue down the jeep track to the first junction (**4hrs 15mins**). L leads down to the visible *stánes (shepherd huts, spring and possible campsite)*, huddled beneath the mass of Pláka, and on to the 1600m col and chapel of Áyios Nikólaos. Continue R, along a new jeep track, which switches to the RH (east) side of the ridge by another pointlessly located signpost. Below is a beautiful beech forest. Looking back you can see why the easternmost peaks of Flidzáni

bear the name Pénde Pírghi (five towers). (This is the place to start the steep, pathless ascent – 1hr round trip – to the 2016m peak of Borléro.)

Borléro in winter: looking south (photo Michael Cullen)

Continue along the track across the southern scree slopes of Borléro to a LH bend, where Lake Plastíras is visible ahead. Here turn R down an old path, which soon makes a faint L/R zigzag. Behind a beech-clad hump to the north is the monastery of Panayía Pelekití (the stone-sculpted Virgin), huddled under a rock face. Ahead (east) are the peaks of Petaloúdha, the LH one sharp and angular, the RH one smoother and rounded, and between them the cleft in the rocky ridge known as the *pórtes* (gates) of the Ágrafa, through which you will leave the mountains. The path enters mixed fir and beech woods, winding steadily downhill to a grassy saddle (**5 hrs**), where another path joins from the L.

Go straight on up (northeast), past a faded sign, looking for the old path just L of the ridgeline. Where the gradient steepens, the path zigzags up the slope until, approaching the first crags of Petaloúdha, it switches from L to R, threading between boulders and stunted pines. Pass through the dramatic cleft of the *pórtes*, slip briefly through a small, rocky defile before escaping to the L and winding down a cow-dung-spattered trail to the saddle between the Petaloúdha peaks (**5hrs 40mins**). (From here the northerly summit – 1770m – is a very steep but worthwhile 10–15min climb.)

Continue down the LH side of the valley, aiming for a pyramidal hill in the distance with a road girding its base (east–northeast). A seasonal stream appears below (though the presence of cattle means puritabs are advisable). The path climbs briefly between junipers, then turns a corner by a multi-trunked juniper (**6hrs**) where, once again, the lake is spread like a turquoise carpet at your feet. You can make out the red-roofed refuge of Elatákos (small fir) on the spur ahead and the small square pavilion of the *paratiritírio* (viewpoint) further down and R.

Follow the path L, soon forking downhill and into the firs. Some zigzags and cairns help the descent. After 15mins pick up a stony track and follow it east–northeast along the Elatákos spur to the red-roofed wooden hunters' refuge (**6hrs 20mins**). It is generally unlocked; inside are six double bunks. You could camp here, but it is only an hour or so to the first of the hotels that have sprung up along the fringes of the lake.

From the refuge, a path shortcuts north to rejoin the track further down, cutting L again after a RH bend to reach the hamlet of Zigoyanéïka in about 45mins. From here you can apparently follow a newly waymarked M2 path direct to **Belokomíti** (**8hrs**); or you can follow the dirt road down for 2km to the main asphalt road circling the lake (**7hrs 40mins**), where the Ktíma Alonáki hotel is 600m to your R (tel: 24410 93420). Here you can order dinner and, by prior arrangement, the owner will drive you down to Kardhítsa next morning for the price of a taxi. There is also the Panorama guesthouse, tel: 24410 94074, at Moúkha 5km east beyond the dam.

Variant for Belokomíti

Just above the hotel a small track descends northwest for 2km (**25mins**) to cross a branch of the lake (this may be flooded in spring). There a path climbs to the village in a further 15mins (**8hrs 20mins**).

Route 13

Asprórema Circuit
from Epinianá (2–3 days)

This is an exhilarating hike into the heart of the Ágrafa's western ridge, where the mountain scenery is at its wildest and most impressive. The first stage follows a beautiful path through the Asprórema (white river) gorge, ending at the scattered hamlet and valley-head of Asprórema (occupied in summer by a handful of shepherds).

From Asprórema you can make a tough circular day hike to Delidhími (2162m), the highest peak in the Ágrafa, or you can press on with the third stage, returning to Epinianá via the rear of the Pláka ridge – another stunning walk, tricky in places. The passage between Koroúna and the pyramids of Sfendhámi is very gratifying – and also a potential jumping-off point for the ascent of Ftéri peak (2126m, not described). The summer settlements of Mérsa and Apidhiá, passed on the descent to Epinianá, are among the most tranquil and scenic spots in the region.

This route can also be used if you want to leave the Ágrafa to the northwest, towards Spiliá monastery, Anthiró and Aryithéa (see Chapter 3).

Stage 1 – *Epinianá (950m) –*
Asprórema (1100m)

Walking time:	4–5hrs, depending on chosen campsite
Distance:	9km
Waymarks:	None
Height gain:	425m
Height loss:	275m
Difficulty:	3
Map:	See Route 12

This is a short day up the valley of the Asprórema. The stretch from Eklisiá to the junction of the Asprórema river with the Skilórema is the most breathtaking piece of path-building in the Ágrafa. There is a choice of places to camp when you reach the scattered hamlet of Asprórema. I would go for the furthest one, as it reduces the distance back to Epinianá via Pláka, and also catches the morning sun.

From **Epinianá** follow the main road (rough-paved) north out of the village. It becomes a dirt road descending steadily, with views R over the upper Agrafiótis to the crags of Koukouroúdzos behind. At the first RH bend, by signposts on the L to Aspróroma and Farángi, continue in the same direction along a small path into the woods. There are some encroaching kermes oaks, but otherwise it is a lovely path. Around **30mins** into the hike you emerge from a stand of firs at a wayside shrine, with views upstream to the peaks of Salayiáni and across the river to the camouflaged buildings of Stáni monastery, huddled beneath an orange overhang.

This monastery, like many in Greece, was supposedly founded when a shepherd discovered a miraculous icon buried here – in this case, that of the Virgin Mary. It had 'walked' here of its own accord from Amfilokhía on the coast when its original church fell to the Turks. The Virgin's birth is celebrated here on 7–8 September, when crowds gather for a night vigil and festival. You can arrange to visit via the secretary of Epinianá, Kóstas Gatzoúdhis, from the Panórama pension.

After a flat stretch through firs, the descent resumes until you cross a stream tumbling down a striated limestone gully. You may see, draped over the fir branches, the single phone line connecting Aspróroma with the outside world. After another sharp LH bend (**1hr 5mins**) – with a fallen tree and boulder adding an extra obstacle – you can see the meadows of Ekklisiá ahead and 100m higher. In a stand of firs ignore a small path forking R and keep L (up) alongside the telephone wire. At **1hr 30mins** reach a flat meadow with a crumbling stone wall a few metres to your L and the single (invisible from here) house of Ekklisiá further L (*perfect camping ground*).

Go up to the foot of the wall and resume west; the path becomes clearer, descending to cross a roaring, year-round stream on crude stepping-stones. The grassy path contours through lush oak and hornbeam woods dotted with hyacinths and wild strawberries. Look out for red-and-white helleborines in June, and the distinctive red Heldreich's lily in July.

At **1hr 55mins** you reach the start of the stone-built section – not much fun for vertigo-sufferers – with stupendous views over the foaming torrent beneath your feet. Past a shrine on the corner (**2hrs 10mins**), the path becomes a broad ledge

chiselled out of the rock face. After 10mins, a second, rusting shrine signals the end of the tunnelled part, though there is still a washed-out plume of scree to be crossed a moment later.

On the opposite bank, beyond fresh scree spills, you can make out the path toiling up abandoned terraces to cross the saddle to the R of a rocky fang. At a small spur the path winds steeply down L to reach the junction of the Asprórema with its tributary Skilórema (**2hrs 30mins**). The concrete footbridge across the Asprórema lies a further 100m upstream but, at the time of writing, the path has been washed away there, so you will have to take your shoes off and cross the Asprórema wherever it is easiest (thigh-deep in spring).

Once across, continue up the far bank to the bridge, where you have two options. Either keep your wading shoes on and follow the watercourse upstream between the jaws of the fang (only practicable after late June); once out of the cleft, keep to the R (true L) bank. Otherwise, take the old path as follows.

Thread very steeply up towards the fang, keeping the grey scree slope initially on your R; then cross this on a well-made trail, and climb to the very base of the fang-rock. Here turn R

In the Asprórema gorge (photo Michael Cullen)

(overgrown) and wind up past an obsolete telephone pole to the saddle (**2hrs 55mins**). Annoyingly the path now descends – though more gently – passing the moss-covered trunks of evergreen oaks before flattening off slightly. Pass above a field (*passable campsite*) with a fading wooden post pointing vaguely at the Kranoúla spring on the opposite riverbank. The river route joins here.

Soon after you enter a grove of plane trees, cross a side stream and – less clear now – bear L before climbing to 50–100m above river level. Cross another rocky outcrop at a saddle with a fir and stone shrine, then plunge back down to river level and keep a stone's throw from the water. Around **3hrs 40mins** you start to climb R away from the river, up a boulder-strewn gully delta, with only a green metal shrine as a pointer. Pick your way up crumbling terraces and wild-oat-covered meadows to a grassy flat top (*possible campsite*), with a ruined house L and the first seasonally inhabited houses of **Asprórema** visible ahead.

Climb a couple of terraces and resume northwest to reach a second saddle with a pair of ruined houses. Between these a path descends to cross the Tsarkórema stream, which has water all year. Climb to the first inhabited house (**4hrs 15mins**), Sanídha, occupied in summer by María Zarkádha and her family.

Asprórema once had enough families to warrant a primary school, while the older children walked down to Epinianá every day for high school. The Zarkádhas were the last family to quit permanent residence, in 1997. Ironically it was the arrival of the jeep track, aimed at making life easier, which allowed them to up sticks and move to the town of Agrínio on the coast, where the other villagers overwinter. Many still come back to these pastures with their flocks from June to October, when the track over the 1700m Tsoúka Sáka pass is open. But their houses are slowly crumbling, with roofs collapsing under the heavy snows of recent years.

A branch of the jeep track runs just above María's house. Follow it northwest up to the main track. Here the suggested route up Delidhími turns sharp R, following the main track up to the base of Tsoúka Sáka.

If you want to push on to the furthest campsite, continue L/straight (northwest) down the main track. At a tributary stream turn L down a very rough track along the L bank. At the main valley cross the stream and carry on up the delta of debris from the Vriská stream, on a faint track. Where this ends (**4hrs 55mins**) there are flat, grassy patches L for camping, and drinkable water from the Vriská stream 50m further on.

Stage 2 – *Asprórema (1100m) – Delidhími (2162m) – Asprórema (1100m)*

Walking time:	7–8hrs (add 1hr for ascent from the east)
Distance:	13km scrambling; 16km from the east
Waymarks:	None
Height gain:	1062m
Height loss:	1062m
Difficulty:	3

Delidhími is the looming peak to the north of Asprórema, the highest in the Ágrafa, with one of the wildest mountain views in the whole country from its summit. The usual ascent is up the gentle eastern slopes from the village of Trováto. However, there are also two little-known ways up from Asprórema, the first via the jeep track and a steep scramble to the Tsoúka Sáka ridge, the second via a forgotten trail linking Asprórema with the valley of Leondíto to the northwest. Because of the scrambling element, I suggest using the first route up (if it looks too steep, you can always opt out and go round from the gentler east side), and the second route – which is quite hard to find when ascending – for the descent.

From **Asprórema** follow the main jeep track southeast, keeping L to pass above María Zarkádha's house (**30mins** from furthest campsite). There is a slight descent past a wooden signpost on the R, Pros Epinianá (which links to the pair of ruined houses at just over 4hrs on Stage 1), whereupon the track resumes its climb. After a few switchbacks, it climbs broadly west, offering views ahead to the ridge linking pyramidal Baldenísi (or Sínoro, 2032m) and Pláka (1852m), halfway along which is a large screefield.

At a **RH hairpin** (**1hr 15mins**), the view extends northwest to take in the twin bulwarks of Salayiáni, linked by a curving saddle and, further R, your return path, seen as a pair

There is no reliable water en route.

of near-parallel lines descending the lower flanks of point 2062. About 10mins later you pass the hut of Kerasiá (cherry tree) and 5mins after that a wooden sign alerts you – as if you needed it! – to the views southeast. If only the money could be spent on waymarking and improving paths instead.

About 300m before the main col, and 200m after a RH bend, by a makeshift hut R, comes crunch time (**2hrs**). Take a look north to the sharp ridge linking Tsoúka Sáka peak with Delidhími – this is the onward scrambling route. There is no path but you will follow faint goat trails across the scree, then bend back and upwards to hit the skyline by a pointy white boulder. This part, frankly, is not much fun; but once you crest the ridge and follow it northwest it becomes more exhilarating and gradually easier underfoot.

If you do not like the look of the scrambling route, continue along the track to the main col at 1700m, shortcut down to the northeast to rejoin the track and follow it L. Ignore the R fork down to Trováto after 2km or so. After a further 1km, opposite a small track forking R, turn L up a path, keeping the gully on your L, which climbs to the southernmost of the three humps east of point 2162. From the grassy bowl below this hump (1920m) the 2162m summit is a short, simple traverse away.

Variant: the scrambling route

From the makeshift hut, climb the spur (Asimórakhi) northeast towards Tsoúka Sáka for 5mins, then plunge down L to the visible trail across the first scree. At the end of the screefield pick out the best goat trail contouring across the sheer slopes, with Tsoúka Sáka looming up R. After a couple of gullies (passable with care) trend R (uphill) on dwindling trails to a grassy ledge with a multi-trunked hawthorn sapling (**2hrs 30mins**). Below you, disused trails surround the Aspróvrisi (white spring), which gushes out of the rocks and gives its name to the whole valley. Cut back R and climb very steeply up the pathless rock-and-grass slopes, with only cream violas and white narcissi to ease the pain, until you crest the ridge by the pointy white boulder below the first hump northwest of Tsoúka Sáka (**3hrs**).

From here turn northwest along or just below the sharp ridge, which compares with the wilder Lake District edges, proceeding with extreme caution as even large rock slabs may be loose. Look out for rusting lengths of barbed wire, which Trováto shepherds erected to reinforce the natural barrier and keep their flocks on the right side of the mountain. You crest a pointed pinkish summit around **3hrs 30mins** (assuming a slow pace), where onward progress to the temptingly smooth and grassy saddle ahead is barred by a 20m drop of unstable bricks. So follow the ridge R for a couple of minutes to a crude stone barrier, hop over this and follow the tiny trail L to the saddle.

From here it is best to make straight for point 2062 to the west – there is no summit as such, just an elbow in the ridge-line. From there follow the ridge easily north to the 2162m highpoint (**4hrs 15mins**), enjoying superb views all around.

To the south lies the craggy jumble of the Koroúna – Ftéri – Liákoura peaks (passed on Stage 3 of this route), to the west – behind unassailable Salayiáni – the long ridge of the Arta mountains, and to the northwest the great bulk of Tzoumérka and Peristéri with their late snow. To the east is the long, greenish ridge of Niála, dotted with firs and scree patches, and capped by the crags of the Pénde Pírghi, Katarakhiás and Svóni (Marathiás). Mighty Veloúkhi (Timfristós) stands southeast, often wreathed in cloud. In between all these, jagged peaks stretch

Looking south from Delidhími (photo Michael Cullen)

as far as the eye can see, broken by the occasional gleaming strip of a lake. Kestrels hover beneath you, their russet bodies and black wingtips strangely colourful from above.

From the peak, drop west down the steep and treacherous slope of loose rocks and tufty grass to the first saddle (**4hrs 35mins**). You can see the path descending north towards the visible houses of Leondíto, then bearing L to join the jeep track at Lakómata. Your onward path is also visible, traversing the western flanks of point 2062. But do not make straight for it; instead, descend west–southwest for a couple of minutes, then east–southeast until the path materialises heading first southeast, then south. It is not in good shape underfoot, but the general route is clear and rarely steep, so that you can make progress once you get your eye in.

At the first spur (**5hrs**; 1850m), the path is unclear; keep R, descend along the spur for under 5mins, passing between two adjacent boulders and, before the scant remains of a shelter, turn sharp L and pick up the continuation of the path. It contours the southwest flanks of point 2062 at 1800m, passing a spring in the lee of a huge boulder. After a low stone enclosure L, you reach the second spur, south of point 2062. Where this breaks into patchy trees below, you can just make out the onward path. Continue a few minutes down the spur, then turn sharp L, aiming for the remains of an oval stone enclosure. Go through this, keep just R of the ridge, then strike R on a faint, rock-covered path. After a couple of easily missed zigzags you pick up the clear line of the upper path seen on the ascent (at the 1hr 15min mark). This takes you southwest to the 1600m line, where you meet the highest junipers. Here the path bears R, passing below a single stout juniper, then across loose rocks, before descending a steep, gravelly spur softened by clumps of vivid aubretia (**6hrs**).

With the trees and vegetation come some route-finding problems. Aim in the direction of the huge hump of Baldenísi. By a boulder, with thicker forest below, bear R. Note the distinctive block of six walled, unused terraces to the R. At the height of the top terrace, you intercept a clear path coming from the northernmost of Aspróréma's houses. Turn L and, with some difficulty, reach a trio of ruined houses, whose low rectangular walls were visible earlier; this is Sfrí on the HAGS map (**6hrs 35mins**). Just beyond these a small, earthy, gravelly path heads steeply down in the direction of the RH end of Pína screefield, passing beneath low firs. Slide L of a slight spur, following the earthy clumps of cattle imprints. It can barely be called a path, but it should see you intercept the northern end of Asprórema's rough jeep track around **7hrs**. This track may be pushed further up in the future; on the 2003 Anávasi map the track stops short of this point, which is marked by three huts.

Turn L and follow the track southeast. Keep downhill, passing the first seasonally occupied houses known as Zoghéika. Cross the white torrent of the Aspróvrisi. Then, for the southernmost houses of Asprórema (Sanídha and so on), continue straight on; for the westerly part (Vriská, 'furthest campsite' and onward route) turn R down the rough track to the main valley. Cross and continue up the far side until the faint track ends, with the furthest campsite on your L (**7hrs 40mins**, 1000m).

Stage 3 – *Asprórema (1100m) – Pláka ridge (1700m) – Mérsa (1250m) – Epinianá (950m)*

Walking time:	7hrs
Distance:	13km
Waymarks:	None
Height gain:	700m
Height loss:	850m
Difficulty:	3

This is a tiring day, with a steep 700m climb at the start and a tricky traverse along the steep, western slopes of Pláka to follow. The afternoon, however, is delightful, particularly the saddles below Koroúna (possible jumping-off point for the semi-technical climb up this peak or the scramble up Sfendhámi) and the path between the shepherds' settlements of Mérsa and Apidhiá.

From the campsite and track-end mentioned above head west, straight up the steep stream-valley descending from Vriská, keeping between the boulder spill (L) and the craggy slopes (R). As long as the houses of Vriská are inhabited, this small path should be clear. Just above a waterslide cross the stream, briefly climb the far bank, resume parallel to the watercourse, then veer L again, away from the stream and into the woods. At level ground with three grey metal water tanks, continue straight up, past a dead tree, where the path splits. The RH option zigzags steeply up to the tin huts of Vriská.

The LH option climbs more gently, across a gully, to a huge fir and ruin, where it bends R through fir saplings to pass a stone's throw south of the tin huts. Either way, at the height of these huts, pick up a path threading east through young firs, then climbing steadily across red gravelly slopes to a beautiful grassy circle (**50mins**). Turn R, following a small path up the spur, with the odd fallen tree and spiny bush to keep you on your toes.

Under a tall stand of firs (**1hr**), bear R on a small but clear path. You pass more firs, then cross a boulderfield, pass between two firs and – less clear now – continue almost level to the remains of a stone sheep pen. On your L the sheer slabs of Pláka rise above the screefields at its feet. Keep climbing gently northwest; the line of the old path is just visible, but the surface is irregular.

About 50m after passing a fir R whose trunk forks at the base, and 50m before reaching the next rocky ridge (**1hr 45mins**), turn sharp L on a barely discernible trail climbing gently south. It may be worth dropping your pack and scouting. The path passes a dead, erect fir trunk, then rises more steeply to reach the meadows below the boulderfield (**2hrs**). There may be other ways of reaching this point, which is unmarked on the Anávasi map except for a widening of the 1600–1650m contour lines.

The onward path leaves from the top L (south) corner of the boulderfield; it is best to head straight up and then L, taking care in case one of the boulders or slabs wobbles underfoot. The path passes a yellow 'No hunting' sign and then (**2hrs 20mins**) crests the ridge between Baldenísi and Pláka summits, which are respectively 1hr and 1hr 30mins hard scramble (each way) along crumbly limestone edges. Curl L and upwards for a couple of minutes (second yellow sign; 1700m) and pick up a faint trail climbing gently south across grassy ledges. The path – discernible but covered in loose rocks – then crosses stony slopes, aiming eventually for the camel's hump of Sfendhámi, just L of the rocky flanks of Koroúna peak. A couple of washouts demand especial care.

After 50mins you pass below a large, cracked band of rock, then round a hump to the R (west), to reach your first saddle at the head of the Skilórema stream (**3hrs 45mins**). The path continues R of the next hump and descends to a second saddle. You can go either way around the next hump, but L is marginally shorter, starting across rusty gravel, passing R of a pointed boulder, then descending awkwardly to a third saddle.

From the third saddle ignore paths descending R to the summer huts of Paloúkia (unless you want to leave the Ágrafa towards Krevátia/Vasilési, or climb 2126m Ftéri peak) and contour L again, past a stone ruin. Below this is a seasonally occupied hut and year-round spring, a hidden spot if ever there was one. Continue over a fir-shaded spur, with the northerly outliers of unscalable Koroúna R, and on to the next saddle in the western lee of Sfendhámi (**4hrs 30mins**). From up close this 1704m peak looks far steeper than before, but is scramblable. You can just see the tin-roofed hut of Mérsa ahead, with the ranges of Timfristós, Kaliakoúdha and Khelidhóna in the distance.

Continue downhill (southeast), just L of the gullyline, making for a visible stretch of whitish path, then aiming to pass below all but the lowest couple of firs. The path levels off through grass speckled with clover and cranesbill. At **5hrs** pass below a weak, wood-channelled spring and above the hut of Mérsa. Here bear L, uphill. After some seasonal trickles comes an uphill stretch with several stone-edged switchbacks. By **5hrs 30mins** you have crested the ridge and moved to the cooler, fir-shaded northern slopes, following a clear, undulating path eastwards. After some grassy meadows – carpeted with daisies in spring – bear R to intercept a dirt road at a hairpin bend, just below a (hidden) stone threshing floor (**6hrs**). About 5mins up to your R is the panoramic summer hamlet of Apidhiá, whose stone houses have fallen into ruin.

For **Epinianá**, continue L, downhill, along the rather dull dirt road. At the third LH hairpin it is easiest to keep L and then turn R at the next junction, following this road all the way into the village (**7hrs**).

Route 14
Khondéïka/Prosiliáko Circuit
from Ágrafa (1–2 days)

Ágrafa village is bounded to the east by the deep gorge of the Sborórema stream and to the south by a slightly wider, nameless gorge descending from the eastern ridge via Khondéïka hamlet (also called Miála). This latter makes for an exciting and wet gorge circuit, feasible as a day trip from July onwards; before that the water levels are too high to be safe. Keen walkers can continue up to the eastern ridge, climb the peak of Prosiliáko which dominates Ágrafa to the southeast, and then descend past Márathos village to the Agrafiótis valley at Karvasarás. The return is either via Stage 2 of Route 12 or by arrangement with a man called Leonídhas in Ágrafa who will come and fetch you in his pick-up (ask for him in any of the cafés; reasonable price).

Stage 1 – Ágrafa (800m) – Lípa (1000m) – Ágrafa via river gorge

Walking time:	3hrs to Lípa/6–7hrs return to Ágrafa
Distance:	5km to Lípa/9km return to Ágrafa
Waymarks:	None
Height gain:	400m
Height loss:	400m
Difficulty:	2/3
Map:	See Route 12

If you plan to return along the watercourse rather than continue directly over Prosiliákos be prepared for some tricky scrambling, and be prepared to get wet. You may want to ask about water levels before leaving Ágrafa, but bear in mind that most locals consider this kind of escapade crazy and will try to dissuade you whatever the conditions!

From the post office and tall plane tree follow the road south, passing Gatis' pension and the church R. Where the road bends L and uphill, turn R down a steep concrete lane. Continue past a RH bend and at the dirt track turn sharp L, descending in the direction of Prosiliáko with a fence on your RH side.

At the junction (now impassable for vehicles), turn L (uphill) and after 50m fork R down the stony bank to find the old path descending in the same direction. Approaching the scree, the original path zigzags R while a smaller trail continues straight on; either way you reach a concrete bridge over the nameless river just below its confluence with the Sborórema. Follow the dirt road upstream and immediately fork L down a bulldozed track into the plane-shaded streambed. This criss-crosses the stream about 10 times all the way to an iron bridge and larger dirt road (**1hr** – more, if you need to wade). Follow this upstream to the pretty, ramshackle houses of Khondéïka (800m), where one family lives in summer.

A path leads upstream, with the help of wooden foot-bridges and planks, to a tin-and-wood pen under the plane trees. Here locate a trail climbing steeply up the scree-filled gully to the south. It is steep going, but worth it in the long run. After 15mins, at the height of the top switchback in the road opposite, the trail bends L and makes for a rocky spur, passing below a forked fir tree.

It levels off by a shrine, with dramatic views over the ravine of creased and twisted rock folds. The steady ascent then resumes, climbing past a couple of gullies and a metal shrine on a stone-clad bend, to a beautiful stone shrine (**2hrs 10mins**). Here the zigzags steepen before straightening out through a southeasterly tunnel of firs. With the huts and fields of Míkra visible ahead beneath the imposing summit of Prosiliáko, descend across a gully (care needed) to a rudimentary wooden gate. Contour across the fields, then drop to a wider path which leads to the centre of the hamlet (**2hrs 45mins**; 1150m). The newly built chapel of Ayios Kosmás is a lovely place to rest (*festival 24 July; water*). ▶

To continue the route, follow the track contouring east, then north, then east again. Ignore the R fork and descend to the wide, stony, east–west valley on whose southern slopes lie the neglected terraces and houses of **Lípa** (**3hrs 30mins**; 1000m).

Return to Ágrafa by the river gorge

Continue a further 1km along the track to a RH bend (**3hrs 45mins**) and here bear L (west) across the fields of Liksoúri

From Míkra there is a direct route up Prosiliáko (I haven't tried it); look down L along the summit ridge to the small saddle before the first shoulder, where a large cairn marks the way up.

(Louxor on the Anávasi map). At the end of these a small path threads steeply down, L of the spurline, to the confluence of two streams (**4hrs**; 870m). The trail used to cross to the R bank and climb westwards along a tiny path known as a *seérma* (wire), but this is now impassable, so follow the watercourse downstream as best you can. There are several low (1m) waterfalls and one higher one (2–3m) which demands careful scrambling, using hand- and footholds underneath or alongside the falling water. A kilometre or more down the gorge (45–90mins, depending on your progress), you come to the deepest pool – typically chest-high at the edges (might have to swim)– after which it opens out and you soon reach Khondéïka. Follow the same route back into **Ágrafa** (**6–7hrs**).

Stage 2 – Lípa (1000m) – Prosiliáko summit (1861m) – Márathos (900m) – Karvasarás (500m)

Walking time:	8hrs
Distance:	15km
Waymarks:	None
Height gain:	900m
Height loss:	1600m
Difficulty:	3

This route diverges from the circuit above at Lípa (possible campsite on the disused terraces by the stream). It is steep and largely cross-country as far as Márathos, the most unchanged of the Ágrafa villages.

From **Lípa** follow the valley upstream, initially west, then curving south. There are traces of path initially, but soon the forest thins out and you just pick your way up the gravelly banks. At the valley fork (1150m), keep L up the less steep valley, which curls R (south) past the springs of the stream. Around 1550m altitude (**1hr 45mins**) you intersect a rough track. If you turn L, you reach the road that runs along the top of Ágrafa's eastern ridge just south of Fidhóskala (snake ladder) summit; this continues southeast past the foot of Kópsi peak to Mavromáta

(14.5km; keep L at the fork after 6km; bus to Karpenísi, more frequently from Dháfni).

For Prosiliáko, cross straight over the rough track and bear R (southwest) up the grassy flanks to the 1861m summit (**2hrs 45mins**), with its vertiginous drop southwards over the valley of Áyios Dhimítrios. Believe it or not, there is an old trail winding down the apparently sheer flanks to the first saddle along the southwest ridge.

Start by following the summit ridge 500m or so northwest from the trig point, then turn L and pick up the narrow path descending steeply west, just R of a slight gully. It enters patchy firs around 1550m, soon bears L and traverses past a boulder-slope to a very ruined stone hut and a weak spring (Lápata Vrísi; **4hrs**; 1420m). From here the path improves, contouring about 100m below the col, then descending westwards towards Márathos. About 10mins from the ruin it bends R down a spur for a few minutes, before resuming southwest. This pattern is repeated 5mins later. After crossing a gully you are best off keeping L (high), though in any event the going gets stonier,

Karvasarás (photo Michael Cullen)

the path loses its comfy bed of fir needles and you emerge onto crumbling terraces. Slither down to join the dirt road by some tin goat huts about 1km northeast of Márathos and follow it into the village, turning R for the centre (**5hrs 15mins**; 900m; accommodation with Mr Peslís, first house on the R – tel: 22370 95869; Greek only).

Follow the main path through the village, past the bust of the rebel Katsantónis (this is his natal village; major festival every Whitsun) to the church of the Taxiárkhes (wonderful frescoes and iconostasis).

From the church continue west and out of the village, zigzagging down the clear path to a wooden bridge over the stream. This climbs the opposite (R or north) bank up to a metal shrine, then levels off around 850m. At **5hrs 50mins** pass the first ruined houses of Yefiráki, one of Márathos' many former satellite hamlets. Bear R along terraces to cross the little wooden bridge which gives Yefiráki its name, then climb briefly. At the next (dry) valley, the process is repeated.

Around **6hrs 30mins** you hit a jeep track at a hairpin bend; keep L and, after 5mins, keep R/straight, across a gully and up past the terraces of Baroútsa (mismarked on the Anávasi map). The track ends by a prominent oak tree on a spur, with the modern, unlocked chapel of Ayii Anáryiri alongside. Here bear R (uphill) past a ruin, possibly following a hose, then sharp L after less than 5mins to pass a rusting shrine. You are still around the same altitude as Márathos.

After the next spur (**7hrs**) you start to descend, levelling off only to cross a scree-filled gully. The path switchbacks down through shady oak woods, keeping R at a small spur, to reach the highest houses of **Karvasarás**. Keep straight on along the fenced path between houses, then drop 10m to the dirt track, which leads north to join the main Agrafiótis dirt road 1km north of Karvasarás bridge (**8hrs**; 550m).

CHAPTER 3
NORTHERN ÁGRAFA:
DELIDHÍMI TO MESOKHÓRA

Áyii Apóstoli: abandoned fields

This section continues the description of the northward route through the heart of the Píndhos mountains. If the traverse is your main objective you need to pick up the route from the summit of Mt Delidhími (see Route 13, Stage 2).

The nature of the terrain is not significantly different from that of the Ágrafa, yet there is an imperceptible change once you cross the watershed represented by Delidhími. The geometry of valley and ridge remains just as complex, and the region is just as cut off from the world. Yet for all that its identity is less coherent.

Although the tarmac is creeping in from east and west, it is still pretty wild country. There is inevitably a fair amount of roadwalking, but mostly on shepherds' tracks and dirt roads. By way of consolation there is also a dramatic day's walking up the riverbed of the Koumbourianítikos, and the possibility of a long rugged traverse of Alamáno and Khadzí at the Mesokhóra end of the section.

Location:	West of the Thessalian towns of Kardhítsa and Tríkala.
Maps:	Anávasi 1:50 000 Topo 50 Northern Ágrafa and Topo 50 Kóziakas-Avghó; NSSG 1:200 000 sheets Kardhítsis and Trikálon; HAGS 1:50 000, sheets Ágrafa, Mouzakion, Mirofillon.
Bases:	Mouzáki and Píli (hotels, restaurants, shops; last chance to stock up before the mountains); Vlási, Mirófilo (taverna/*maghazeé*); Leondíto, Petrotó, Kalí Kómi, Moskhófito, Polinéri (*maghazeé*); Spiliá monastery (visitors' dorms, plus meals).
Access:	Daily buses from Athens to Tríkala and Kardhítsa and on to Mouzáki for Vlási and Píli for Mesokhóra. The service into the mountains is now infrequent.

Aryithéa

1435m

PETROTÓ

KARYÁ

Route 15

Petrotó

KOUMBOU

N

0   1   2 km

Map 8
DELIDHÍMI – MESOKHÓRA
Route 15 (stages 1 – 4)

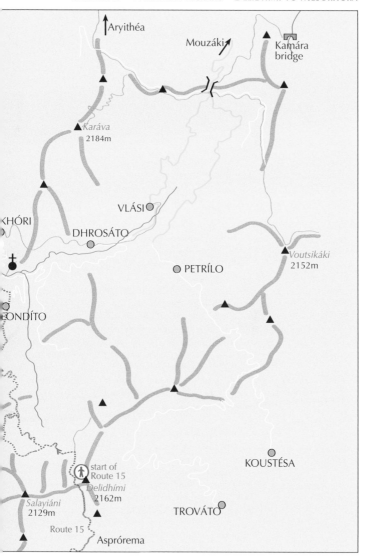

↑Aryithéa

Mouzáki↗

Kamára
bridge

Karáva
2184m

KHÓRI

VLÁSI○

DHROSÁTO

○PETRÍLO

Voutsikáki
2152m

✝

●

○

EONDÍTO

KOUSTÉSA

start of
Route 15
Delidhími
2162m

Salayiáni
2129m

TROVÁTO

Route 15

Asprórema

117

Route 15
Delidhími to Mesokhóra

Stage 1 – *Delidhími (2162m) –*
Leondíto (1000m)

Walking time:	3hrs 30mins
Distance:	11.5km
Waymarks:	None
Height gain:	None
Height loss:	1160m
Difficulty:	2

Access to Delidhími on the north side is from the village of Leondíto; 9km on a rough but beautiful shepherds' track to the last sheepfold at Lakómata, and about 1hr 30mins from there to the col below the summit.

From the summit of **Mt Delidhími**, drop down to the col at about 2000m just to the west. I have not done the descent from the col, but you can see the line of the path with the naked eye. It is also shown on the Anávasi map (with a brief description) descending steeply almost due north, passing a water trough, to meet a clear transverse path (E0288920/N4344500) crossing the grassy slopes between two spurs just below the 1700m contour (estimated time from the col **30–40mins**).

Turn west or L on the transverse path. Cross a dry gully and bear R along the opposite flank, then up and over a sharp little spur, cutting back L down a good rocky path on the west flank to the shallow gully below. Here bear R and down to the shepherds' hut at Lakómata (**1hr**; E0288364/N4344572; 1525m; *spring; campsite*).

From Lakómata there are two possibilities. One is to follow the track, contouring west for 30mins beneath the distinctive horn-like peak of Salayiáni, passing a spring on the L, to a second sheepfold with a solid little cottage on a piece of level ground at the locality known as Méghas Stanós, E0287091/N4346821 (1540m; *possible campsite*). Bear R at the fork shortly after. The track contours north along the slope

for about 600m, before zigzagging precipitously down into the woods at a locality called Niáles. At the bottom zigzag (**2hrs**), a disused track comes in from the gully to your R. **This is the alternative route from Lakómata**, which is followed by leaving the track just after the Lakómata hut and heading north-west down across the bracken-covered slopes to the site of the abandoned hamlet of Ghíka on the spur, where to your L you pick up the end of the disused track to Niáles (saving 20–30mins).

From Niáles, continue down the track to **Leondíto** in about 1hr 30mins (**3hrs 30mins**). ▶

Mt Delidhími (left) and Salayiáni (centre) from the north

Leondíto is a lovely but hardly flourishing little place, with a seasonal *maghazeé* on the square. Road access is from the Koumbourianítikos valley via Vlási and Mouzáki.

Stage 2 – *Leondíto (1000m) – Spiliá monastery (Moní Spiliás; 850m)*

Walking time:	1hr
Distance:	3km
Waymarks:	None
Height gain:	0m
Height loss:	150m
Difficulty:	2

Spiliá monastery

Head north from the square along the road. On the L just past a walled spring and opposite the church (R below the road), a track cuts diagonally up to the L to some houses. Beyond the houses is an area of flat grassy ground, once a field, supported by a stone terrace wall. The path for the monastery of Spiliá follows along below the wall, bearing round to the L/west and into the fir forest. In 2004 it had just been cleared. It is an easy-going route, in and out of small gullies and over intervening spurs, sticking pretty much to the 900–1000m contour except for the last stretch where you descend about 100m into a deeper gully before a steep climb up to the **Spiliá monastery**.

The modern annex is rather an eyesore, but the site and the old buildings sitting atop a sheer-sided crag jutting over the Koumbourianítikos valley are spectacular. There are now a couple of resident monks, so you can ask for accommodation and food.

Variant
The Koumbourianítikos valley: Vlási (1050m) –
Dhrosáto (1100m) – Spiliá monastery (850m)

Walking time:	4hrs 45mins
Distance:	12.5km
Waymarks:	None
Height gain:	350m
Height loss:	550m
Difficulty:	3

Use this route if you are coming into the mountains from Mouzáki. The bus will take you as far as Vlási.

The route follows the deep, enclosed valley of the river, which rises as the Petriliótikos on the slopes of Voutsikáki (2152m) and Karáva (2184m) and becomes the Koumbourianítikos as it flows west. The best walking stretch is between the villages of Dhrosáto and Petrokhóri on the north flank of the valley on a long-disused but fairly clear section of the old mule road. The descent to Petrokhóri, however, has become dangerous; it would be wise to follow the alternative proposed. Voutsikáki and Karáva, both rather rounded and featureless on this side, can be climbed from the Áyios Nikólaos col (see below).

Leave **Vlási** by the road, heading down towards the valley bottom. Just below the last houses a section of E4 cuts across a field (sign in the middle) on an unclear path down to the river and road bridge. Over the bridge turn west on the road (being tarmacked in 2004) and follow it along the narrow fir-clad valley where the river runs between fantastically contorted rock strata to the first RH junction. Here a subsidiary track doubles sharply back R and down to an old stone bridge (**1hr**).

Cross the bridge and continue up the track to the village of **Dhrosáto**. Go through the lower level of the village to the point where the track ends at a chapel (**1hr 30mins**). From here the old path continues along the stony slope covered with prickly oak scrub, contouring or climbing slightly. It is still pretty clear, though no longer used. After crossing two runs of scree the path zigzags up beneath reddish, friable crags to a marked col in the narrow end of a rocky ridge running down off the Spitáki peak to the north (**2hrs 30mins**). This is the highest point of the path (about 1140m) and a great viewpoint. In front of you is the village of Petrokhóri, with the monastery of Spiliá to the west. To the south across the ravine of the Petriliótikos/Koumbourianítikos river you can see up the Leondíto valley to the ridges of Delidhími.

The path continues contouring along the valley flank until it meets the riverbed below Petrokhóri in another 45mins. From here you can either go up into the village or cut L/south across the abandoned terraces below it to meet the dirt road and descend, cutting off the loops, to the Khani Nasióka *maghazeé* back in the Petriliótikos/Koumbourianítikos valley (**3hrs 45mins** by this route).

You need to be very careful on this last section of the route, as nearing the riverbed the path crosses two steep gritty gullies where it has virtually disappeared. You can barely get a foothold, and a fall would be long and unpleasant. According to locals it is safer to descend via the chapel of Profítis Ilías on the ridgeline about 120m beneath the col mentioned above. From here there is a path both to Petrokhóri and down to the Nasióka *maghazeé*, both of which are used by villagers celebrating the saint's feast day on 20 July. To reach the chapel, continue past the col until you can see it, then cut back down to the L through the scrubby trees: it takes about 30mins from chapel to *maghazeé* (**3hrs total**).

From the *maghazée* follow the riverside track west to the bridge, cross to the true L bank and continue, uphill now, to the sharp LH bend where the monastery comes into view (**4hrs**

15mins). Just before the bend a bulldozed track climbs up L on to a scrubby spur, crosses the crown of the spur to the R and leads into the stony bed of the stream descending the long ravine on the east side of the monastery crag. Head up the streambed for about 100m where, at the foot of a plane tree, you can see the remains of the stone revetment that supported the old path. From here you follow the old path zigzagging up past a spring at the top to the **Spiliá monastery** (**4hrs 45mins**).

Additional routes, including ascent of Karáva and Voutsikáki

The road from Mouzáki to Vlási reaches its highest point (1540m) at the col of Áyios Nikólaos, where three worthwhile hiking routes begin. All are marked on the map, although I have not checked them. One – reasonably well signed and described as ecological – leads northeast on the old mule path to the bridge at Kamára in 2hrs. A second – unmarked – heads east, then south on to the narrow summit ridge of Voutsikáki (2152m; 2hrs 15mins), whence you can continue following the long Tébla ridge, ending with a descent to the village of Neráïdha close to Lake Plastíras in a further 3hrs. A third route (marked with red paint) sets off west from the col, following a track through the beech woods for about an hour, joins up with the E4 for a short distance and then heads south on a good path, veering gradually south-west up the bare slopes of Karáva (2184m; 2hrs 30mins). Continuing on the track with the E4 would bring you to Aryithéa in the next valley in about another 2hrs 30mins. In theory the E4 also passes through Vlási. An E4 sign in the village indicates 'Aryithéa 5hrs', but I was unable to find the start of the path, and none of the locals seemed to know about it either.

Stage 3 *– Spiliá monastery (850m) –*
Koumbourianítikos riverbed (550m) –
Petrotó (700m)

Walking time:	5hrs
Distance:	12km
Waymarks:	None
Height gain:	250m
Height loss:	300m
Difficulty:	3

There are two possibilities for this stage. The tedious one – although as always the scenery is beautiful – is to follow the dirt road, which now runs high along the west flank of the Koumbourianítikos valley. The more interesting route (water level permitting) is to follow the riverbed; straightforward when the water is low, but a very different proposition, for example, after a violent night's thunderstorm.

Looking west from the monastery you can see an isolated two-storey house on the ridge of a steep-sided spur at eye level about 2km away. Follow the track from the monastery gate, crossing a gully and keeping L at the only junction (with the 'main road'.) At the house turn off the road to the R. Leaving the house on your L, go down a path which follows the top of the spur. The path is clear until it begins to bear down to the L, descending the L flank of your spur through woods of prickly oak.

At the bottom you come out by a small lake formed in 1963 by a massive landslip. The track (which leads eventually to Petrotó) runs alongside the lake and round its head, where mounds of moraine-like débris hold the water back from spilling into the Koumbourianítikos valley below. Cross over the track at the head of the lake, and keep well over to the L side of the steep stony slopes leading down to the river, to the L of the big steep gully that has opened up. There is no path and it is a bit of a scramble. You reach the river at **1hr**.

Once in the riverbed follow the water downstream on the L bank. When the river is low it is easy going. Even in the narrows – where it is deeper and faster – you can generally make your way round on the bank.

The riverbed is wide, and both banks are lined with plane trees. The valley is deep and traps the heat in the middle of the day; the glare from the white stones is pretty uncomfortable. It is best to make an early start; the bulk of Karáva gives you shade until about 10am. There are few signs of life any more. You see the odd ruined cottage. It is a lonely spot, the sense of isolation heightened by hearing nothing but the sound of the rushing waters. After about 50–60mins the river widens and you feel less enclosed.

At **3hrs** you come to a confluence with a river flowing from the northeast along another wooded gorge, a beautiful spot. Keep L, following the L bank of the combined streams.

Not long after you pass some idyllic summer sheepfolds deep in the shade of the bankside planes.

After 3hrs or more in the riverbed you come to the works area for one of the tunnels for the River Akhelóös diversion project (see below). Leave the riverbed and climb out through the works area on the R bank and up the track to the now tarmac road by a fork (**4hrs 30mins**), where a dirt track climbs steeply uphill to the R for Petrotó. There is a ramshackle but wonderfully friendly *maghazeé* by the fork. **Petrotó**, a pretty and partly derelict old village (**5hrs**), lies 2km up the track. The *maghazée* is on the R on a terrace overlooking the road just past the church.

The River Akhelóös diversion scheme

From the edge of Petrotó you can look down into the start of the finest stretch of gorge in the entire course of the Aspropótamos/Akhelóös river. The landscape has been totally disfigured by engineering work, part of a scheme to dam and harness the waters of the Akhelóös for hydroelectric production and irrigation in the plain of Thessaly. Work has been going on at enormous expense since 1987, in violation of the international RAMSAR convention on wetland conservation and of a Natura 2000 protection order for the fauna and flora of this region. The EU long since withdrew funding, and Greece's own supreme court has more than once ruled the scheme illegal.

The work already completed includes a 180m-high earth dam at Mesokhóra, a hydroelectric plant at Glístra, various tunnels and lines of pylons. For the moment (in 2004) work seems to have stopped. But the worst is still to come: the construction of another dam below Petrotó. This will block the mouth of the gorge, causing the river to back up and form a lake, thus destroying the grandeur of the landscape and flooding the riverside land further upstream. The inspiration for the scheme was clearly political: to secure the votes of the farmers and prosperous towns of the Thessalian plain. But the cost will be the destruction of perhaps the finest stretch of river landscape in the whole country. Protest! Write to your MEP.

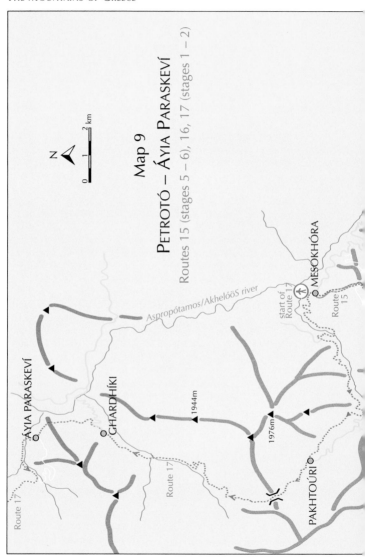

Map 9
PETROTÓ – ÁYIA PARASKEVÍ
Routes 15 (stages 5 – 6), 16, 17 (stages 1 – 2)

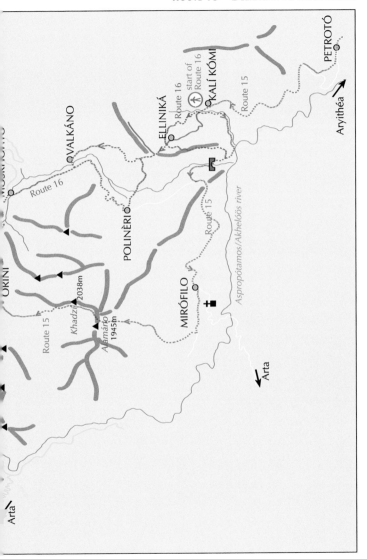

Stage 4 – *Petrotó (700m) – Kalí Kómi (600m)*

Walking time:	3hrs
Distance:	10km
Waymarks:	None
Height gain:	100m
Height loss:	200m
Difficulty:	2

The only section of path that survives leads up to the little col above **Petrotó**, cutting off the westward loop in the road. Carry on up the cobbled lane/*kaldereémee* by the *maghazeé*. There is a stone shrine as big as a bus shelter just over the col. In front of you the ground drops away into the deep winding gorge of the Aspropótamos. On the opposite flank you can see the beautiful little Séltsou monastery. Once on the road it is a 3hr tramp to Kalí Kómi. From the last col – by a recent mobile phone mast – you look down into a surprisingly lush and very enclosed little valley. The last section of the old path began here on the R of the road and led down to the shrine at the entrance to the rather scattered village of **Kalí Kómi** (**3hrs**). If it is overgrown (I did not attempt it in 2004), you will have to follow the loops of the road.

The road to Kalí Kómi

For the *maghazeé*, continue straight along the road from the first houses towards the church. There are no shops or accommodation in Kalí Kómi. If in need of any help, ask for Dhimítris Kotsónis and mention Tim's name.

Side trip from Kalí Kómi

There is a lovely walk down through the over-arching canyon formed by the Armatolíki – the Kalí Kómi stream – into the Akhelóös gorge (**30–40mins**), with some wonderful deep pools for swimming. There is an even narrower canyon, Váïna, a short distance downstream on the same bank of the Akhelóös, by which you can return to Kalí Kómi. When you come out of the narrow stretch of the defile, scramble up the valley side through overgrown fields to rejoin the dirt road just before the last col above Kalí Kómi.

Stage 5 – *Kalí Kómi (600m) – Paliokámara bridge (480m) – Mirófilo (740m)*

Walking time:	3hrs 30mins–4hrs
Distance:	11km
Waymarks:	None
Height gain:	580m
Height loss:	460m
Difficulty:	3
Map:	See Routes 15/16

It is possible to walk from Kalí Kómi over into the next tributary valley to the west, head up that tributary stream for a short distance, and then climb up west through a locality marked as Khirólaka on the map to join the Polinéri – Mirófilo road. It is a bit of a scramble as there is no longer a clear path, but it remains much the shortest route to Mirófilo. Also, linked up with a traverse from Mirófilo over Alamáno and Khadzí, it makes a demanding but much more interesting continuation of the route to Mesokhóra. The more direct route through Elliniká, Valkáno or Polinéri, and Moskhófito is practically all roadwalking.

From the point where the Armatolíki stream joins the Akhelóös (see sidetrip above), turn R upstream on the R bank (true L) for

The Akhelóös river

a few hundred metres to where a wooded spur bars the way ahead, pushing the river out to the L. Make your way up the flank of this spur to a small saddle just back from the rocky bluff that terminates it, known variously as Kástro or Áyia Karakounisíou after a long-vanished monastery.

Here you cross the end of the now-faint trail coming down off the spur from the village of **Elliniká**, Kalí Kómi's neighbour. Cut down to the Polinéri stream as best you can and head upstream for a short distance until you come to what is possibly the oldest bridge in Greece (AD1241, according to my researches), arching across the narrows between rocky crags (**35mins**). It lay on the long-vanished 'road' from Árta in the west to Tríkala in the plain of Thessaly. You may have to wade here. Keep upstream on the true L bank (R to your line of march) until the true R bank is clear, then cross over.

Make your way upstream through overgrown riverside meadows and fields for about 1km (20–25mins), then begin to climb L up towards the Polinéri – Mirófilo road which contours along the slopes about 400m higher up. Aim to reach it about 500m north of the 90° bend to the west (E0273527/N4360830; 924m, **2hrs**), where a steep scrubby spur runs down to the river. There is a goat pen and a patch of stony open ground about 30mins below the road. Turn L and follow the road into **Mirófilo** (about 6km; **3hrs 30mins–4hrs**).

An alternative (which I have never taken) – if you cannot find the route up through Khirólaka – would be to keep following the true R bank of the river until you reach the end of a still-clear path climbing gradually up to the village of Polinéri – with, of course, a longer walk on the road to get back to Mirófilo.

The road leads into the central core of **Mirófilo** where there are two or three *maghazyá* close to the *plateéya*, where the village's dynamic president (*próedhros*) Yiórgos Ráptis has his offices. He does not speak English, but will go out of his way to help if you make yourself known to him and mention Tim's name.

In 1945, after Greece's liberation from German occupation, this *plateéya* witnessed an event that perhaps changed the post-war history of the country. The decapitated head of Aris Veloukhiótis – Communist leader of Greece's biggest wartime Resistance movement – was displayed here by the government-sponsored bands that had ambushed him in the Fángos ravine on the opposite side of the

Aspropótamos. Full-blown Civil War broke out not long after, and lasted until 1950. Had he lived, Greece might have ended up behind the Iron Curtain like its Balkan neighbours.

One thing not to be missed in Mirófilo is the 14th-century monastery of Áyios Yióryios 30mins down the road towards the Aspropótamos, which here re-emerges from its gorges.

Stage 6 – Mirófilo (740m) – Vromerí (1900m) – Mesokhóra (850m)

Walking time:	6hrs 20mins
Distance:	15km
Waymarks:	Signposts and paint blazes from Khadzí onwards
Height gain:	1150m
Height loss:	700m
Difficulty:	3
Map:	See Routes 15/16

Mirófilo's summertime shepherd population mostly keep their flocks on the southern slopes of Mt Khadzí in the area known as Alamáno, about 3hrs from the village.

From the *plateéya* follow the concrete road west, and bear up R at the fork shortly after. It becomes a rough track which contours along beneath the steep mountainside for about 1km to a plane-shaded stream gully where a concrete ramp forks uphill to the R. Turn up here and follow the track up into the mouth of the ravine coming down from Alamáno. Where the track peters out beneath a steep rock section (**1hr 30mins–2hrs**), the old path continues up the R flank of the ravine and into the grassy cwm where the sheepfolds lie beneath the 1900m Vromerí ridge (**about 3hrs**). Aim to hit the ridge just east of the 1945m high point.

At your feet a deep valley opens up, bounded on the north side by a sharp rocky ridge with the path to Mesokhóra

heading clearly north. Drop down into the valley, heading for the intermediate ridge at E0268849/N4365757 (1674m), reached in 30–40mins (**3hrs 40mins**). About 5mins later you come to a signed fork in the path (E0268843/N4365908, 1668m). Back to the R one branch leads up, into and round the scree cirque that leads to the obvious col below the sharp 2038m peak of Khadzí towering above R (about 1hr to the top; red paint). Straight ahead leads to Mesokhóra.

Keep along the spine of a grassy ridge, with a gully R separating you from the western scree slope of Khadzí. Another 15mins brings you a first small col, a further 5mins to a second, opposite the end of the main Khadzí ridge to your R (**4hrs**; E0268860/N4366650, 1598m). There is a red diamond sign on the bump L. Continue north, traversing across the grassy east-facing slopes in front of you; be careful not to lose too much height. There are black-and-yellow paint blazes as well as signposts.

After 50mins (**4hrs 50mins**), at a col leading to the northwest side of the ridge, turn R down the ridge to a lone tree (3mins) just above a lower col where a shepherds' track passes. Bear 30° up the grassy ridge ahead to the top of the knoll (red diamond; E0269220/N4368075, 1464m) and continue along the spine of the ridge. At **5hrs 10mins** reach a prominent stone

Khadzí summit to left, Vromerí ridge centre background

133

cairn (E0269654/N4369016, 1416m) with a fallen 'To Khadzí' signpost. Continue down the now broad ridge known as Malórakhi just slightly west of north for another 20mins until you come down to a track at E0269789/N4370014 (1230m). Here turn R and continue down to a crossroads by a shrine at Stavrós. A signpost points south back to 'Khadzí 4hrs 15mins', and north down a path following the west flank of the ridge in front to join a track that leads past the village cemetery into **Mesokhóra (6hrs 20mins)**.

There is a new *maghazeé* in the centre of the village run by Spíros Kokális (tel: 24340 31200). He speaks a little English and will do his best to help you out with accommodation or any other problems. He is one of a new breed of younger men choosing to return to village life.

Route 16
Delidhími to Mesokhóra: Alternative route from Kalí Kómi – Mesokhóra

Stage 1 – *Kalí Kómi (600m)* – *Elliniká (900m)*

Walking time:	1hr 30mins
Distance:	4km
Waymarks:	None
Height gain:	340m
Height loss:	80m
Difficulty:	3
Map:	See Route 15

These villages are about as far from the modern world as it is possible to get in Greece today. They lie at the innermost end of the slowly shrinking network of the earliest dirt roads. It is far from unpleasant to follow the road up to Elliniká, but the path still exists and it is worth making the effort to find it.

Follow the dirt road past the *maghazeé* and down to the river. Cross the bridge. The road bears R. At the first sharp L bend (5mins from the bridge), by a red-roofed house R, keep straight ahead on a small track, signed Armatolíki. You come to a chapel. Ignore the track to the L; continue past the chapel and into the bed of the stream that flows down from Elliniká. Cross over and turn L up the R (true L) bank. The path is no longer clear. Keep close to the stream at first, only working uphill R after 5–10mins. The path meanders through scrub, past an ancient shrine and up a collapsed, partly subsided slope on to the spur that forms the R flank of the stream gully. There are still a couple of inhabited cottages among the trees (**45mins**). (If you climb up from the streambed too soon you will reach some open 'fields' on top of the spur. Keep north up the spur, rounding a copse by the R. Bearing back to the L and slightly downhill, you will come to these same cottages.)

The remains of a wide, well-made *kaldereémee* lead up to touch the edge of a track by an inhabited cottage and sheepfold. The path continues uphill to the L of the track. Cross it once, then immediately again, continuing uphill, bearing L, then R, passing a modern chapel on the L (**1hr 10mins**). The first houses are visible ahead. You come out on the track once more and follow it into the village by the church and *maghazeé* (**1hr 30mins**).

Side trip from Elliniká to Karakounisíou/Paliokámara bridge

Walking time:	2hrs (one way)
Distance:	4.5km
Waymarks:	None
Height gain:	70m
Height loss:	550m
Difficulty:	3

Continue on up the road from Ellíniká for about 10mins. On the crown of a RH bend you come to a blue Leader sign ('Karakounisíou Bridge 8km'), announcing the allocation of EU funds for the restoration of this ancient bridge. The project, needless to say, has never been completed.

The old road to Paliokámara bridge

Rather than walk along the track (which branches L here) it is possible to find the old path. It begins on the R about 100m from the start of the track and winds diagonally L up on to the ridge, from where you look down on the village of Polinéri and the Khirólaka locality (through which you need to pass if you take the variant for Mirófilo).

Keep along the ridgeline, or just below to the L. Much of it is a scratchy sheep path now, leading gradually down to a conspicuous telephone mast. Cross to the R (west) side of the ridge and keep descending diagonally L. Sections of old cobbles are still visible. Gradually the path peters out and you have to cut down to the messy end of the new Leader track. Keep down L into the trees from the end of the track, passing some ruined houses. Stay on the ridgeline as far as possible – or slightly L – until you reach the *kástro* where the old monastery is supposed to have been. Cut down R to the river and back upstream a few hundred metres to the bridge (**2hrs**). To continue to Mirófilo, see Route 15, Stage 5.

Stage 2 – *Elliniká (900m) – Valkáno (700m) – Moskhófito (800m), by road*

Walking time:	3hrs
Distance:	9.6km
Waymarks:	None
Height gain:	360m
Height loss:	460m
Difficulty:	2

Apart from the first 30mins above Elliniká this is all dirt road, although the section between the Mavrovoúni col and Valkáno is no longer regularly maintained.

From the church continue along the road for a short distance, then take the path R between the first two houses on the R (*water as you climb clear of the top of the village*). The path sticks closely to the foot of the stony slopes of Mavrovoúni, with a gully L. The road is also over to the L. After about **30mins** rejoin the road at a distinct col at 1160m, where a kind of natural amphitheatre opens ahead, leading down L into the Aréndas river valley below Polinéri. The dirt road continues, contouring round the head of this amphitheatre to another col exactly opposite, where the long winding descent to Valkáno begins (**1hr 45mins**). The tarmac starts here. Cross the river by the bridge just below the village and turn R at the junction with the Polinéri – Moskhófito road. Follow this all the way to **Moskhófito (3hrs)**.

Variant: Elliniká (900m) – Moskhófito (800m), via Polinéri (800m)

Walking time:	2hrs 15mins
Distance:	4.5km
Waymarks:	None
Height gain:	460m
Height loss:	520m
Difficulty:	3

On the greater part of this route – from the Mavrovoúni col to the river below Polinéri – the going is rough and the path unclear, although the general direction is not; you can see your destination.

The route is the same as Stage 2 as far as the Mavrovoúni col above **Elliniká (30mins)**.

A stream rises in the grassy amphitheatre that opens below the col. A path runs down to it, following a line of telephone poles. There is a spring. Turn L downhill, following the L bank of the stream as far as a ruined cottage under the trees. Just below this cross to the R bank of the stream. The path winds quite steeply down the stony, slabby slope of the peak known as Korfoúla that closes the RH side of the gully. Keep fairly low down, close to the stream. The path is scarcely used any more.

There is a rocky spur above R. Where the stream gully begins to open out below this spur, the path traverses R to the first tree (about 30mins from the col; **1hr**). It continues R towards the R edge of this spur, where it winds more directly downhill among scrubby hornbeam and what are clearly remnants of cultivated land. Keep descending, with the deepening stream gully well to your L, until you reach the edge of a big reddish landslip. Polinéri village is visible on the opposite slopes of the valley ahead. Traverse R round the top of this landslip and down on a fairly clear path to the river (**1hr 40mins**), where you cross over by a log bridge anchored in a plane tree. It is about 30mins up the other side to the *maghazeé* in **Polinéri**; turn L when you reach the road (**2hrs 15mins**).

To continue to Mirófilo (13km by the road), keep on south. For **Moskhófito** (6.5km), turn R when you first reach the road in Polinéri.

Stage 3 – *Moskhófito (800m) – col (1250m) – Mesokhóra (800m)*

Walking time:	4hrs
Distance:	9km
Waymarks:	None
Height gain:	500m
Height loss:	400m
Difficulty:	2

A rather tedious section of dirt road, passable after Oriní only for a four-wheel drive vehicle. It may still be possible to cut off the loop through Oriní by leaving the road immediately after the Platanákia bridge, going a little way upstream, then crossing to the true L bank of the river and heading northwest towards the col where you would rejoin the track. This is the way the path used to run, but I have not attempted it for many years.

Follow the road westward up the ravine of the Aréndas river towards the heart of the Khadzí massif, crossing the river at Platanákia and again at the hamlet of Oriní (**1hr 15mins**). From Oriní the track winds north up into beautiful fir forest on a shallow col at about 1250m. From here it is level pegging to the crossroads at Stavrós (**3hrs**).

See Route 15, Stage 6 for the descent to **Mesokhóra** (**3hrs 40mins**).

CHAPTER 4

THE ASPROPÓTAMOS

This chapter covers the country north and west of Mesokhóra and the valley of the River Aspropótamos (known more formally as the Akhelóös), whose headwaters lie just beyond the village of Khalíki. It is the most southerly extension of Vlach territory in the Píndhos, its people referred to (by other Vlachs) as Aspropotamítes.

Gardhíki

The Vlachs are a pastoral people, semi-nomadic until the 20th century. The largest surviving community have their home in the northern reaches of these mountains. Today they are citizens of the Greek state and their culture daily becomes more and more indistinguishable from the Greek, but their really distinctive feature has always been their language, which is Latin, not Greek, akin – though for reasons of nationalistic rivalries this is extremely controversial – to Romanian.

Their villages number about two dozen and are scattered from Pakhtoúri northwards to Aetomilítsa on the slopes of Mt Grámos on the Albanian frontier. In the old days the possession of flocks made the Vlachs relatively rich. Their control of the wool trade extended their commercial influence throughout much of the Balkans, and they founded banks and trading houses as far away as Vienna and Odessa. Because of their strategic position – in particular astride the Katára pass above Métsovo, the principal east–west trade route across the Píndhos – they enjoyed favourable tax status under Ottoman Turkish rule, and the town of Métsovo became a sort of *de facto* Vlach capital. The substantial houses of villages such as Kalarítes and Siráko still bear witness to this former glory.

In spite of obvious decline, the flocks still return in summer and in the *maghazyá* you can still hear the elderly speaking in their unfamiliar tongue.

The Píndhos Traverse continues on a mix of footpaths and little-used tracks. The best route from the walker's point of view would lead to Anthokhóri and on to the main Yánina – Métsovo road about 18km west of Métsovo. The more direct route to Métsovo now entails a whole day of walking on tracks or dirt roads.

Location:	East of Yánina, capital of the province of Epirus (*eépeeros*), and south of Métsovo.
Maps:	Anávasi Topo 50 1:50 000 Pindus: Koziakas – Avgho and Topo 50 1:50 000 Pindus: Peristeri, Kakardhitsa, Tzoumerka. HAGS sheets Mirófillon, Kastanéa, Ágnanda, Prámanda; Road Editions Epiros/Thessaly 1:250 000.
Bases:	Gardhíki, Kalarítes, Khalíki (rooms, tavernas); Pakhtoúri, Matsoúki, Meshokhóra (*maghazée*); Métsovo (all amenities).
Access:	Daily buses to Métsovo from Athens, Thessaloníki, Yánina and Kalambáka. Daily flights from Athens to Yánina. Occasional buses from Yánina to Ágnanda, Prámanda and Kalarítes and from Píli to Mesokhóra.

Route 17
Mesokhóra to Métsovo

Stage 1 – *Mesokhóra (800m) – Pakhtoúri (950m) – Souflí col (1700m) – Gardhíki (1100m)*

Walking time:	6hrs 25mins
Distance:	17.5km
Waymarks:	None
Height gain:	1075m
Height loss:	725m
Difficulty:	3
Map:	See Routes 15/16

Note Figures calculated from the Pakhtoúri turning.

If at all possible, get a lift or take a taxi for the 8km from Mesokhóra to the turning for Pakhtoúri, where the path begins. The road from Mesokhóra has been completely disfigured by a huge earth dam, and the Aspropótamos reduced to a pathetic greenish ooze. Once past the dam the landscape improves dramatically, but you are still trudging the road and these extra hours make reaching Gardhíki in a day a pretty demanding task. You could break the journey by camping, or possibly even find some kind of accommodation in Pakhtoúri.

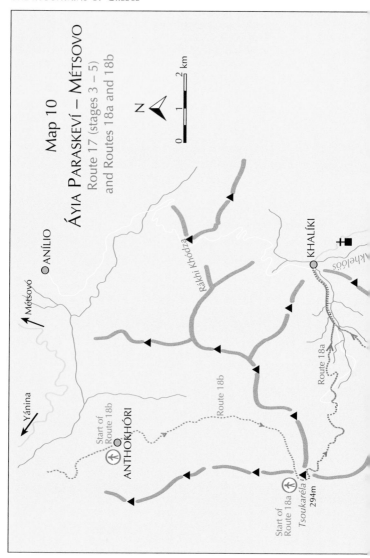

Map 10

ÁYIA PARASKEVÍ – MÉTSOVO

Route 17 (stages 3 – 5)
and Routes 18a and 18b

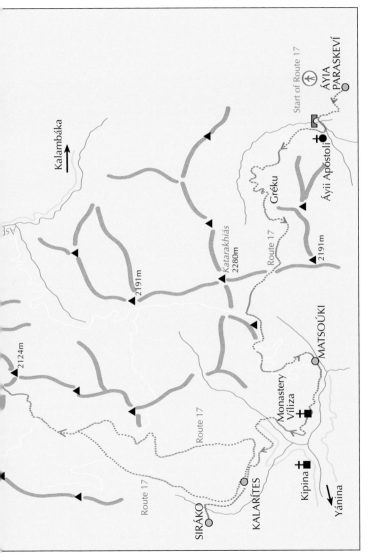

From the Pakhtoúri turning onwards, however, you enter a different world. The old path – albeit little used – still exists, climbing a lovely tributary gorge through abandoned terraces to the village. There follows a stiff climb on a shepherds' path to a 1700m col, then a long descent through fir forest to a tributary of the Aspropótamos, finishing with a short uphill trudge into Gardhíki.

In the angle of the turning to Pakhtoúri is a wooden kiosk sheltering a spring. Turn R here up the road, with the stream below R. You soon come to a LH hairpin, with a spring and shrine beneath plane trees R. A rough track leaves the crown of the bend (R), ending after a few metres at a concrete bridge, which crosses the stream to a cluster of stone cottages. Turn L up the path, keeping below the cottages. The path ascends this R flank of the valley (true L bank of the stream) almost all the way to Pakhtoúri. At **about 50mins** cross a small tributary stream descending from your R by a collapsed wooden bridge. The path remains pretty clear in spite of the encroaching scrub. Keep climbing past old terrace walls and across the remains of long-abandoned fields. With the main stream far below L and craggy heights above R you cannot go far wrong.

At **1hr 10mins** come to a bridge across the main stream to your L, just below the village of Pakhtoúri. Cross and turn L under trees on a path that soon becomes a dusty scramble; it has been destroyed by goats. Scramble up R to the top of the steep bank, where you turn back R along the upper edge of the stream gully to the first houses and up to the square/*plateéya*, where there is a *maghazeé* and fountain.

Pakhtoúri lies tucked in under the steep green ridge of Souflí. The route on to Gardhíki lies over the distinctive col at the L or western end of the ridge, northwest of the village.

Leave the square by the top side, turning L along the concrete road to the basketball and football pitches just outside the village (**1hr 30mins**). Between the two pitches on the RH side of the road there is a spring. Here a path (not marked on the Anávasi map) leads R between the pitches. After a few metres it begins to climb steeply up the nose of a wooded spur, zigzagging back and forth. In 10mins or so it passes L on to the R flank of the valley which leads eventually to the col you are aiming for. Winding steadily up, it works its way back to the nose of the spur at a point where you look back down over

Path to Pakhtoúri

the village. From here it continues up the line of the spur and into the fir trees. At **2hrs 10mins** the path reaches the top of the ridge and levels off along the R flank of the LH gully. Directly above you now are the wildly contorted rock strata of the Soufli ridge that separates you from the Gardhíki valley.

At **2hrs 40mins** you pass a stand of sycamore trees, then some giant firs; you are approaching the head of the gully. On the far side, in a grassy clearing among scattered beech trees, is the shepherds' hut that was visible already from Pakhtoúri. Another 10mins bring you across one stream, curling L round the head of the gully, losing height slightly now, to a second stream at E0262508 /N4373499. The hut is now in front of you and slightly L. The pass to Gardhíki is up the grassy gully to the R and above.

There is no one clear path up the narrow gully to the col, which forms an unmistakeable V between two grassy heights. Keep towards the L flank and a steady 45mins plod will see you there (**3hrs 30mins**). The views are spectacular, both northwards to Kakardhítsa and back to the south over the Ágrafa.

On the col another steep grassy gully opens immediately at your feet, leading down to a track at the bottom where the trees begin. Traverse along the L flank, without losing too much height, until you can see into the next valley where there are a number of sheepfolds, then zigzag down R through scattered scrubby trees to the gully bottom and a forest track (**4hrs 20mins**; E0262033/N4374725; 1370m).

Turn R on the track, which winds down through open grassy fir woods, cutting the corners as often as possible. After about 40mins – on the R of the track on a LH bend above a gully – you come to a grassy clearing with a stone-walled spring beneath fir trees, and a long wavering waterfall off the wooded crag R. Just over 10mins later, on another LH bend, pass a small shrine L with a waterfall R. The track continues down, winding back and forth through the fir forest, to the river (**5hrs 35mins**), where there is now a concrete ford (be careful crossing when the river is high).

Turn R on the far side, following the river bank and ignoring an uphill turn to the L above a sheep pen. At **5hrs 55mins** you reach the first houses of the almost deserted (except in summer) village of Athamánia (Moutsiára, by the old name). A further 30mins uphill on the tarmac brings you to Gardhíki (**6hrs 25mins**), once a very substantial village, now largely deserted. The *plateéya* is just above the road to the L, with several *magazyá* and a small hotel. ▶

It is possible to continue north along the Aspropótamos to Khalíki in a couple of days, but it is all tarmac. You can also exit the mountains here, by taking the road east to Pertoúli and Píli.

***Stage 2** – Gardhíki (1100m) – col above Gréku spring (2050m) – Matsoúki (1100m)*

Walking time:	7hrs 45mins
Distance:	20.5km
Waymarks:	None
Height gain:	1150m
Height loss:	1100m
Difficulty:	3
Map:	See Routes 15/16

This is a long hard day, not because of any technical difficulty or danger, but simply because of the distance and the ascent. There are a couple of places where you need to pay particular attention to navigation: one is finding the bridge just a few minutes west of Tzioúrtzia/Áyia Paraskeví, the other is crossing the col between the Gréku spring and Krithária. For most of the day you are in open country and can see clearly where you are going. The route crosses the watershed of the Aspropótamos and enters that of the Arakhthós, which drains the outer, western flanks of the Píndhos from Métsovo to Árta.

Follow the tarmac road northeast out of the village for about 800m. Where the tarmac begins to descend towards the Aspropótamos valley (**15–20mins**) turn L on to the dirt road that cuts across the shoulder of the prominent little bluff ahead. The road passes an elaborate wayside shrine, and descends north at a gentle gradient to the village of Àyia Paraskeví (still more commonly known by its old name of Tzioúrtzia – pronounced a bit like Georgia), lying in the narrow valley of a tributary stream. Make your way L-wards down through the village towards the mouth of the rocky defile in the valley bottom by the church of Áyios Yióryis (**1hr 5mins**). A path leads into the defile and immediately crosses a bridge to the true L bank of the stream.

Turn uphill L. The valley bottom is filled with plane trees. The path climbs parallel to the river past some walnut trees and remains of old terraces (**1hr 15mins**), while a steep fir-clad slope rises on the opposite bank. Past the terraces, with a red arrow painted on a rock, keep down to the L until you come to a goat pen where more red arrows point you onwards and up to the R. Ignore them and cut down L to the river to find a bridge. Cross and turn L, winding up a steep path to join the end of a rough forest track that climbs steadily in a southwesterly direction up the R flank (true L) of another stream gully.

At **1hr 38mins** ignore the track going straight ahead (L) off a RH hairpin and keep on up through scattered fir trees. At 1hr 52mins you join the main track from Tzioúrtzia used by the shepherds (E0262933/N4382821) and turn R. After 5mins you come to the stone chapel of Áyii Apostóli (1150m) beside the track on the edge of some grassy fields with a spring and cattle trough nearby. Immediately above the chapel fork R on the track, turning your back on the big stream gully you have been following and heading north, then northwest, through the firs back towards the now deep valley of the Tzioúrtzia stream, known as Kalí Piyí.

At **2hrs 27mins** ignore the small track branching R and slightly downhill as you exit from the trees. Ahead is a big expanse of grass with a tin-roofed shed on the crest of the spur opposite that you could see from Tzioúrtzia. Steep grassy slopes grazed by sheep and cattle enclose the valley in front of you. About 30mins later you reach the shed, with a spring right on the crest of the ridge behind it (E0261750/N4385036) at around 1400m. The area is called Pláka. Behind the shed the Kalí Piyí valley swings sharply west.

The gradually deteriorating track continues up the slopes above the shed in long zigzags. The old mule road has completely disappeared, and unfortunately it is generally easier to follow the track than make your way across the steep slope, cutting off the loops. As it gains height the track heads into the upper part of the Kalí Piyí valley high on its L flank. At **4hrs** you reach the copious Gréku spring on the L of the track at an altitude of 1739m, with a dedicatory plaque (E0260326/N4384557).

The track, now very rough, continues in an almost southerly direction towards what appears to be an obvious shallow grassy col a short distance ahead. A rough branch bears R to

Tzioúrtzia: start of the path to Matsoúki

Matsoúki from the col above Krithária

a couple of derelict-looking shepherds' huts on the opposite side of the now shallow valley. The correct route lies up the slope behind (west) of these huts, cutting back slightly to the north to cross the western ridge at a point almost exactly due west of the Gréku spring (and not visible from the track where you are). The old path only becomes clear when you reach the col on this western ridge at the low point just north of the 2141m peak and just south of the 2280m Katarakhiás peak at about 2010m (E0258708/N4384554).

The obvious col in front of you, with another shepherds' hut at about 1950m, is in fact a distraction. When you get there it clearly does not lead to the main western ridge that you need to cross to reach Matsoúki. If, like me, you make this mistake, bear R or west away from this col towards the big rocky 2141m peak, crossing the grassy lower slopes of an intervening smaller rounded height on your R until you reach the dead ground between the two. Here bear R (north) again and follow the gully between the two heights. Then either scramble L-wards up to the western ridge when the opportunity arises or – easier if you are well loaded – dip down into the grassy bowl that opens at your feet, then follow a line of grassy bowls and clear stony gullies leading back up to the real col below Katarakhiás (**5hrs 50mins;** my error must have added a good 30mins).

From the col you look directly down on Matsoúki 1000m below in the valley bottom. About 400m in distance below the col, and 250m lower in altitude, a shepherds' track crosses the slope heading south towards Kakardhítsa, passing a very prominent pink-roofed sheepfold on a grassy spur. A path zig-zags down this spur to the valley bottom and into Matsoúki. It is a good deal shorter than the route of the old mule road (now overlaid by a dirt track), which I followed. It might be worth a try.

The line of the old mule route is clear from the col, tra-versing northwards along the western slope of Katarakhiás, to a shepherds' hut with a water trough about 1km distant at a locality called Krithária on the Anávasi map. Towards the end you slither and slide rather steeply down to the hut (**6hrs 15mins**), where you join the shepherds' track and turn R. After a few minutes you come to a more important dirt road and turn L to begin the long zigzagging descent to Matsoúki (7–8km if you stick to the road). You are traversing at a gentle gradient the steep east and south flanks of a spur whose peak is marked on the map as 1811m.

As you round the nose of the spur after about 1200m, and look down on the road looping like a coiled spring beneath you, leave the road and cut straight down the obvious dry steep gully descending almost due west. It is not difficult, although there is no real path. When you reach the road at the bottom at around 1415m (**7hrs 15mins**), turn L. Keep your eye open for further shortcuts. After about 500m you catch a glimpse of the red roof of the chapel of Áyios Nikólaos. Before you reach the chapel, turn off the road to the L and bear south, then slightly southeast across abandoned fields and terraces. Keep to this side of the valley; you are saving 1.5–2km. You can see the first roofs of the village below. Rejoin the road at a cross-roads by a spring and cattle trough (**7hrs 45mins**). Bear R, and in a few minutes enter the village.

Matsoúki is another reasonably prosperous Vlach shepherding village, with some 18,000 sheep on the village pastures in summer. There are three or four cafés and a taverna by the newly renovated *plateéya* and church. At the time of writing there are no formal rooms to stay in, but if you ask someone will provide at least a space for you to spread out your sleeping bag.

Stage 3 – *Matsoúki (1100m) – Víliza monastery (1000m) – river (750m) – Kalarítes (1150m)*

Walking time:	2hrs 45mins
Distance:	8km
Waymarks:	Sporadic red paint and signposts
Height gain:	450m
Height loss:	300m
Difficulty:	3

Leave the village by the upper tarmac road. Below and ahead is the deep gorge formed by the Hidden River, the Kriméno Potámi, that runs down off the slopes of Kakardhítsa. On the first LH bend a newly paved and signposted path heads R along a ledge below the crags to the **monastery of Víliza** (*moneé Veéleezas*) clearly visible on a spur about 1km west. The paving comes to an end after 5mins and the path, clearly marked by red paint splodges, continues up and down above a precipitous drop to the monastery (**35mins**).

The monastery buildings occupy a natural grassy belvedere above the gorge. If you climb the slope behind you can look down into the courtyard and get some idea of what life in such a place must have been like for a small community of monks (*spring water from a tap by the walnut tree in front of the main building*).

From the monastery the path continues, bearing R, along the contour into oak woods and becomes less and less clear. After about 6mins there is a fork. Do not go straight ahead; fork L downhill. There are red marks on a rock just over 8m down. To the L below you are thickening oak woods. Do not lose too much height, and do not go down into the woods. There are red marks, but they are hard to see among the encroaching scrub. Keep along the contour after the initial short descent, moving R-wards round a grassy spur, below and along a stretch of broken and rusting wire fence. Then descend to a little walled pathside spring (**50mins**; E0254347/N4383657; marked on the map).

The path continues descending gently to an open grassy spur with a blue tin shrine (E0254176/N4383218; alt.900m).

Down a short stone ramp with a red arrow, on a very overgrown terrace just below it, is a collapsed stone hut jutting out
over a confluence of valleys, with the village of Kalarítes at
around 1200m on the opposite slope to the west. You have
reached a natural belvedere. You cannot go any further in the
direction you have been following; the ground ahead falls
steeply away. Turn 90° R (north) along the top of what must
have been a terrace wall. The overgrown path disappears into
apparently impenetrable vegetation after 20–30m. Push through
the tunnel of bushes, on all fours for 20m. At the other end the
path is faint but clear once more, running along a sort of grassy
ledge, descending slightly but remaining pretty much on the
contour line around 850m except for two brief sections of
descent.

At **58mins** the path makes a sharp L turn downhill, doubling back on itself for 3–4 mins before making a R-hairpin by
a fallen signpost and continuing northwards along the contour, faint but always followable. Cross a dry gully (**1hr 9mins**)
beneath some big rocks (red paint) and, 20 mins later, by
another signpost, the path makes a L-hairpin, followed by a
R-hairpin and descends to a high arched stone bridge (**1hr
30mins**) across the river, boiling away in a deep shady defile
beneath.

Cross over and turn R. The path climbs up above the true
R bank of the river until, after 5mins, you come to a place where

*The shrine and path
from Víliza, just visible
towards the bottom of
the nearest wooded
ridge*

Kalarítes

you can clamber down to the water: a wonderful spot to bathe.

Shortly after, the path veers L uphill away from the river. There are frequent red paint spots which you need to follow carefully. There is no clear path and the route winds steeply back and forth until reaching the main road to Kalarítes by a large road sign (**2hrs**), declaring grandly that the route you have just had such difficulty following is the 'Matsoúki Pedestrian Itinerary 3 hours' (*spring 100m down the road L*).

Turn R at this signpost and follow the tarmac for about 45mins to the entrance to the village (**2hrs 45mins**). Simple but comfortable accommodation is available with Napoléon Zánglis, who runs the *maghazeé* just uphill from the square (mob: 6972265961), and with Pávlos Patoúnis (mob: 6973778206) who lets rooms in an old village house at the eastern edge of the village (where you came in).

Kalarítes is one of the loveliest and least-known villages in Greece, standing on the rim of a deep, trench-like gorge. Until recently it was only accessible on foot – an hour's steep climb up a zigzagging cobbled stairway (*skála*) from the river below – but still worth a look. Partially restored but now scarcely inhabited, it was once extremely prosperous, enriched by the wealth of its renowned gold- and silversmiths who monopolised the jewellery business in Ali Pasha's 18th-century Yánina. The original Bulgari jeweller began his career here.

Side trip to Siráko (1hr)

If you have time try to visit neighbouring **Siráko**, an equally dramatic village, whose prosperity was based – among other things – on making capes for Napoleon's navy. It is an hour's walk away on the other side of the gorge via a steep and airy path – not suitable for anyone troubled by heights.

There are further interesting hiking possibilities in the Tzoumérka and Kakardhítsa massifs a little to the south.

Stage 4 – *Kalarítes (1150m) – Tris Pírghi (2000m) – Khalíki (1200m)*

Walking time:	7hrs 30mins
Distance:	16km
Waymarks:	None
Height gain:	1000m
Height loss:	900m
Difficulty:	3

For the first leg of this stage – some 3hrs 30mins – there is no escaping the track used by the shepherds going to and from the sheepfolds at Kourkoúmbeta on the southern slopes of the Peristéri massif. It is normally quite easy to arrange a lift. There are two possible tracks – with not much to choose between them – one passing to the east, the other to the west of the ridge directly behind Kalarítes. According to the Anávasi map there is also a ridgetop path for about half the way to Trís Pírghi, though I have never tried it.

The route starts at the upper edge of the village. The track heads first east, then due north along the eastern flank of the Profítis Ilías ridge, for just over 6km (about **2hrs**). Here on a RH hairpin (at about 1550m altitude) turn L off the main track where it turns sharply east and continue north on a lesser track over on to the west side of the main ridge. (The Anávasi ridge route starts about 1.5km further east by the Nikoúltsa spring.) Keep heading north more or less on the contour for about 1hr until

As far as Trís Pírghi the landscape is dry and barren, but once you are on the path at Valtonéri and over the ridge it becomes much more dramatic and interesting.

you have turned the base of the Souflomíti peak to your R. The track is heading slightly east of north. Before it begins to swing west towards Kourkoúmbeta, leave it and head northeast up the wide cwm R, cut by the numerous stream gullies that give the locality its name: Valtonéri (marshy).

Variant: the western track

For the western track leave the village via the chapel of Áyios Athanásios. The track climbs gently but steadily for about 1hr 30mins. When you reach the RH bend that reveals for the first time the full sweep of the mountains above Kourkoúmbeta, the track begins to descend. About 500m beyond this point a path slants up the bank R. If you miss it, keep on down into the gully ahead, and where it begins to veer L head up the gully R aiming for the shepherds' hut on the knoll above, and thence for the track described above (which passes behind it).

As you cross Valtonéri – *mootshiára* in Vlach – the line of the old mule trail is still visible as it makes for the low point in the ridge, Trís Pírghi (**4hrs 30mins–5hrs**). Three cairns used to mark the point where it crossed over, but only one was standing in 2004; snow had taken care of the others.

A section of the old road below Stournára

From the ridge the old path zigzags L, then R down to the shepherds' track traversing the slope directly below Trís Pírghi (E0255590/N4392864; 1862m). Khalíki lies at 40°, out of sight, in the hollow where three valleys meet.

Cross the track. The path drops down at 40° to meet the line of the stream in the wide, shallow gully below. (*The spring, which gives rise to the stream – and does not dry up – lies 150m along the track R and about 50m below it, E0255730/N4392862.*) Follow the path due north beside the probably dry stream to a point where it passes through a narrow rocky defile (E0255804/N4393445; 1753m) and descends, bearing 40°, to join the track again. Keep L down the track. You can see a sheepfold ahead and below the track to the R. Continue along the track for nearly 20mins, then bear steeply down R to the fold, which lies on a jutting shoulder above a deepening stream gully at a place called Stournára (**5hrs 55mins**; E0256287/N4394169; 1584m). ▶

From Stournára you need to get down into the deep gully to the east of the sheepfold. The general direction is about 66°. It is the route of the old mule road, but care is required in finding the loops of the path. Pass the fold, dropping down east towards the void, as it were, but be careful not to pass below the wall of big stones that you will encounter. The path remains on the upper side of this wall, bearing 90° L down a kind of natural funnel between the rocks. It then bears R and descends through various zigzags. You need to end up on the grassy, bracken-covered knoll (E0256502/N4394210; 1469m; **6hrs 15mins**) above the stream and below the copse of beeches enclosing the waterfall to your R.

When you reach this knoll, bear R towards the foot of the waterfall where you will find a good path bending back L at 30° along the true L bank of the stream and entering a beech copse. There are clear remains of the old cobbled mule road here, leading out into the open again and along the upper edge of another group of beeches. The stream is below R. On your L is open grass and bracken at the foot of the steep slope leading up to the Stournára track. Head 40°, towards the beginning of the fir woods, keeping 40–50m above the stream.

Enter the woods at **6hrs 30mins** and continue, losing height steadily, on a clear path under the trees, still on the L flank of the stream gully, for about 15mins. Here you can see that the old path bore off L-wards across the line of the spur you have

The track continues, bearing first west, then east, to Khalíki in about 10km; keep R at any junctions until you get down into the valley.

been descending, but has been damaged by logging. A fainter, twisting, stony path bears off R and down the rib of the spur to meet a good dirt track (E0257046/N4395020; 1304m; **6hrs 55mins**) between the stream you have been following and its junction with the main river running down to Khalíki. Turn L on the track and in a few paces come to a ford.

Coming up The general direction from the ford is 130° until you reach the rib of the spur. Above the R bank of the track you will see a slight path running L-wards. After a few paces you come to a fork. Take the L branch and after 30m head uphill towards the end of the spur, bearing 164° until you find the beginning of the faint stony path described above. You reach the proper path after about 200m.

From the ford follow the track to its junction with the main shepherds' track to the sheepfolds on Peristéri and turn R, following the true L bank of the river. At the entrance to **Khalíki** village one road forks uphill L and leads to the upper side of the *plateéya*; the lower road brings you in just below the *plateéya* (**7hrs 30mins**).

At the north end of the village the Hotel Levéndis is open all year round; contact Sotíris Levéndis, tel: 24320 87239 and

Khalíki: the church

24320 87755. The same family also owns the *maghazeé* that overlooks the square. The existence of the hotel makes Khalíki an attractive proposition as a base for a few days from which to explore the Peristéri massif, doing day walks, for example, to Trís Pírghi, Tsoukaréla, Peristéri's highest peak, and the source of the Aspropótamos. Khalíki is another seasonally inhabited Vlach shepherd village.

Stage 5 *– Khalíki – Métsovo*

It is still possible to walk directly from Khalíki to Métsovo, though most of the route described in the original edition of this book has been superseded by a dirt road. It is about 20km long, rough but beautiful: passable in dry conditions, though hardly suitable, for an ordinary car.

A better walking route, which will bring you out on the main Yánina – Métsovo road at Votonósi (11km west of Métsovo), is to head west from Khalíki, crossing the col below Mt Peristéri, then veering north down the valley to the village of Anthokhóri, about 6km by road from Votonósi. Our route description runs from Anthokhóri to Khalíki, so you would need to reverse it – not difficult, as you can see where you are going pretty much all the way.

The road route: Khalíki (1200m) – Hódja's ridge (1650m) – Métsovo (1050m)

Walking time:	5hrs
Distance:	16km
Waymarks:	None
Height gain:	800m
Height loss:	1000m
Difficulty:	3

It is still possible, if you decide to go this way, to avoid some of the road work. Head north out of **Khalíki** following the west (true R) bank of the Aspropótamos, keeping to the riverside footpath until the river divides at the spot known as Paliomonástiro. Here the main river makes an almost 90° turn R (east). Take the LH stream (straight on/north), keeping to its true R bank.

This is the way the old mule path went. A little way along you come to another dividing of streams. The path crosses the LH stream and winds up the rocky ground separating the two. It is not clear whether you are following a path or a rain gully, but provided you aim for the road – you can see the embankment above – you cannot get lost. When you hit the track, turn uphill. The view gets more spectacular the higher you go; look way back down the Aspropótamos valley over a long perspective of ridges and peaks.

At E0259693/N4398458 (1528m) the road crosses the spine of the spur in a sharp LH bend, with a small shrine on the R. Just round the bend the path is traceable again; it climbs up on to the spine of the spur and follows it uphill, with the road below R. Follow the spur all the way up (with the road always on your R) to the pass (E0259116/N4399367; 1634m; **2hrs**) known as Hodja's Ridge (*rákhee tóo Khódza*). On a knoll L are two lonely beech trees, the highest for miles around. In a high wind they make the most eerie screeching noise, audible long before you can see them. Far to the northwest towards the frontier with Albania you can make out the bulk of Mt Gamíla.

At the highest point of the pass you can either continue R-wards down through the forest on the dirt road, or try to follow the line of the old mule trail, in which case you branch L off the road and head straight down the gully in front of you. (I have not been down here for many years, but you can see where you are going, so there should not be any great difficulty.) Drop quickly down towards a wide expanse of mountain meadow known as *to mandreé too Khódza*, Hódja's sheepfold. At first the path follows the R side of the gully below a bank of beeches. Lower down – where the gully opens into the upper reaches of the meadow – it crosses to the L of a small stream and winds down in the general direction of a sheepfold located on the downhill edge of the meadow, close to the upper limit of the fir forest. Enclosing the meadow to the west is a low ridge, to the east a stream gully, which gradually deepens into a considerable ravine debouching at its lower end into the River Rónas. The river and the Métsovo dirt road on its further flank are what you are aiming for.

You reach the sheepfold at **2hrs 30mins**, now served (as far as I can tell from a distance), by a track leading down into the main Rónas valley past come ancient cottages and crossing the river by a concrete bridge. On the other side you rejoin the Khalíki – Métsovo dirt road. Turn L and follow along the north flank of the valley to Anílio, Métsovo's twin, reached about 1hr 30mins after leaving Khódza's meadow (**4hrs**). **Métsovo** itself lies on the north side of the deep ravine separating the two towns. A good *kaldereémee* connects them, but it is a long haul down and up after a hard day (**5hrs**).

NOTE For the best footpath route to the Yánina – Métsovo road, reverse Routes 18a and 18b.

The Vlach town of **Métsovo** is something of a metropolis in mountain terms. It is practically the only town in Greece which has made a conscious effort to preserve its traditional architecture, costumes and customs. The result – sadly, though perhaps inevitably – is that it has become a rather over-commercialised tourist attraction. That means, however, that there are several hotels and eating places, banks, shops and transport connections, which make it a useful hub for mountain activities.

The town has long been a prosperous centre of the Vlach wool and muleteering business, and the weaving trade still flourishes. The engineering works all around are creating a modern version of the Via Egnatia, the famous Roman road that linked Italy with Byzantium and the east. The historic Zygós (now Katára) pass from Epirus to the plain of Thessaly (which Julius Caesar crossed on the way to his victory over Pompey at Farsala in 48BC) will soon become redundant, as the new road will go through a tunnel. There was a Turkish customs post on the pass until World War I, which shows how recent the modern Balkan frontiers are; it was only in 1913 that Métsovo and Yánina, Epirus's capital, became part of the Greek state.

Route 18a
Mt Peristéri/Tsoukaréla (2294m)
Descent to Khalíki (1200m)

Walking time:	3hrs 5mins; (coming up) 5hrs
Distance:	9.5km
Waymarks:	Occasional red arrows
Height gain:	(coming up) 1094m
Height loss:	1094m
Difficulty:	3
Map:	See Route 17

To make a day walk of the climb to Tsoukaréla, Peristéri's highest peak, get some-one either in the hotel or *maghazeé* in Khalíki to put you in touch with the shepherds who have the highest sheepfold at Verlínga (1950m), where the track ends. They will willingly give you a lift up in the morning.

When you get to Verlínga, you will see that immediately behind the shepherds' hut a stream runs out of a little rocky defile. The spring from which it rises is just out of sight over the rise at E0253462/N4395702 (2000m). To the west, across green, well-watered turf, and after a 30min climb up grassy slopes with no clear path, you reach the obvious col (E0252865/N4395904; 2145m) where the south ridge from the summit ends. It is a 15min climb up the ridge over broken turf and following a line of stone cairns to the summit (**1hr** from the hut), with stupendous views in every direction. You also get a clear view down the route to Anthokhóri, along the L flank of the valley that descends northeast and north from the foot of the north face. ◀

For Anthokhóri, bear down diagonally R/northwest from this col to join the track visible below, follow it R/down to where it ends by a sheepfold below the north face of Tsoukaréla; then reverse Route 18b.

To return to Khalíki, descend to the south col described above in 15mins. Bearing southeast at 106° drop down to the spring at E0253462/N4395702 (see above). Traverse 200m R, cross a second stream and turn down a dry gully L at E0253576/N4395565 (2013m). You are just above the Verlínga sheepfold. Don't go down to it, but bear diagonally R towards an open grassy plateau, where a natural gully funnels you down to a lower level (red arrow on rock at E0253973/N4395356; 1934m; **50mins**) at 125° with a large rocky bump blocking the view ahead. (Coming up: the defile above the sheepfold is at 305°.)

At the foot of the bump bear R and then round to the L, keeping the bump L (red arrows); the twisty rocky height of Méghas Trápos is in front of you. Go down through a chaos of boulders, where some 10m of the old cobbled road survive, to E0254292/N4395330 (1899m) at the foot of the boulder slope (**1hr 15mins**). The way ahead is not clear: turn L at 330° up a grassy gully for a few minutes, then R and downhill across open grass to the track, visible below. Hit the track by a large boulder at E0254464/N4395496 (1779m). (The boulder is marked with a red arrow pointing L towards the Méghas Trápos peak for those coming up.)

Cross the track. The path continues on the other side, following below the track, bearing R and down into and along the bottom of the gully by the stream to a red arrow. Bear L across a flat grassy area contained within a wide bend in the track. Cross the track again where the stream crosses (two red arrows; E0254792/N4395316; 1721m; **1hr 30mins**). Below the track the path continues bearing slightly L. It almost joins up with the track again, then bears away R (remains of the old *kaldereémee* visible) and down pretty much due east to the *stroónga* (sheepfold) at Krithária, cutting off a considerable loop in the track. I rejoined the track at E0254945/N4395391 (1075m) in order to avoid the congregation of dogs at the sheepfold. I followed the track down to the fork (not shown on the map) about 300m north of the sheepfold (**1hr 50mins**).

Keep straight ahead (east) at the fork along the flank of the deep gully that opens below the Krithária *stroónga*. The old path follows parallel and lower down the slope, passing just above the scar of a landslip. After 300m the track makes a sharp L hairpin round the spur (E0255628/N4395485; 1623m). Leave the track here and turn R down the line of the projecting spur until you rejoin the main path (**2hrs**), heading L.

A few minutes later you come to a noticeable juniper bush with red-and-white plastic strips hanging from it (E0255950/N4395350; 1530m). Here the path starts to zigzag down L-wards towards the bottom of a deepish gully with fir trees growing either side (**Note** The Anávasi map marks the path, wrongly, as continuing on the south flank of the gully.) At the bottom of the gully (plastic strips and red arrow), cross to the L bank and descend east into the firs. After less than 10mins pass through a grassy clearing. Less than 15mins later you emerge into a patch of bracken and on to the track at E0256708/N4395569 (1469m). (*Coming up, turn R at this point. The point at which the path enters the firs is marked by two long strips of red-and-white plastic hanging in the trees.*)

Turn L and downhill on the track. A short way along, the path bears down L again through a rough corridor between the trees, while the track bears off R. Meet the track again (**2hrs 30mins**) at E0257060/N4395467 (1301m) by two stone cairns. (*Coming up, turn R here and stay close to the bank of the track for 100m before bearing R up the gully between the trees.*) Turn L on the track (the next shortcut, signed by big red paint marks, is very overgrown). Keep on round the next sharp L bend till you come to the more open ground at Kraniés, with the remains of old terraces planted with cornel trees. Here stone cairns mark the start of the old route (the line of the path is visible) down across the grass and through the trees to rejoin the track (which has swung off L) and follow the willow-lined river into the village (**3hrs 5mins**).

Route 18b
Ascent of Tsoukaréla
from Anthokhóri (1050m)

Walking time:	4hrs 30mins
Distance:	8.5km
Waymarks:	none
Height gain:	1244m
Height loss:	(going down) 1244m
Difficulty:	3
Map:	See Route 17

After the initial climb out of Anthokhóri – once you have passed above the 1396m knoll and left the shepherds' track – the paths are not very clear; let yourself be guided by the gradual southwesterly curve of the Goudouváka ravine. Do not lose any height, and do not gain height too quickly either.

From the uppermost *maghazeé* in Anthokhóri – where the bus stops and turns round – take the lane leading uphill R beside the school. Cross the stream and leave the track, turning uphill to the R. Past a watering trough, keep up to the R by a large rock. In a few minutes you hit the track again. Turn R and continue immediately up L under a prominent bluff. In about 20mins you reach the track again, crossing a narrow neck of ground behind the bluff, from where you can see ahead and L into the main ravine. Go briefly L on the track, then take the R or upper fork, which leads to a hut, then a sheepfold and watering trough by a lone thorn tree (**1hr**).

From the fold continue straight ahead on the R flank of the valley across stony turf cut by minor gullies draining the

Approaching Tsoukaréla

treeless ridge above. The path is slight, but relatively clear and climbs gently. Pass to the L just below a second trough and in a further 15mins, rounding the spur which has been blocking your view ahead, skirt the upper edge of some trees. Turn R straight uphill for a few paces. You can now see ahead up the main ravine to the high jagged ridge leading to the summit of Peristéri, not yet in sight. Bear off L again and cross a stream below a sharp rocky peak on the R.

You are now heading into the mouth of the upper part of the ravine. At **1hr 55mins** the path veers L into the bottom. Head up R, descending gradually towards the stony ravine bed. Occasional faded blotches of red paint mark the way. Half an hour's plod brings you to a grassy hollow (**2hrs 30mins**) and an apparent impasse. Ahead the gradient steepens.

To your R a steep smooth slab of rock is cut by a loose, pebbly passage – that is the way. In a few moments you emerge on top of some heavily fissured rock pavements. Keep steadily R-wards and upwards, between and over a series of rounded bumps, and very soon Peristéri/Tsoukaréla itself comes into sight, closing the L side of the ravine. At the RH edge of its base is a distinctive col, scarred by a bulldozed track. Passing a stone-paved pond in a hollow, aim straight for the col. Just below it is a sheepfold (**3hrs 30mins**).

For the summit, follow the shepherds' track to the col, pass through it and, where the view opens out again, head southwards up the slope L to the col below Tsoukaréla and follow the cairns north up the ridge (**4hrs 30mins**).

CHAPTER 5

THE NORTHERN PÍNDHOS
MÉTSOVO TO THE ALBANIAN BORDER

The Flénga lakes and Vália Kálda

This chapter covers the heavily forested mountainous country – the last redoubts of the Píndhos brown bear – stretching north from Yánina to the Albanian frontier. It is cut by two enormous ravines – Víkos and Aöós – and dominated by three of Greece's highest mountains: Gamíla (2497m), Smólikas (2637m) and Grámos (2520m), the latter right on the frontier. Much of it is Vlach territory.

The chapter includes a description of the last stage of the Píndhos traverse from Métsovo to Mt Grámos, with a separate section on Mt Smólikas. For Mt Gamíla and the Zagóri see Chapter 6.

Location:	Between Yánina and the Albanian border.
Maps:	Anávasi Topo 50 Pindus Valia Kalda 1:50 000 and Topo 50 Pindus Zagori 1:50 000; Korfes sheet 155 for Smólikas and sheets 157 and 158 for Grámos 1:50 000; Road Editions Epiros/Thessaly 1:250 000.
Bases:	Métsovo (all amenities); Samarína (hotel, rooms, tavernas, summertime shops); Kefalokhóri (hotel, taverna); Vovoúsa, Dhístrato, Áyia Paraskeví, Aetomilítsa (rooms, taverna); Foúrka, Dhrosopiyí (maghazeé); Palioséli (taverna).
Access:	Daily flights and buses from Athens to Yánina, and buses on to Métsovo and Kónitsa; less frequently to the villages.

Route 19
Métsovo to Mt Grámos

Stage 1 – *Métsovo (1050m) –*
Flénga Lakes (1950m)

Walking time:	4hrs
Distance:	12km
Waymarking:	Inconsistent: mostly P1 signs on trees
Height gain:	650m
Height loss:	250m
Difficulty:	3

Just above Métsovo – where the road climbs up to the Katára pass – is an extensive plateau, Politsiés, famous summer pastures for the Vlach shepherds. It is here that the Aöós, one of the main rivers draining the northern Píndhos, has its springs. These have been dammed to form an artificial lake, bounded to the northeast by the 2000m ridge of Mavrovoúni, Flénga and Aftiá, with a refuge at about 1800m overlooking the lake.

There are a number of ways to start this section. The **Mavrovoúni refuge** at E0255876/N4414264 (1829m) is the first objective. It is accessible by road: 14km on tarmac, 5km on a pretty rough track.

It is possible to walk it, though you cannot avoid 5–6km of tarmac. Coming out of **Métsovo**, turn R and climb northwards, past the small ski station, to the edge of the plateau where a minor road branches L for the Aöós dam. The National Park brochure rather optimistically marks a path, but just strike off this minor road in a northerly direction, aiming for the junction on the road along the north shore of the lake (E0256400/N4411600). It is 2–3km across grassy undulating ground. From this junction a track leads north for about 1km before turning into a path, clear at first, that heads broadly north to join the track to the refuge (all marked on the Anávasi map).

A compromise solution is to take a taxi out of Métsovo to the start of the refuge track at E0254400/N4412900. From

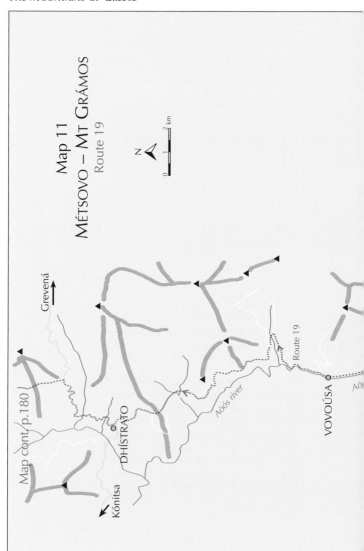

Map 11
MÉTSOVO – MT GRÁMOS
Route 19

N

0 1 2 km

Grevená

Map cont/p.180

DHÍSTRATO

Kónitsa

Aóös river

Route 19

VOVOÚSA

Aóö

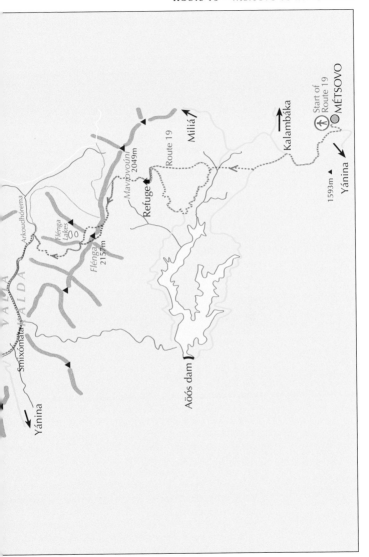

there it is a steady slog in a northeasterly direction for **1hr 15mins** to a fork by a (probably dry) spring, where the track for the refuge doubles back L/northwest. It is another 15mins to the refuge (*camping*), normally locked, but with a well-protected porch for shelter. The views over the lake and away to the southern Píndhos are superb. The nearest sure supply of water is the spring on the far side of *páde la láklu*, the Vlach name for the green meadow 15mins higher up the track behind the refuge (where there is also a cowman's hut).

From this meadow follow the track northwest, then north, through a rather desolate landscape scattered with felled and rotting trees to its end at E0256187/N4415742 (1956m; gentle gradients). About 100m ahead there is a P1 and a red diamond on a tree. Bearing W290°, then 280°, descend a shallow grassy gully round the head of a deeper gully to a spring at E0255730/N4416139 (1920m; **2hrs 45mins**). Continue uphill and L-wards at 280° and over a small saddle into another broad grassy gully at 308°.

At **3hrs** you reach the head of this gully at E0254681/N4416510 (1963m). Ahead grassy ground with scattered trees slopes down into the start of a substantial valley descending north–northeast to join a forest track in about 50mins, which after about 1200m joins up with the Miliá – Vália Kálda track. (I have not done this route, but it is almost certainly the easiest and quickest way to join up with the E6 path that runs the length of the Vália Kálda valley to Vovoúsa.)

To reach the lakes, keep straight ahead on the L flank of the declivity ahead, but more or less on the contour for about 10mins. You can see a yellow P1 sign in a clump of young pines some way L above the faint path. The rounded stony Flénga peak is now straight ahead. Once past the clump of young pines climb steeply L up on to the narrow neck of land (E0255248/N4416413; 1997m) that serves as a bridge to the rising southeast ridge of Flénga, and turn 90° R. You can now see the artificial lake again below L.

Either continue over Flénga, following the line of the ridge and descending on the far side just past the lakes or – at the point where the Flénga ridge begins to rise (**3hrs 20mins**) – turn steeply down R to join a clear but unsigned rocky path (E0253942/N4416786; 1962m) traversing through box scrub north and northwest round the flank of the peak to a rocky shoulder at E0254037/N4417053 (1968m) at the edge of a red

boulder scree. Go down to the R for 30–40m, L across the boggy ground in the hollow below and up the opposite side, bearing L to a dead pine by a seepage. Passing a spring at E0253881/N4417414 (1979m), climb the slope ahead to the rim of the grassy cwm (**4hrs**) in which lie the two small jewel-like Flénga lakes: a beautiful campsite.

Mavrovoúni refuge: looking south over the Aöós lake to Mt Peristéri

Stage 2 – *Flénga Lakes (1950m)* – *Vovoúsa (1000m)*

Walking time:	5hrs
Distance:	15km
Waymarks:	Occasional P6, red paint and small cairns down to the river, then E6 and black and yellow paint
Height gain:	200m
Height loss:	1200m
Difficulty:	3

171

A beautiful section of path that takes you through the remote and heavily wooded Vália Kálda – Vlach for 'warm valley'.

From the crest of the ridge enclosing the western side of the lakes, keep west for 200m, then bear down north into the trees and the gully opening below. You may have to cast around to find the start of the path. The first 700–800m was under snow cover when I did it, and my first GPS position is E0252838/N4418256 (1757m). Allow **30mins** from the lakes.

The path descends north down the narrowing spine of a spur in mixed forest of beech and black pine between two streams. After 10mins look for a P6 fixed to a tree. Small cairns, occasional red paint and plastic strips mark the way. At **50mins** cross to the true R bank of the RH stream. Be very careful here, for the path – at least in spring – can be invisible, obscured by young beech growth, fallen leaves and boulders, and there are no markings.

After crossing the stream continue for 30–40 paces before bearing gradually L at about 30°. Don't go too high above the stream (into an area full of big boulders) and don't lose height either. Keep more or less on the contour, climbing very slightly. In 5mins you come through the dense beech growth on to a slope with more mature, widely spaced beech trees mixed with black pine, and suddenly the path becomes clear, 'lined' by fallen trunks. It levels off along the contour above a steep grassy slope covered with pines. After 10mins pass a grassy dingle R, with a P6 on a tree L (E0253093/N4419202; 1522m). There follows a gentle descent through open pines on the steep grassy L flank of a spur to reach and turn a corner at E0253055/N4419474 (1513m; P6; **1hr 7mins**).

From heading south, the path veers east and down to emerge on the open grassy nose of a spur (P6; **1hr 12mins**), overlooking the Arkoudhórema river in the valley bottom and a stand of big burnt pine trees. Continue descending east, traversing across a slope and over a small shoulder (**1hr 17mins**), bearing south then northeast. A few moments later you come to a pathside spring in a clump of beeches, emerge into pines, bearing 50° and zigzag steeply down to a second spring (**1hr 26mins**). Bearing 30–40° you drop down to a wooden signpost at the junction with the E6 path (**1hr 30mins**). For Vovoúsa,

Vália Kálda: crossing a stream in spring

turn L and follow the E6 along the true L bank of the Arkoudhórema.

To the R/east, the E6 leads in a couple of minutes to a wooden bridge, then on to a path that turns into a forest track. The track follows the river bank to its confluence with a stream flowing in from the L, which it crosses by another wooden bridge a few moments later and emerges in a wide and beautiful meadow by a junction of rough tracks (about 40mins). One leads to the village of Kraniá (guesthouse), the other to Miliá, both about 20km away.

Following the E6 signs (either yellow squares or black-and-yellow paint blazes) downstream, cross one tributary stream descending from the south, then a second (E0252607/N4420455; **1hr 55mins**). After a few minutes of level going beneath the pines, climb up and over a short sharp rise before continuing again on a flattish stretch on a clear path to reach the river bank (**2hrs 20mins**). Cross the river and turn downstream on the opposite (true R) bank for 50m, where, by a large black-and-yellow arrow, you climb up L-wards. After about 10mins pass through a grassy clearing (**2hrs 30mins**) some way above the river bank, and begin a steady climb to the top of a pine-clad spur.

The path turns immediately downhill to reach a stream a few minutes later with a waterfall R (1150m). Cross over and climb steeply up L to the edge of a landslip (**2hrs 40mins**), then up R round its top edge and, gradually losing height, traverse down to a large signpost on a tree on the crown of the spur above **Smixómata** (confluence of the Arkoudhórema and Aöós rivers; **3hrs 5mins**). It indicates **Vovoúsa** to the R, Katafíyio to the L and Vália Kálda in the direction from which you have come.

Vovoúsa via the Aöós west bank

The easier route.

Turn L and continue down to the bank of the united streams, the Aöós. Turn L down the bank to the water's edge. About 50m upstream there is a yellow Katafíyio sign on your side, plus another on the opposite (true L) bank. Cross the river (almost certainly a boots-off exercise) and take the path up R, which brings you in a few minutes to a clearing in the trees and the start of a forest track (**3hrs 35mins**). Follow the forest track beside the river, ignoring a L fork after 15mins, until you reach the main tarmac road (**4hrs 12mins**). Turn R. The Katafíyio stands in a riverside meadow some 500m along on the R; it is a hotel, with uncertain opening times, and not a refuge (in spite of the name). It is about 3.5km into **Vovoúsa** (50mins; **5hrs**).

Vovoúsa via the E6 and Aöós east bank

Turn R at the **Smixómata** signpost. In 10mins you come to the edge of a big scree slope. Cross over and a few moments later traverse a steep open slope. At **3hrs 35mins** (E0249606/N4420503) the path descends to the river, where you turn R and follow the water's edge for 5mins beneath scree slopes. Climb back into the woods, bearing gradually more north than west through open pines. The path is often obscured by box and heather. Cross a little stream by a patch of open water and 10mins later you will be opposite the Katafíyio hotel on the far bank (**4hrs 10mins**). About 10mins later cross a stream with an E6 sign on a pine tree close to the main river. In another 5mins cross a flat meadow and re-enter the forest (**4hrs 30mins**). Shortly after go straight across another stretch of meadow, cross a stream and start to bear L downhill towards the bank of the Aöós, through a tunnel of greenery and into a riverside clover meadow with old cherry and fruit trees (**4hrs 42mins**). Cross the meadow in a straight line to meet a grassy track which passes a riverside sawmill, then some sheds, and brings you out on the tarmac by the road bridge. Keep straight along the road and into **Vovoúsa** (**5hrs**).

A much more interesting route, but the path is not well maintained; keep a sharp lookout for the E6 signs.

Vovoúsa is a tiny and very remote village, despite the recent asphalting of the road. I recommend Sofía Stangoyianni's guesthouse (tel: 26560 22846) on the R just after the high-arched bridge, and Angelos' taverna (tel: 26560 22841) a little further along on the L. Sofía's son, Andónis, is an officer for the Pindhos National Park and runs the information centre at the end of the village (tel: 26560 22003; email: pevovousas@germanosnet.gr).

Stage 3 – Vovoúsa (1000m) – Dhístrato (950m)

Walking time:	5hrs 20mins
Distance:	16km
Waymarks:	Red-and-yellow signposts, infrequent for first hour; lying on the ground or burnt where most needed
Height gain:	550m
Height loss:	700m
Difficulty:	3

Leave the village by the dirt road that leads north up the R flank of the Aöós river valley towards Perivóli. About **10mins** from the Vovoúsa bridge leave the main dirt road and fork L downhill on a rough forest track (yellow-and-black paint marker on tree). Continue along this little-used track through riverside meadows – which are slowly being overgrown by scrub – and into forest of black pine. The track begins to climb. At **30mins** you pass a red and yellow sign on the L. Forest stretches as far as you can see. ◀

The track begins to bear east away from the Aöós high on the flank of a tributary valley. At **45mins** keep down L on a logging track. Opposite on the far side of this valley is the locality known as Paliomonástiro, a grassy conical hill with a short white column and the remains of a wooden cross on top; legend has it there was once a monastery here. At **1hr 5mins**, on

There were fresh bear prints along the track through the riverside meadows when I last walked it.

Vália Kálda: fresh bear prints at Paliomonástiro

a RH hairpin, a track cuts down L. It is the first L fork you have come to and is easily missed; there is no sign, but there may be a couple of cairns. In 5mins you come to the river, turn downstream for 20m and cross on to a track heading L (due west) up the opposite bank. After a steepish climb through open pine woods you reach a more important forest track (**1hr 20mins**, E0248991/N4428025). There are no signs, but turn L on the track. Very soon you come to some E6 signs pointing down L towards the river you have just crossed.

Another 10mins bring you to Paliomonástiro (**1hr 35mins**). There is an expanse of meadow either side of the track. The hillock with the white column is just to your L. The track climbs steadily for a while, then descends. You are heading north and just west of north up the east flank of the Aöós valley. Behind you down the valley two pink roofs – just visible – mark the position of Vovoúsa.

At **2hrs 10mins** ignore the track that turns downhill L (now that they are not really needed there are numerous red-and-yellow signposts). The going is steadily uphill. After 10mins you pass a spring R. Ignore the L fork a few minutes later by an E6 and red/yellow signs and keep on uphill. Just past the point where the track begins finally to lose height again an E6 and red/yellow signs point L down some wooden steps on to the old path (**2hrs 45mins**; E0246753/N4431136; 1198m).

The path – well marked – winds down steeply through tall pines towards the mouth of a red, rocky defile where a tributary stream of the Aöós flows down from the northeast. In 20mins you reach the bottom of the slope by some sycamore trees and emerge from the woods on to a path that traverses R round a rocky spur till it reaches the bank of the stream in a tunnel of willows and greenery (**3hrs 15mins**). Cross the stream and go straight up the grassy slope opposite, bearing L uphill along the R flank of a second stream gully to a quite substantial half-finished building (**3hrs 30mins**). There is a forest track just above R.

Leaving the building on your L, keep up a grassy slope bearing L-wards (do not get on to the road). You come to the stream (**3hrs 40mins**) and climb steadily up on grassy ground through open pines with a steep pine-clad spur L. You are in a sort of gully, with a dry gully R. There are numerous red/yellow signposts, most of them lying in the grass, so not easy to see until you are right on top of them. The wood becomes denser, and after about 25mins you emerge on the forest track in an area clear of trees (no sign to mark the path for those coming down). Go up the track (red/yellow signs) and round the LH hairpin, then leave the track and head R up the very steep grassy bank above (more signposts).

The path winds up very steeply through pines that have been badly burnt in a forest fire to reach the top of a narrow wooded ridge by a now broken shrine (**4hrs 40mins**). There are plenty of signposts on the way up (though many poles have lost their red-and-yellow discs). On a clear day there is a fine view of Smólikas from the ridge.

From the ridge a clear path leads R-wards down to the continuation of the track you have left below (an E6 sign marks the path for those coming up). Turn R on the track, past a spring and cattle trough, and continue in a northwesterly direction along the R flank of a broad gully where once there were fields. A sign R marks the line of the old path which runs along above the track, through a stand of pines, to rejoin the track by a pink-roofed chapel just above the village of **Dhístrato**. Either follow the track round or cut down by the chapel, then down into the gully below and back up to the track. If you have followed the path, turn L along the track for a short distance to the first LH junction (signposts). Turn down L and you come

Dhístrato

to a shrine and big white cross by the first houses of the village (**5hrs 20mins**).

A neatly paved road leads to the *plateéya* where there is a café and rather overpriced hotel. An E6 sign points R to Samarína (4hrs 30mins). The best place to stay is with Stéryios Góghos (rooms 25 euros), tel: 26550 24810 or mob: 6974303076. He has a taverna directly opposite. There is a bus to Kónitsa four days a week; a taxi to Greverá – back on the mainline bus routes – costs about 40 euros.

There is nothing special to keep you in **Dhístrato** (or Breáza, as it is still called by many Vlach speakers). It is pretty and green. Mt Smólikas (Greece's second-highest peak at 2637m – and badly damaged by fire in 2000) rises across the intervening valley of the Samarína river. No one was hurt in the blaze, but friends reported that the fire advanced at terrifying speed, setting off a veritable firework display of exploding munitions left in the ground since the end of the Civil War in 1949.

Stage 4 – *Dhístrato (950m) – Samarína (1420m)*

Walking time:	5hrs
Distance:	Approx 15km
Waymarks:	Red-and-yellow signposts
Height gain:	800m
Height loss:	500m
Difficulty:	3

As the crow flies Samarína lies 10km due north of Dhístrato/ Breáza. There are no detailed maps of the area available, so it is impossible to know the precise distance. The figures below are only approximate.

Leave Dhístrato by the tarmac road to Mt Vasilítsa (ski station) and Greverá. You round the head of a deep gully below the village, and after **20mins** pass a shrine L by the beginning of a rough track. This is where the path from Dhístrato comes out (red/yellow marker). Everyone, however, advises that it is best to stick to the road for this first section.

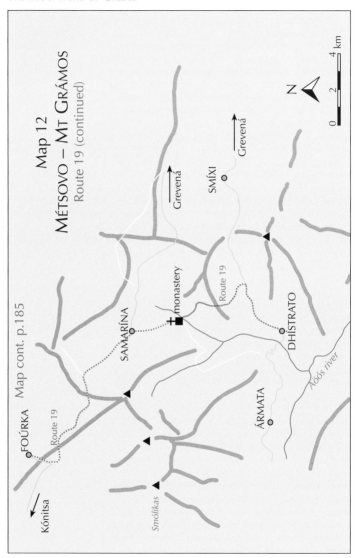

Map 12
MÉTSOVO – MT GRÁMOS
Route 19 (continued)

Past a trout farm you begin a long uphill slog on the road, with pine forest either side. To your L is a big gully, which forces you to gain a considerable amount of height before you can get round it. Keep your eyes skinned around the **1hr** mark; a couple of minutes later a rough logging track climbs into the pines L of the road. There are two E6 signs, and 50m into the wood a red/yellow sign (E0246439/N4436655; c1200m).

The track leads into a grassy clearing, where the way becomes unclear. Bear L across the clearing and down through open pines. There is a faint path. Look for a black-and-yellow paint mark and begin to climb the steep stony slope of the spur ahead, with no clear path. You reach the line of the spur at E0246084/N44370447 (1275m). Turn back to the R, zigzagging upwards to reach the crown of the spur at E0246096/N4437107 at **1hr 30mins**, where there is a red/yellow signpost.

Continue up the ridgeline. From here on the path is fairly clear and signed all the way. At **1hr 38mins** bear off the ridgeline to the L to round the head of the big gully to your L (E6 and red/yellow signs). Be a little careful traversing earth banks here.

At **1hr 48mins** cross a stream and 10mins later, on the top of a spur, go up R. About 50m later traverse an open stony slope to come out on another spur at around 1550m (**2hrs 5mins**) above a conspicuous tall dead pine tree. Continue traversing to reach a spring by a fallen pine (E0245988/N4438139; 1484m; **2hrs 17mins**) and on, losing height now, to a wooden bridge over a stream (**2hrs 32mins**). Climb L and up to the top of a bald spur (**2hrs 42mins**), where you get your first glimpse of Samarína's monastery, Ayía Paraskeví, standing on the edge of an expanse of meadow clearly distinguishable amid the surrounding forest.

About 20mins later you begin a steep zigzagging descent of a pine-clad spur to reach the bottom and traverse R, winding back and forth, descending all the while, in the direction of the river and monastery meadow. A few minutes later enter gentler grassy ground, and come to a wooden bridge over a stream by a spring. Shortly afterwards, down a series of wooden steps, you reach the main Samarína river at **4hrs**.

Cross the heavy wooden bridge and turn R up the true R bank of the river. A few moments later turn L and climb steeply up the bank through the pines – more wooden steps – to reach

The path to Samarína, Mt Smólikas in the background

a dirt track (**4hrs 6mins**). Turn L and at the first L-bend leave the track and turn R up the grassy slope of the meadow, past a sheepfold (beware the dogs, if it is in use), to the low stone church of Áyios Sotíras (**4hrs 20mins**). It possesses wonderful 18th-century frescoes, although it is unlikely to be open. At the apse end is a copious spring. For the actual monastery buildings turn R at the church, cross the stream and follow the track to the end – only 100m or so. For Samarína, turn L at the church up a couple of zigzags on to the forest road (L takes you back to Dhístrato in 20km) and turn R, climbing gently, first through pine woods, then beech, until you reach Samarína (**5hrs**).

Situated at an altitude of over 1400m **Samarína** is the highest village in Greece, its name almost a household word because of a famous folk song. Wars and the ravages of time have destroyed practically all the old buildings, the most notable survivor being the church of the Panayía on the green below the *plateéya*, with wonderful frescoes and a carved iconostasis (festival on 15 August, when Samarína fills with thousands of visitors and the *maghazyá* all hire gypsy bands to entertain them in a wild cacophony of music and merrymaking).

It is the most flourishing of all the Vlach sheep villages, with 50–60,000 sheep on the summer pastures. It used to be deserted over the winter months, but the improvement of the road means that the hotel now stays open and winter tourism is beginning.

For accommodation: Hotel Samarina (tel: 2462 095216/095352) at the top of the village; nice rooms above the Anthoúlis taverna (tel: 2462 095378, evenings) in the top R corner of the *plateéya*, and with Lákis Avéllas (tel: 2462 095278) at the year-round café/taverna in the bottom R corner (opposite the cigarette kiosk). If you need basic information ask Lákis; he is used to working with English walking groups (though his English is basic).

Stage 5 – *Samarína (1420m) – Gréklu ridge (1600m) – Foúrka (1350m)*

Walking time:	3hrs 20mins
Distance:	12km
Waymarks:	None
Height gain:	200m approx
Height loss:	250m approx
Difficulty:	2

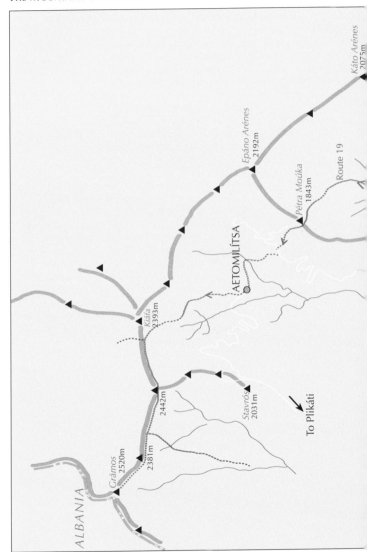

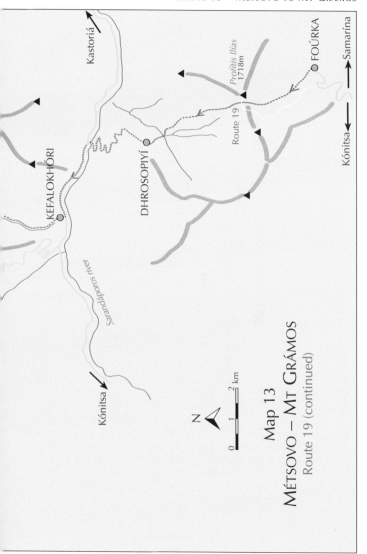

Kastoriá

Profítis Ilías
1718m

FOÚRKA

Samarína

Route 19

KEFALOKHÓRI

DHROSOPIYÍ

Kónitsa

Sarandáporos river

Kónitsa

N

0 1 2 km

Map 13
MÉTSOVO – MT GRÁMOS
Route 19 (continued)

The incumbent mayor of Foúrka talks of clearing and waymarking the old path between Foúrka and Samarína and between Foúrka and Áyia Paraskeví; for now you have to take the road.

> Follow the dirt road, which leads northwest out of **Samarína** up the treeless valley of the Samarína stream. In about **1hr 30mins** you reach the Gréklu ridge. The valley is full of sheepfolds, so watch out for the dogs!
>
> Once on the ridge, turn L. You are in beech woods all the way, with magnificent flowers in late May and June. After 1hr 30mins, still on the ridge top, you come to a crossroads by a shrine. To your L the road drops into the valley of Áyia Paraskeví. Turn down R for **Foúrka**, which you reach in about 20mins (**3hrs 20mins**). There is a *maghazeé*; ask here about accommodation.

Stage 6 – Foúrka (1350m) – Profítis Ilías (1650m) – Dhrosopiyí/Kántziko (1000m)

Walking time:	2hrs 40mins
Distance:	8km
Waymarks:	None
Height gain:	300m
Height loss:	650m
Difficulty:	3

Foúrka is enclosed to the northwest by a wooded ridge, on the end of which is the chapel of Profítis Ilías, clearly visible from the village. Your immediate objective is a shrine on the ridge below and L of the chapel. The path is only intermittently clear, so you will need to use this low spot below the chapel to keep yourself on course. There is no waymarking on either the Foúrka or Dhrosopiyí side of the ridge, and nobody goes this way on foot any more. Navigating is nonetheless not too difficult, and it is lovely country.

> Starting from the *maghazeé* opposite the church, head uphill and turn R on the concrete lane just above, bearing L almost

immmediately on a dusty lane. Pass two new shrines on the R, and 20m later bear off R. There is an old shrine half-hidden under a bush L. The general direction to the col below Profítis Ilías is 324°.

A reasonably clear path brings you in 5mins to the edge of a beech wood (E0239142/N4450115; 1413m). Inside the wood the path is clear and broad; you are obviously on the old mule road. Very quickly you come to a fork; take the R branch and cross a dry gully by a gnarled old pine. At **12mins** you emerge from the trees onto a grassy slope with scattered pines. Bear up to the L. After 5mins you pass above a small pond and just below the edge of the beech wood (bearing 310° here). In a further 5mins cross a small stream (E0238537/N4450616; 1483m). At **27mins** you are rounding a rocky spur just above the edge of beech woods (E0238542/N4450845; 1482m). Bear up L, then R past two big dead fallen pines and cross a dry gully (bearing 350°).

At **34mins** cross another stream gully with pines along its banks (E0238374/N4451147; 1482m), then another, lined by beech trees. About 5mins later you reach a cattle trough (*poteéstra*) with a paved apron in front (E0238418/N4451383; 1526m; **43mins**). The **Profítis Ilías** chapel is visible at 18°. Climb up the bank beyond the *poteéstra* in a L-wards direction on to the grassy slopes above and head up to the ridge, aiming for the col L of the chapel. On the ridge (**1hr**) you will find a small tin shrine (E0238394/N4452171; 1647m) beside the rough track leading to the chapel. The view extends away northwest to the ridges and peaks of Mt Grámos.

At your feet, grassy ground slopes down to the edge of beech woods 300–400m away. A rough track runs down off the ridge to your L and crosses to the R below you, passing a shepherds' hut and sheepfold at the edge of the trees. Head R-wards down towards the fold and (**1hr 5mins**) bear R on the track to a second, lower hut, which you leave to your L. Continue down the track to the first sharp LH hairpin on open ground just above another band of beech trees. Leave the track and cut straight downhill/north through the beeches – only a short distance.

You come out on the upper edge of a big expanse of sloping meadow (**1hr 15mins**). About 5mins below you (E0238398/N4453067; 1482m) is an old concrete *poteéstra*/water trough. Immediately below it is a very degraded track that has

Dhrosopiyí and Mt Grámos seen from the Foúrka path

been transformed into a stream gully running across the open grassy slope. Follow this gouged out channel L to reach the remains of another track. Here turn R and downhill at 334° towards the pines. (If for some reason you cannot find the water trough, no matter; the western edge of the meadow is bordered by a sizeable ravine and the general direction of the path to Dhrosopiyí – Kántziko, by the old name – is north and slightly west of north down the top of the spur that forms its R flank.)

In a few minutes (**1hr 30mins**) you are heading down into the pine woods at 344° (E0238232/N4453296; 1457m). At **1hr 40mins**, at E0238223/N4453597 (1390m), you are on to the big main spur; general direction north (340°–350°). Be careful not to be drawn down to the R into the grassier, more open stretches. In 5mins you reach a grassy clearing with two large heaps of stones just to the L of the spurline (E0238206/N4453842; 1348m); turn L into the clearing, then R and down again. At **1hr 55mins** you can see the village almost dead ahead. A further 5mins brings you to a ruined stone hut just L of the path (E0238037/N4454149; 1254m). At **2hrs 5mins** you reach a kind of rocky 'nose' (E0237944/N4454378; 1198m), where the path veers down to the L.

At **2hrs 17mins** bear slightly off down the L flank of the spur and a couple of minutes later bear down L again at 240°, passing a second ruined hut (E0237629/N4454627; 1075m), heading towards the gully bottom, which you reach among big boulders (E0237532/N4454853; 1016m; **2hrs 25mins**). For those coming up, there is a faint red arrow.

Cross the stream and bear L at about 300° across open ground. The first houses of Dhrosopiyí are now in sight. At **2hrs 30mins** cross a second stream and bear R across a field, passing a cement-block stable, and on to a track. Past three or four old stone farm buildings you come to the first modern house, where you fork R, then R again at the next junction and down to the village square (**2hrs 40mins**).

Dhrosopiyí is pretty and quiet, with only a small permanent population. It has never recovered from being at the heart of the Civil War battles, when the Greek Communist rebels/*andártes* made this area their last stronghold. Most of those who would have been the grandparent generation today emigrated.

Stage 7 – *Dhrosopiyí (1000m) – Kefalokhóri (700m)*

Walking time:	2hrs 30mins
Distance:	9km
Waymarks:	None
Height gain:	0m
Height loss:	300m
Difficulty:	2

You are moving into the heart of the Grámos massif from here on: sparsely populated, thickly wooded and slightly spooky. The name Grámos had immense emotive power for the older generation of Greeks. For the political Left it meant a heroic last stand against the forces of evil; for the Right it symbolised the scheming wickedness of Bolshevism and of Greece's hated Communist neighbours.

For such reasons – and lying as it did on the Iron Curtain frontier – Grámos was for a long time a no-go area. Now it is a conveniently remote and 'leaky bit' of the border for the many Albanians who want a clandestine route to the relative riches and freedom of Greece.

Without a lift to assist you on this stage, you are faced with some 5km of tarmac, albeit downhill, from Dhrosopiyí to the Sarandáporos river and the main road. The old path has disappeared. Turn L on the main road. After 4km you reach the new village of **Kefalokhóri** 200m R of the road on the bank of a tributary river. A consolation is the unexpected and comfortable taverna/hotel Fasoúlis (tel: 26550 81481).

Stage 8 – *Kefalokhóri (700m) – Aetomilítsa/Dénsko (1400m)*

Walking time:	3hrs 45mins
Distance:	12km
Waymarks:	Sporadic red paint
Height gain:	800m
Height loss:	100m
Difficulty:	3

From the village cross the bridge to the true R or west bank of the river, and head north for about 1hr (4km) on a rather tedious track towards the abandoned village of Likórakhi until you come to a concrete bridge and ruined mill. About 10mins past the bridge (**1hr 10mins**) you come to the confluence of two streams running out of deep gullies. The track to Likórakhi leaves the valley bottom here and doubles back and up in a sharp RH hairpin with a shed on the bank on the corner.

Leave the track here and turn down L to the stream and cross over. Bear back to the L on the opposite bank on a rough path, climbing on to the spine of the spur that separates the two streams. Bear up R, following the spine of the spur, keeping rather to the top of the LH gully and passing a couple of ruined buildings and continuing on up through

once cultivated fields, all the time sticking to the top of the flank of the LH gully.

After about 35mins you come to a patch of meadow with a ruined stone hut (E0235355/N4462909, 1205m). Bear 30° up a bank to meet a track (**1hr 55mins**) traversing across the slope to a red-roofed shed visible over to the L. Cross the track and bear 340° on a very faint track up to a watering trough in a grassy hollow (**2hrs**; E0235375/N4463194, 1276m). Continue uphill at 30–40° for about 10mins on to a sort of a plateau covered with heaps of old stones and unkempt fruit trees (E0235699/N4461720). A wooded slope rises from its upper limit.

Head for the northwest corner of the plateau, marked by some big beech trees, where a path goes in under the trees and crosses a dry streambed. Bear R and quite steeply uphill. There are several cattle paths, both just in the edge of the pine trees and more out in the open to the L in a sort of open grassy gully; take any of them. At the top of this steep incline there is a large red-and-white arrow on a stone on the ground (E0235028/N4463696; 1463m; **2hrs 18mins**).

Ruins of Likórakhi: the path to Aetomilítsa follows the spine of the LH spur to the patch of open ground directly below the central skyline crag of Pétra Moúka

Cross an open field with two isolated wild pear trees, bearing 310° to a very rough track and turn R. About 5mins later on the R of the track is a dry rocky gully lined with beech trees (E0234733/N4463910; 1433m). Turn R into the mouth of this gully and almost immediately L round the first beech tree, bearing 300° west (red paint on a stone). The prominent triangular crags of Pétra Moúka are at 90° R.

Across grassy ground with scattered trees pass a pond some 30m R, with a disused sheepfold just above it. Shortly afterwards (**2hrs 35mins**; red diamond waymark) come to a deep-cut grassy stream gully flanked by pine trees. Cross over, bearing R into the edge of a wide meadow. Turn sharply uphill to the R aiming for the low point in the skyline at 300°, passing a big isolated pine tree with a red paint dot at the start of the worn gully-like path leading to the saddle. From the saddle (E0234268/N4464131; 1500m) bear off R, gradually losing height – the path quite clear here – and contouring gradually R and north to a patch of meadow with an old and distinctive cattle trough made of linked, dug-out pine trunks (E0234009/N4464727; 1515m; **2hrs 46mins**). About 40m above it a shepherds' track runs west to meet the Aetomilítsa

The buildings of Aetomilítsa

road. The path continues across open grassy slopes among well-spaced pines until it joins the track at E0233692/N4464939 (1508m). Turn L and follow the track to the junction with the dirt road to Aetomilítsa (**3hrs**; E0233749/N4465348; 1470m), signposted Arénes, Lianotópi, Grámo. Turn R and keep on to **Aetomilítsa** (**3hrs 45mins**).

The road leads straight into the village square, where you will find the *maghazyá*. For the guesthouse, take the L fork 200m before the square. This road forks in turn; the guesthouse is at the end of the lower branch, the church at the end of the upper. You can camp in the churchyard; there is a spring/fountain 100m away. The only transport out is going to be a lift.

Aetomilítsa/Dénsiko lies on the edge of a wide cwm where a tributary of the Sarandáporos rises. It is derelict, only occupied in summer when the Vlach shepherds bring up their sheep. In the battle for Grámos in 1949 the Communist C-in-C, General Márkos, had his HQ in the village. Many of those who were in their teens or older in 1949 spent more than 30 years in exile in various parts of the old Soviet Union.

Stage 9 *– Aetomilítsa/Dénsko (1400m) – Mt Grámos (2520m)*

Walking time:	4hrs 30mins–5hrs
Distance:	11km
Waymarks:	None
Height gain:	1120m
Height loss:	0m
Difficulty:	3

The Albanian frontier runs along the top of the ridge just west of peak 2520. Straying across it may not have consequences as dire as they would have been before the collapse of Communism. Nonetheless, be very careful not to wander into Albanian territory.

Aetomilítsa is enclosed to the north by a wide horseshoe ridge, which curves from Kiáfa peak in the east to Gkésos peak (2186m) in the west. There is a path up the R flank of the valley behind the village to the col west of Kiáfa (**2hrs 30mins**), whose summit is littered with Civil War debris. From there the path curves round west to meet the remains of an old military road (**3hrs**), which you follow for about 45mins to a small spring (a L turn on this track takes you south to the Civil War memorial at Stavrós). The summit, a scree cone known simply as 2520, is another hour or so northwest along the ridge (**4hrs 30mins–5hrs**), from where you look down on the Albanian frontier, the erstwhile Iron Curtain, following the crest of the north–south ridge just 100m below.

There is a route down to the village of Plikáti in the valley immediately south of the summit, in 3–4hrs. I have not done it, but it follows the R flank of the steep gully draining due south from peak 2520 to the main valley floor, and thence along the course of the main river until you meet with the track leading up to the village.

Route 20
Mt Smólikas Traverse

Smólikas (2637m), Greece's second-highest summit after Mt Olympus, is a big bulk of a mountain, in the main rounded and grassy or forested, craggy only in the centre of the summit area. The forest is mostly black pine, interspersed with beech on the colder north-facing slopes and giving way at the higher levels to the rubbery-barked *róbolo* or Balkan pine. Because of its centralised bulk, sharply defined by deep valleys all round, there is a marked sense of airiness and distance, with long views. These are especially dramatic from the south side facing the crags of Gamíla, where a narrow, winding road connects a string of badly depopulated and surprisingly green villages, served four days a week by a bus from Kónitsa. There is also a very rough dirt road crossing the Aöós from Vrisohkhóri, which you could walk.

The crags of Gamíla seen from Mt Smólikas

Stage 1 *– Palioséli (1100m) – Smólikas refuge (1750m) – Dhrakólimni (2000m) – summit (2637m)*

Walking time:	5hrs (+ 2hrs 15mins if you descend to refuge)
Distance:	Approx 8.5km
Waymarks:	Fair; red-on-yellow, red paint, green hut symbol to refuge, thereafter random red paint and occasional signs
Height gain:	1537m
Height loss:	0m
Difficulty:	3

The path is relatively well marked as far as the refuge. Khrístos Stratigópoulos, the first manager/tenant of this brand-new stone building, speaks English. He is an enthusiastic naturalist and environmentalist, one of a new generation of Greeks beginning to take a serious interest in the mountain regions.

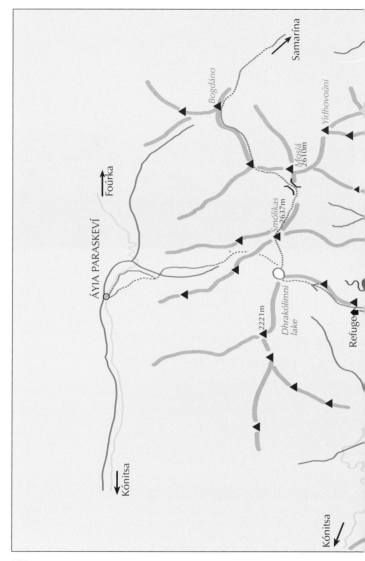

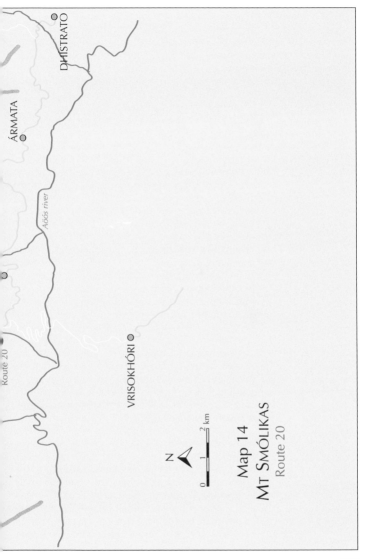

DHISTRATO

ÁRMATA

Aóös river

Route 20

VRISOKHÓRI

N

0   1   2 km

Map 14
MT SMÓLIKAS
Route 20

THE MOUNTAINS OF GREECE

From the refuge to the Dhrakólimni (Dragon Lake) tarn the going continues to be an easy but steady plod, in open forest to around 2000m. From there to the summit, however, is painful: a steep climb on loose rock, best done without a full pack. If you are going on to Samarína you just have to grit your teeth. If heading for Áyia Paraskeví I would strongly recommend leaving the bulk of your gear by the tarn.

In the middle of Paliƈséli a large plane tree shades a fountain and the main church, with a paved *plateéya*, the commune office and a taverna beside it. On the opposite side of the road – and just below it – is a *maghazeé* called Barba Míhos.

On the R immediately after it the old – and largely defunct – path from Vrisokhóri joins the road. On the L a concrete lane climbs past a newly renovated chapel and divides almost at once (red-on-yellow waymark and green hut symbol). Take the L fork. You come very soon to a concrete bridge over a stream. Keep R on the R bank (true L) of the stream. At the last house, just before a wooden bridge, an arrow points R – Προς Καταφυγιο/*pros katafeéyo*: to the refuge. Go up here, passing on the R a restored and red-painted *dristélla* – a chute for pummelling/fulling newly made rugs and blankets with water. Keep close to the stream. You come out on a dirt track. Turn L for 30m, then sharp R up a walled 'ramp' (waymarks) to a red-roofed fountain and shrine, bearing the date 1868 (**10mins**).

The deepening stream gully is now on your R. Two minutes later, past an oak tree bearing red and green waymarks, the path traverses L away from the stream, turns back R and climbs to a *freyátyo* or manhole cover (village water supply). A few moments later it emerges on to abandoned fields, with a hut L. Up the R side of the fields it brings you out on the dirt road to the refuge (E0234082/N4437519; **25mins**).

Turn R up the road, cutting off the corners when you can. After a few minutes, at a RH bend, there is a red dot on a tree R, together with red and green waymarks. Cut off the corner here. A few moments later look for a faded sign on a dead tree L of the road. Bear L at 335° on what remains of a faint stony track; you can see a waymark on a tree about 100m ahead. A high wall-like rocky ridge encloses all this area on the R.

At **40mins** bear up slightly R at 350° over open grass on a very faint line of path. The road is about 50m to your R. Soon after cross a broken-down terrace wall. Keep bearing slightly

R, at 352°; there is a red mark on a tree 100m ahead. Cross a small stream, bearing L and up for 50m to a red-roofed hut by a cattle trough (E0234201/N4438447; red marks on trees). ▶

About 50m higher up to the L through long grass and reeds you reach the road again. Turn L for 50m and scramble up the stony bank to the R (**47mins**; red waymark and green hut signs). The path runs parallel to the road across a grassy slope through open trees towards a ridge. At the top of the first slope bear R, then sharply L up to the small col (E0234046/N4438896; **57mins**).

Turn 90° R up the ridge into the forest (frequent waymarks). The path bears L off the ridge to traverse along a steep slope through the trees. At **1hr 5mins** cross an open grassy clearing along its lower, L edge to a much bigger clearing with a sheep-fold, where a track leads L to the dirt road. Go straight up the wooded slope behind the sheepfold to the old wooden refuge of Náni (**1hr 20mins**, E0234406/N4439674; 1710m) where there is a copious spring and just beyond a wide grassy clearing beside the dirt road, which makes a good campsite. The path continues uphill through the pines behind the hut at 70°, marked by the occasional red tin disc or blue plastic ribbon, and brings you in 5mins to the newly opened *Katafeéyo Smólikas*/Smólikas refuge (1750m; Khrístos Stratigópoulos, mob: 6946670565; www.smolikas.com; *beds and meals*), where the dirt road ends.

From the refuge head northeast down on to the path, which is marked by ancient red discs and paint splodges. Turn R and in 5mins come to a big spring (*last sure source of water*). Turn R and begin to climb, winding steadily up a spur through beautiful open grassy pine woods. In 20mins (**1hr 40mins**) you reach a grassy hollow where a red arrow on a tree indicates the way, straight up through the middle of the hollow to a small saddle where you look out over the Aöós valley. A curling red arrow on a rock indicates that the path doubles back L, climbing through trees to a little rocky shoulder with a view back to Mt Trapezítsa above the town of Kònitsa (**1hr 50mins**).

Traverse R-wards beneath a rocky knoll to an open grassy col, where you bear L (a sign at the foot of a pine tree). Another 10mins bring you to an open red-stony shoulder where you get your first view of the conical summit of Smólikas. Heading northward at 24°, in line with the peak, you reach another

Nearby is a spring, *ee vreésee too toórkoo*, named to commemorate an attempt by a Turk to shoot an icon of the Virgin Mary; his gun exploded and the Virgin remained unhurt.

Smólikas: the 2637m summit

wide grassy shoulder (**2hrs 25mins**). Cross it, heading north, and in a couple of minutes meet the path coming up from the R from the village of Pádhes (red square on a yellow ground; E0236168/N4440326; coming down, be careful not to be seduced by the new-looking sign into bearing L towards Pádhes). There is a sheepfold below R and one of the rare O3 signs. You are heading north on the L flank of the deep main gully draining south from the peak.

At **2hrs 42mins** there is a spring 5m below the path on the R, which in late summer may be no more than a seepage. After a long stretch of gentle gradients you are approaching a saddle (E0235922/N4441023; 2050m) where a yellow sign-post indicates Pádhes 2hrs, Dhrakólimni 15mins, summit 2hrs. Turn R up the ridge and begin to climb. You emerge above the treeline and continue L-wards, then bearing R to reach the Dhrakólimni tarn at **3hrs 15mins**. Surrounded by gentle grassy banks it makes a lovely campsite, as does the grassy cwm just below it to the north, should you require a more sheltered spot. The views northwest to Mt Grámos and south to the alpine crags of Mt Gamíla are already spectacular (although not as fine as from the summit itself).

The path for the summit begins in the southeast corner of the tarn, dodges behind a stony hillock, then zigzags steeply up a fierce slope (red on yellow waymarks) for 30–40mins before the gradient eases on a long grassy slope. A long line of posts marks the route over well-cropped turf. It veers well out to the L, before returning R and up to the summit (**4hrs 30mins**). Stick to the path; the gradient is much easier.

From the summit in the clear light of early morning you may be able to see the highest peak in Greece, Mt Olympus, away to the east, as well as far back to the south from where you have come. Clear or not, you can certainly see the route ahead to Samarína (Stage 2a).

Stage 2a – *Descent to Samarína (1420m)*

Walking time:	4hrs (ascent 6hrs)
Distance:	Approx 10km
Waymarking:	Occasional paint and cairns
Height gain:	200m
Height loss:	1400m
Difficulty:	3

For most of the first 3hrs the route runs above the treeline in an airy inhospitable landscape of shattered rock where you are unlikely to encounter anyone. You may see flocks of sheep lower down either side of the ridge, especially to the south where you pass above the deep and beautifully forested Vália Kérna – its lower reaches tragically destroyed by fire in 2000 – between the Mosiá and Bogdáno peaks.

East of the summit the ground drops steeply into a wide cirque with Smolikas's second summit, Mosiá, dominating the eastern end. You can see the section of the path to Samarína, known as Skála, climbing across the scree below it.

Late in the year water may be in short supply, so come prepared.

To reach it, drop down the steep ridgeline (red paint) from the summit, then follow the ridge along, keeping R of and below it until you come to a small tarn (dries out). Turn diagonally R down the gully which drains the tarn until you reach level ground by the ruins of a stone sheepfold. On your L is a

Smólikas: the cirque below Mosiá

big gap in the ridgeline, known as Lemós (**45mins**). Here you join up with the regular Pádhes – Samarína route, which passes through this gap and down into the cirque.

A paint splodge marks the start of the united path. A few minutes later you pass a pool on the L fed by meltwater from a patch of snow that survives right through the summer. Follow the paint blazes across the bottom of the cirque, then L-handed up the steep rock stair of Skála towards the top of the height with the trig point. Near the top there is a spring under a rock R of the path.

At **1hr 25mins** reach the top of the stair. Ahead stretches a broad, flat-topped ridge of reddish gravel with a line of small cairns descending diagonally R across it. In the middle distance, ahead and slightly R, are two pointed wooded peaks. On your R the ground drops into another deep cirque – the Válía Kérna. The route runs L of the rim of this cirque to its further end, where it traverses R beneath the two wooded peaks and crosses a saddle to the R of the second one.

Follow the cairns to the end of the flat-topped ridge (**1hr 33mins**), where the path turns down a rocky couloir, levelling out at the bottom into a dry gully. Keep R of the gully.

At **1hr 55mins** leave a lone stunted pine on your R. Keep down L away from the rim of the cirque. In 15mins you come to the first trees, on the L. The path passes L-handed round the back of a bump. After 10mins bear R to traverse across the face of the wooded peaks seen from the 'red ridge'. At **2hrs 35mins** turn up L by some big trees and over the col between Bogdáno peak L and Gorgólu R. Samarína village lies at the foot of Gorgólu.

The path bears R as it crosses the col. At **2hrs 45mins** there is a spring in a gully L of the path, known as Bogdáno. The trees hereabouts are Balkan pines. A little further on the path crosses a second stream, then winds down R-handed into the trees.

At **3hrs 5mins** pass the Soupotíra spring in a grassy clearing. Keep on down through the woods, until after about 40mins you emerge on to the bare slopes directly above Samarína. It is only a few minutes down to the first building, the improbably large Samarína Hotel, built with donations from Samarína's *emigré* sons in the United States (**4hrs**).

For information about Samarína see Route 19, Stage 4.

Stage 2b – *Descent from Dhrakólimni (2000m) to Kerásovo/Áyia Paraskeví (950m)*

Walking time:	2hrs 50mins
Distance:	Approx 8km
Waymarking:	Spasmodic
Height gain:	0m
Height loss:	1050m
Difficulty:	3

From the northeast corner of the tarn, drop down into the grassy cwm below where there is a sheepfold. Cross the grass to the northeast corner to pick up a path that is not so much well marked as well trodden; there is no road and the shepherds have to come and go from their fold on horseback. They do not like it and keep agitating for a road. For the moment, however – and luckily for walkers – their appeals are falling on deaf ears.

From the rim of the cwm (about **25mins** from the tarn) the path loops down into trees on the R flank of a deep gully with

For the return to Dhrakólimni from the summit of Smólikas, see Route 20, Stage 1.

a river in the bottom. After about 20mins the gradient eases and the path crosses a long (in height) but well-stabilised stretch of scree. About 10mins or so later it bears R away from the river gully at 326° and starts to descend more steeply. At **1hr 10mins**, descend along the L edge of a grassy clearing. In 10mins you pass a bigger clearing on the L of the path with a wooden hut, and shortly after the village comes into view for the first time at 340°. The path heads northeast at 40°, then switches to a long reach at 280°.

Pass a third grassy clearing to the L, with piles of old stones, followed by a fourth, also on the L, in a hollow, by an O3 sign. A few moments later you come to a spring. Heading in a northerly direction pass a clearing with the remains of old terraces. Cross a narrow bridge of ground between two gullies and, at **2hrs 5mins**, you come down to the corner of open fields (E0236120/N4446117; 12226m) with a stream in willow trees L and a second stream in willows R. ◀

The route from here down into the village lies across long abandoned fields. There are paint marks all the way, but not always obvious; keep your eyes skinned, especially in open grass.

Turn R across the grass for 80m to the further stream (spring just on the other side), bear L for 100m and you come to a big boulder L of the path, marked with red paint dots. About 10m further on a red arrow on the ground points L. Turn L, following the red dots (straight ahead is the path to the chapel of Profítis Ilías; see 'Variant: Profítis Ilías link to main path'). Your direction is 344°; the willow-filled stream course is on your L and you are walking along the top of an old terrace wall. About 5mins later, at the edge of a group of trees, turn R at 30° and continue to a junction of paths in the middle of a field (E0236012/N4446723; 1198m**; 2hrs 17mins**). Turn 90° L. For 2mins walk uphill, then the path levels off and starts to descend quite steeply at 336°. It is quite broad, with a gully below to the R. At **2hrs 30mins**, at a small saddle (E0235732/N4447390; 1116m), turn 90° R.

The path descends first through a tunnel of hazel with a barbed wire fence R and an old orchard below, then bears L down a narrow spur, with the village houses visible below. A water channel crosses the path at right angles. Step over and carry straight on downhill on a narrow sunken path between old stone walls and overgrown gardens till you hit the road by a telegraph pole marked with a red arrow and a hollow red diamond (**2hrs 50mins**; E0235678/N4448033; 1010m). You are in the village, about 15mins walk up from the square and *magazyá*.

The owner of the *Smólikas*, on the road just above the square, speaks some English and offers food and accommodation (tel: 2655-024215). The best place to camp – apart from the fields mentioned above – is either at or on the track to the chapel of Profítis Ilías. From the square it is 30–40mins walk along the road, heading east out of the village. Well past the last houses and just after a big cement-block stable on the L a dirt track leads R across old terraces to the chapel (E0236492/N4447125) perched on a jutting spur at 1052m above the river and surrounded by forest. There is a spring and a wide level 'parking' area, where the shepherds from Smólikas leave their vehicles.

Variant: Profítis Ilías link to main path

A well-trodden path used by the shepherds starts from the L edge of the 'parking' area and goes up through the trees and across some abandoned fields at 226°. Where the fields come to an end, turn L up through the pines on to a very rough track, then turn R. At **15mins** the climb becomes steeper; 5mins later you come to ruined terrace walls and an open grassy area R. Shortly after you reach the boulder which marks the junction with the main path from the village (see above).

Cheesemaking in a sheepfold

CHAPTER 6

ZAGÓRI AND MT GAMÍLA

In the Víkos gorge (photo Michael Cullen)

Of all the mountainous areas of mainland Greece, the Zagóri probably offers the best combination of natural wilderness and eco-sensitive development. At its heart is the massíf of Mt Tymphi/Gamíla whose uplands conceal limestone pavements, deep swallow holes, alpine pastures and a lovely tarn, Dhrakólimni (Dragon Lake). Bordering Gamíla to the west is the dramatic limestone gorge of Víkos, whose 1000m cliffs make it one of the most impressive in Europe. To the east lies the deep forest-clad valley of the Aöós dividing it from neighbouring Smólikas, the second-highest peak in the country.

Most unusually for Greece, the region's handsome stone-built villages have been carefully protected and even the paths are maintained and waymarked to near-Western standards. An unexpected highlight are the graceful arched stone bridges, which have survived from the region's 18th- and 19th-century heyday, when the 46 villages of the Zagóri (*zaghorokhórya*) enjoyed a privileged tax and trading status within the framework of the Ottoman Empire. Happily for the walker, many of the old cobbled mulepaths that facilitated this commercial activity survive to this day.

The chapter describes a flexible circuit, offering three to seven days of moderate or harder walking, combining the best of the scenery with the best of the cultural heritage, as well as a higher-level two-day backpacking route over the dramatic Gamíla ridge and down the wooded flanks of the Aöós.

Location:	The northwestern province of Epirus, 1hr drive north of the regional capital, Yánina, close to the Albanian frontier.
Maps:	Anávasi Topo 50 Pindus Zagori 1:50 000; Road Editions Epiros/Thessaly 1:250 000.
Bases:	Yánina (big city: all amenities); Kónitsa (hotels, shops, bank); Pápingo (hotels, tavernas, refuge); Tsepélovo, Monodhéndri (hotels, tavernas); Arísti (hotels); Kípi, Vrisokhóri (rooms, taverna); Skamnéli ((hotel).
Access:	Daily flights and buses from Athens to Yánina; buses from Yánina to Kónitsa and occasionally to Tsepélovo, Skamnéli, Arísti, Pápingo.

Route 21
Zagóri Circuit (3–7 days)

If you have a full week follow the six stages as described, but do Stage 1 as a day hike out of Tsepélovo, then the alternate Stage 1 as your first point-to-point stage. If you have less time, combine or omit Stages 1 and 2. If you want (or have) to avoid staying at the refuge, it is possible to do a long day hike from Pápingo to Dhrakólimni and back, before leaving the mountains via the Stage 4 route.

Stage 1 – *Tsepélovo (1100m) – Vradhéto (1300m) – Belóï viewpoint (1400m; optional) – Kapésovo (1100m) – Koukoúli (900m) – Kípi (800m)*

Walking time:	5hrs (+1hr for Belóï detour)
Distance:	15km (excluding detour)
Waymarks:	Red paint splodges (Tsepélovo to Kapésovo)
Height gain:	500m (excluding detour)
Height loss:	800m (excluding detour)
Difficulty:	3

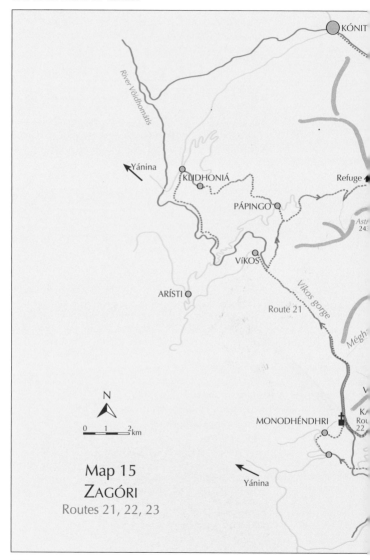

KÓNIT

River Vóïdhomátis

Yánina

KLIDHONIÁ

PÁPINGO

Refuge

Astr
24?

VÍKOS

ARÍSTI

Víkos gorge

Route 21

Mégh

N

0   1   2 km

V

K
Rou
22

MONODHÉNDHRI

Map 15
ZAGÓRI
Routes 21, 22, 23

Yánina

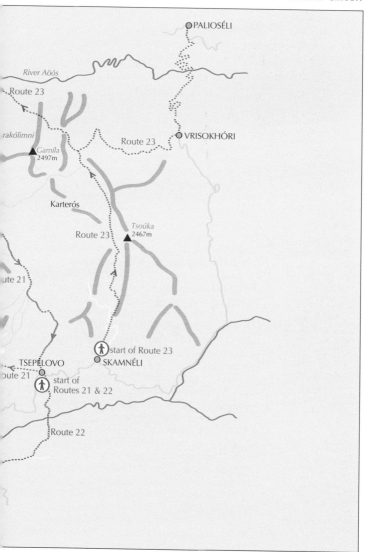

PALIOSÉLI

River Aöós

Route 23

rakólimni

Route 23

VRISOKHÓRI

Gamíla
2497m

Karterós

Tsoúka
2467m

Route 23

te 21

start of Route 23
SKAMNÉLI

TSEPÉLOVO
oute 21
start of
Routes 21 & 22

Route 22

This route usefully links Tsepélovo with the impressive cobbled stairway or *skála* that winds up to the hamlet of Vradhéto, Beloï (with its breathtaking views of the gorge) and the foothill villages of Koukoúli and Kípi.

From the main square and plane tree of Tsepélovo, follow the wide, cobbled path which passes R of the church, descends to cross a bridge (spring R) and then climbs L-wards. At a R curve (**5mins**) turn L along a small path (faint red dot on rock L) descending gently between brambles.

At the streambed continue upstream for a few minutes to a denser clump of walnut trees. Here, turn sharp L up the far bank, keeping uphill. There are several faint goat trails, but aim for the high crag top L of the steep mini-ravine west of Tsepélovo. You should soon cross the bottom of a boulder spill, where the large border stones of the old path are just visible. The goat trails tend R, while the red-dotted route carries straight on, passing above a larger hawthorn tree and climbing steeply through pine saplings to rejoin the original path.

Bearing L, the path improves and zigzags up, at times cut into the rock, past an old stone shrine (**30mins**), before deteriorating again as it traverses to meet the gully floor beneath the high crag. Approaching the gully, ignore the red dots ahead and turn sharp R along traces of the old path, which resumes L and improves again. After a section along the gully bottom, you come out on a jeep track, with the crude chapel of Áyios Yióryios 250m L.

Follow the track straight (west) up to a grassy saddle (**1hr**) with wide, fern-covered terraces and a dewpond. From the saddle, turn 90° R (north–northwest), up the slope. After about 8mins ignore a promising rock-bordered trail which bears R and instead strike L (still north–northwest) up a slight gully dotted with junipers, keeping your eyes peeled for red dots and the occasional cairn. This small, rocky trail, used only by a few trekking groups, climbs steadily for 20mins to reach a beautiful, square-bricked cairn and ruined shrine (**1hr 30mins**).

The path now descends slightly, aiming for a clump of trees on the northwest skyline, to cross a gully amid rough-blocked limestone pavements. Briefly follow the west bank beneath a fenced-off pine plantation, then re-cross and climb the gravelly slabs, bearing L at the top to reach the clump of plum trees (**1hr 45mins**). Just beyond these you intersect the road (now surfaced) to Vradhéto at its junction with the unsurfaced turn-off up to Kazárma and Méghas Lákkos. Purists could follow the unsurfaced track uphill for 10mins and then the path L to Vradhéto, but my preference is to amble down the surfaced road, enjoying the views and easy going. After nearly 4km/1hr (**2hrs 40mins**), there is a side road L into the shepherds' hamlet of **Vradhéto**.

For the onward path to the Skála Vradhétou you need to fork L and immediately turn sharp L again along a gravelly path (green SKL painted on the tarmac).

Variant: detour to Belóï viewpoint

Keep R/straight along the road, which soon loses its surface. After 5mins turn L down a path (signed Belóï 15min) leading clearly and fairly levelly north, then northwest. This descends between rock stacks to reach the viewpoint, a fabulous balcony over the Víkos gorge, with just a low wall separating you from the 800m drop.

For the Vradhéto steps, return to the side road mentioned above. Follow this uphill and, just before the main road, bear R onto a gravelly path heading east just below the road (green SKL on the tarmac).

Recommended, but it will add up to an hour to the timings below.

You soon pass a wooden sign R, 'Skala, Agios Athanásios'. After 5mins (**2hrs 45mins**), fork R down the smaller path (red dots) and pass a stone's throw beneath the secular-looking church of Áyios Athanásios. Reach the lip of the Mezariá ravine – a tributary of the Víkos – and the switchbacks start, 39 in all, descending 1100 steps. ▶

After 30mins (200m) descent you cross a pair of bridges over the Mezariá streams, then climb up a section of new paving and a stretch of jeep track, until you reach the asphalt Vradhéto road just above its junction with the main Kapésovo – Tsepélovo road (**3hrs 30mins**). (A brown 'Skala Bradetou' marks the start for those doing it in reverse.) Go down to the main road; Kapésovo is 400m R.

The Vradhéto steps are without doubt the most impressive and most photographed section of Zagorian mulepath. Until 1973 they were Vradhéto's sole link with the outside world.

If you are doing this stage as a day trip from Tsepélovo, take the afternoon bus (c. 15.45 Mon/Wed/Fri) or walk or hitch back to Tsepélovo from here (6km). There is a sign after 3km to the abandoned 18th-century monastery of Rongovoú (600m).

If you are continuing to Kípi, turn L at the main road and immediately R up a rough jeep track, passing below two rectangular churches. About 10mins later drop steeply down to rejoin the road and turn L. Follow it for about 1km and, just before a RH bend (**4hrs**), turn L on to a dirt road (no signpost). This leads all the way down to Koukoúli in 2.5km, but there are two worthwhile shortcuts. The first comes after 5mins, dropping L off the road, across open ground and past a water reservoir, to rejoin the dirt road in 7–8mins. The second is also on the L, but much shorter, passing a hut.

The dirt road joins an asphalt road at the southeast edge of Koukoúli (**4hrs 30mins**), near a café in the shade of a giant plane tree. It is worth exploring this tranquil, car-free village, with its proud stone mansions and the region's finest botanical collection at the Lazarídhis Exhibition. Afterwards, follow the asphalt road south for 5mins to reach a bench beneath a fir tree on the R. Opposite this a small path climbs the L bank of the road (flimsy wooden sign 'Steps of Koukoúli to Kontodhímos/Lazarídhis bridge') and crosses a clearing into the woods. It then threads through the oaks in an easterly direction, either on the level or gently descending, for 10mins.

At a broad band of shattered shale underfoot (**4hrs 45mins**) bear R, then L (waymarks resume). It becomes a paved *skála* (zigzagging path), passing a camouflaged shrine under a rock face on the L and descending more steeply to the riverbed. Here the path heads R (downstream) and across the single-arched bridge, built in 1753 by Tólis Kontodhímos, interpreter at the French Embassy in Constantinople. On the far bank a narrow path leads R to the modern road bridge 200m west of Kípi (**5hrs**). Follow the road L into the village centre.

Stage 2 – *Kípi (800m)* – *Vítsa (900m)* – *Monodhéndhri (1050m)*

Walking time:	3hrs, excluding detours
Distance:	8km
Waymarks:	O3 (red diamond on white square) as far as Mítsios bridge
Height gain:	300m
Height loss:	50m
Difficulty:	1

Follow the main road west out of the village, across the Vikákis stream (R is the Kontodhímos bridge and walking route from Koukoúli). About 500m from the village, fork L down a dirt track descending to the triple-arched stone bridge of Plakídha or Kaloyerikó.

Do not cross the bridge. Water level in the river permitting, continue downstream along the R bank through willow saplings (O3 red-on-white diamonds). After 100m you are forced into the boulder-filled riverbed, with dramatic rock stacks overhead. Follow this carefully downstream for 1km to the single-arched Kókoros bridge and adjacent road bridge (**45mins** from Kípi). Only in winter, and after very heavy rains, will this involve river-crossings or wading, in which case you are best off following the road from Kípi, keeping L, to the Kókoros bridge.

Again, inviting though it is, there is no need to cross, but continue along the R bank, passing walnut trees (red waymark), and then a series of riverside ledges and a cave shelter. Under tall oaks (**1hr**) fork L to continue along the valley floor, through flower- and thistle-filled fields, and then along a stony path. At **1hr 15mins** a paved path from the Koukoúli road joins from your R and shortly after this you reach – and cross – the last bridge of the day, the well-preserved Mítsios span (1748). Downstream lies the full length of the main Víkos gorge (but the first 2km are pathless and boulder-strewn, which is why I recommend approaching from Monodhéndhri).

Head back up the L bank for 100m before starting the zigzagging climb known as the Skála Vítsas. The path is well built, the gradient steady and the waysides bursting with wild flowers in May and June. After a good 30mins' climb (**2hrs**) you reach the first houses of Vítsa and, at the church of the Virgin Mary, keep R to emerge on the *plateéya* of Káto (lower) Vítsa, with its vast, spreading plane tree. Continue 100m west to the main road and follow this straight/R for 100m. On your L a cobbled lane leads up to the *kióski*, the covered belvedere alongside Áyii Pántes (All Saints) church, which makes a good picnic spot. Opposite this is the 17th-century church of Áyios Nikólaos, with its broad yard and porticoes.

To continue to Áno (upper) Vítsa and Monodhéndhri, take the upper of two cobbled lanes, passing above this church. You emerge on the asphalt road serving Áno Vítsa and follow this up to the junction with the main Monodhéndhri road

(**2hrs 35mins**). Opposite is the rather unlikely site of a Geometric (9th–4th century BC) settlement, with the remains of a dozen houses and two graveyards nearby.

Follow the road towards **Monodhéndhri** and fork R (lower road). About 700m after this you can bear L up a cobbled path, a shortcut into the village centre (**3hrs**). For the disused but spectacular monastery of Áyia Paraskeví (15mins), continue to the huge plane tree, with Kikítsa's taverna ahead, and the beautifully frescoed church of Áyios Minás R. Turn L (north), signed to 'Víkos gorge' and 'Áyia Paraskeví monastery'. The broad, paved lane leads after 1km to the 15th-century gate. There is a heart-in-mouth viewpoint over the gorge, with even more giddying views if you climb the steps to the L and follow the old trail – basically a ledge in the sheer cliffside, with a wooden bridge and a walled gate at strategic points – to the hermits' caves.

Stage 3 – Monodhéndhri (1050m) – Víkos gorge (500m) – Pápingo (950m)

Walking time:	6hrs 15mins
Distance:	14.5km
Waymarks:	O3, red diamonds on white, except for first hour
Height gain:	500m
Height loss:	600m
Difficulty:	3

The Víkos gorge is the jewel in the crown of Zagorian hiking, over 12km long (and this only the middle section) and dwarfed by cliffs rising 500–1000m above the riverbed. Best of all, you usually have it to yourself. From the magnificent turquoise springs of the Voïdhomátis river the route climbs to Pápingo, for easy onward access to the Astrákas refuge and Mt Gamíla. But it is quite possible – easier and shorter, in fact– to climb out to Víkos village, which has a simple pension and road access to Arísti (for the lower Víkos gorge walk). Either way, take plenty of water and watch out for snakes, attracted to the pools of the riverbed.

The Víkos gorge from the Pápingo end (photo Michael Cullen)

From the central plane tree (Kikítsa's taverna), head east up a cobbled lane (not the lane heading north to 'Vikos Kanyon'). Two signs give slightly optimistic times to Pápingo (6hrs) and, in Greek only, to Kípi (2hrs) and Víkos village (4hrs 30mins). Past the public toilets on your R and then the large church of Áyios Athanásios, whose grounds would make a reasonable campsite, the lane becomes gravelly.

Ignore yellow signs pointing L to 'Grounia Z7' and R to 'Ag Apostoli'. Pass between the unfinished open-air theatre and its unused outbuildings (all EU-funded). The rough-paved path zigzags down through hornbeam and other deciduous trees, speckled with autumn crocus, hellebores and cyclamen in late September and October. Pass a shrine R (**15mins**); views ahead to the cliffs of Mezariá side canyon herald a steeper, more relentless descent, but the cobbles are firm and the path shady. Approaching the gorge bed (**45mins**), ignore small paths forking R (for Kípi) and continue straight on, passing a low rock face on your L. You are now in the depths of the canyon, 300m vertically below Áyia Paraskeví monastery.

From here the path, well-blazed with O3 red-on-white diamonds, follows the L bank of the gorge, at times next to the riverbed, at times climbing over rocky shoulders, all the way to the Voïdhomátis springs 10km downstream.

After a beautiful stretch 50–80m above the gorge floor, descend iron steps to the dry bed, keep along the L bank (O3

Do not be tempted into the bed itself, a jumble of enormous boulders interspersed with scummy, seasonal pools. The path demands some care, but is maintained every spring and should be easily passable.

waymarks) and climb again past the worst of the scree slopes. This ascent climaxes at a narrow saddle beside a rocky outcrop (**1hr 35mins**). The descent which follows is steep and slippery. You pass an overhang and a rocky ledge with tree-trunk bridges before climbing through gentler woods.

The sound of running water and a metal sign 'Eos Papigkou' (**2hrs**) announce the turn-off R to the junction of the Méghas Lákkos and Víkos watercourses, where a clean stream flows year-round. Known as Klíma, it is the only drinkable water until the Voïdhomátis springs. It is possible – though trail-less and hard work – to continue up the Méghas Lákkos to the high pastures of Gamíla in 5–6hrs.

Return to the main path and continue northwest, past flat, shady ground at the base of a moss-covered boulder-spill. After the stone shrine of Áyia Triádha on the R (**3hrs**; *unreliable well-spring*), the going improves, with semi-open meadows affording views up to the soaring pinnacles R. Later, a knuckle-line of rock gendarmes climbs the L slope. At **3hrs 45mins** you earn your first views up to Víkos village, appearing as a single house atop the lowest knoll of the LH ridge, where this descends into woodland. Shortly after this a plane-mounted O3 plaque points R, alongside the riverbed, for the easily missed trail to Pápingo.

For Vikos

The main path, intermittently paved, climbs gradually L between twin hawthorn saplings (more paths down to the river in case you miss the earlier fork); then past a smaller R fork which leads in 10mins down to the ex-monastery of Panayía; then, more steeply, up to the asphalt road at the southern end of **Víkos** hamlet (**5hrs**).

The O3 route follows the riverside to some huge, grey, rounded rock-buttresses on the R bank (**4hrs 10mins**); you will see O3 waymarks pointing up the R slope.

Voïdhomátis springs

Outside midsummer, this is the point where the subterranean aquifers of the Voïdhomátis well up into an icy, clear and surprisingly forceful stream. Dye tests have revealed that the water takes over a week to filter through the 1200 vertical metres separating the springs from the Épos and Provatína sinkholes above.

The Voïdhomátis springs (photo Michael Cullen)

From the rounded rock buttresses follow the O3 path up the steep R (northeastern) slope. In the afternoon sun, the relentless, zigzagging ascent through sparse Jerusalem sage shrubs is a killer, so take it gently. A massive granite finger (**4hrs 45mins**) makes a good rest spot, with views over the lower, impassable section of the gorge. Beneath huge orange cliffs – the first of the towers of Astráka – the path crosses a scree slope. After a short descent you pass beneath a pretty overhang R, before resuming the climb towards Pápingo. On your L comes a dramatic drop to the ravine separating Mikró from Meghálo Pápingo.

Shortly after this (**5hrs 40mins**), by a wooden sign in Greek, the path forks: L (downhill) goes to Meghálo Pápingo, R (uphill) to Mikró Pápingo. The former descends past the Stefóvrisi spring (trickle) to cross the ravine and climb to Meghálo Pápingo in 30mins (**6hrs 10mins**), emerging across the road (south) from the large village church. The latter twists uphill through old fields at the foot of the towers (O3 waymarks), bears R at a stony shoulder and climbs even more steeply to a pair of walled springs at the southern limits of **Mikró Pápingo**. Cobbled lanes lead you into the village centre (**6hrs 15mins**).

Stage 4 (optional day hike) – Pápingo (950m) –
Áno Kleidhoniá (900m) – Káto Kleidhoniá
(400m) – lower Víkos gorge (450m) –
bridge below Arísti (450m)

Walking time:	5hrs 30mins
Distance:	12.5km
Waymarks:	Red paint to Káto Kleidhoniá; occasional red-on-white arrows (in lower Víkos gorge)
Height gain:	300m
Height loss:	800m
Difficulty:	3

The lowest reaches of the Víkos gorge are extremely picturesque and often overlooked. Despite their more modest scale, the sheer reddish cliffs, plane-shaded banks and enticing blue-green pools scoured out by the icy Voïdhomátis river make it a hike well worth fitting in if you have time. The best way to do it is from Pápingo (the route described below), but there is an alternative via the rather overgrown path from Arísti described under Route 22.

From Meghálo Pápingo church follow the cobbled lane north, and at the fork keep L (Odos Anagnastopoúlou). At the junction in front of Pension Koúlis, run by Koúlis Khristodhoúlou (the EOS rep who maintains the local trails) turn L (red arrow). At the next junction, with the Hotel Saxónis R, keep R along Odos Daska, which becomes a dirt track and leaves the village. You pass the wayside chapel of Áyios Athanásios (L), ignoring small forks off the main track.

At the end of the track (**20mins**) continue down the L bank along a path which crosses a gully (often dry) and climbs back up the far bank. Less than 10mins above this gully, fork R (flimsy sign 'Clidonia'). The path climbs past a shrine, enters a grassy corridor and eventually dips to cross the deepest of the gullies draining the western flanks of Lápatos (**1hr**). Follow the red waymarks carefully as they thread through the scrub. Pass a stone's throw below two adjacent firs, then cross the last gully (a small path joins from pastures R) and climb to cross a slight spur (blue sign 'Kleidonia', **1hr 30mins**). Soon the path widens and descends southwest towards an aerial, offering views back to the towers of Astrákas and the Víkos gorge.

At the humming cellphone aerial and adjacent chapel, pick up a dirt road looping down and R into the near-abandoned hamlet of Áno Kleidhoniá (**2hrs**). Continue through the village, forking L where the road surface changes from paving to asphalt (sign to 'Ayios Athanásios') and you will stumble upon a panorama which matches any in the area: the combined floodplains of the Voïdhomátis and Aöos rivers laid out in a patchwork at your feet, with the looming bulk of Mt Nemértska in Albania beyond, and to L and R the endlessly intersecting dips and peaks of row upon row of mountains. From the flat rocky ledges below the chapel (**2hrs 10mins**) a red-dotted path heads briefly R before starting its long series of switchbacks down the steep hillside to Kalívia Klidhoniás. The name means 'huts of Klidhoniá' and, until last century, were temporary winter quarters. The path is generally well waymarked and defined, apart from a clearing where you keep R, though loose rocks make the descent quite treacherous. At **3hrs** you pass a locked chapel and a weak spring, then slip between cliff and boulder to reach the highest inhabited house of Kalívia.

Follow the concrete track downhill (blue fence R) and, after 100m, at the junction, continue L/straight, downhill (R leads through Kalívia to the main road and bus stop). Where the track ends by a vine-covered garden, continue along the path which drops to cross a dry, boulder-filled gully and climb

The lower Víkos gorge (photo Michael Cullen)

to a livestock shelter (**3hrs 15mins**). Here follow the jeep track L, climbing slightly before descending to join a larger road, with the stone bridge of Káto Klidhoniá 100m L (**3hrs 30mins**). It is a beautiful spot, marred only by the occasional passing coach party.

Do not cross the bridge, but follow the well-made path up the L (true R) bank. It soon loses its paved surface and slips along the river's edge in the shade of semi-submerged plane trees. At times rough underfoot, the path climbs over some rocky flanks and descends to a bracken- and plane-filled meadow enclosed in a loop of the river (**4hrs 20mins**). In the middle a path leads L up 100 steps to the dilapidated monastery of Áyii Anáryiri, a worthwhile 5min detour.

From the meadow the path continues up the river's true R bank, curling L (east) and climbing up on to a series of rock ledges with caves above, in which some of Greece's earliest Stone Age tools and bones have been found (15000–9000BC).

Shortly after this come some unexpectedly steep and high climbs – up to 80m above the river – over densely wooded spurs. The small path is signalled by occasional cairns and red-arrowhead-on-white signs, and can be slippery after rain. Around **5hrs 15mins** drop for the last time to the now wide river banks and continue south, following a network of tracks through plane woods, to join the Arísti – Pápingo road at the first hairpin east of the river bridge, by a barrier (**5hrs 30mins**). The bus for Pápingo currently comes past around 15.30 Tues/Fri.

Stage 5 – Pápingo (950m) – Astrákas refuge (1900m) – Dhrakólimni Lake (2000m) – Astrákas refuge (1900m)

Walking time:	5hrs (3hrs to refuge; 2hrs round trip to lake)
Distance:	5km to refuge (+ 6km round trip to lake)
Waymarks:	O3 (red-diamond-on-white) and orange or red dots and arrows to refuge
Height gain:	950m to refuge (+ 300m to lake)
Height loss:	300m from lake to refuge
Difficulty:	3

A well-used path leads up to the EOS mountain refuge (*staffed; 8 euros for/members of a national mountaineering club, 10 euros for non-members; meals*), perched on the 1950m-col below Astráka peak and visible from the Pápingo villages. It is essential to book ahead in season: Koúlis Khristodhoúlou, tel: 26530 41335/41115/41484 (fax), or c/o Koúlis' pension in Meghálo Pápingo. Failing that, contact Kóstas Tsoúmanis, tel: 26530 41257/41892 (fax) or c/o Hotel Dias in Mikró Pápingo. It is a panoramic location and a handy, often sociable, base for exploring the uplands of Mt Gamíla – most impressively, the alpine tarn of **Dhrakólimni**.

From Mikró Pápingo car park and plane tree follow the cobbled lane ahead (south) and then L, passing Hotel Dias L. At the junction keep L (signs to 'Refuge 3hrs, Provatina cave 3hrs, Drakolimni 4hrs, Gamíla 5hrs'). Leave the village and pass the covered spring of Avraghónios and shrine of Áyios Pandeléïmon R (**10mins**; *possible camping spot under plane tree*). This is the first of four springs which irrigate your ascent and which sometimes shelter yellow-bellied toads. Shortly after this, fork R (sign to 'Katafiyio') and wind uphill through juniper, oak and hazel, following occasional red dots/orange arrows (and droppings from the pack animals which service the refuge).

After the next spring (Andálki, 1220m; **45mins**; sign to 'Refuge 2h20') the path switchbacks up stony, eroded slopes and the trees thin out, making it hot work. An hour later pass the unreliable spring of Tráfos (1550m; sign to 'Refuge 1h20') and veer slightly away from the dry gully L, zigzagging uphill (ignore the shortcuts used by those descending). About 15mins above Tráfos (**2hrs**), there is a R fork to Astrákas peak and Provatína 'cave'.

You could spend an extra night at the refuge and bag Astráka (2432m) on a 5hr circular route. It is a reasonably clear cross-country trail, accurately marked on the Anávasi map.

Provatína

At 405m deep this vies with various Mexican *cenotes* for the title of deepest straight-drop sinkhole in the world. Another contender is the Épous (or Épos) sinkhole, almost directly above the Voïdhomátis springs; this has been measured at 447m, but not in a straight drop.

Ignore this fork (it is possible to shortcut and miss it anyway) and continue northeast towards the clearly visible refuge. Another 15mins brings you to the fourth and last spring, Koúrna

Astráka and the path to Dhrakólimni (photo Michael Cullen)

(1800m), and a final 25min slog sees you at the col, with the refuge just to your L (**3hrs**). To the east the ground drops away abruptly to a perfectly flat *loótsa* (seasonal lake), with shallow, muddy waters in spring and colourful algae in autumn. There are some shepherds' huts and *lákes* (meadows) visible to the L. You can also see the path to Dhrakólimni winding lazily up the grassy slopes to the northeast.

For Dhrakólimni, continue down the abrupt east slope along a steep and rocky path. After 10mins ignore the R turn for Gamíla and Tsepélovo (G painted on the rock) and continue straight on (D for Dhrakólimni), descending to the north end of the seasonal lake. Find a small red-dotted path climbing east over a rocky hump (aim just R of a prominent rounded boulder on the skyline), then descending northeast over grassland to some boggy turf (35mins).

There are several drinkable springs here. From the easternmost one follow the previously visible path, climbing steadily northeast up the grassy spur with the sheer scarp of Plóskos R. Another 45mins should see you through a V in the rim of the tarn (2000m), where you would expect it to drain out. But its reed- and snow-fringed waters are plentiful, clear and surprisingly unglacial. Climb the cairned summit on the far side (2050m) for the views over the Aöós valley to Mt Smólikas (which has a namesake Dhrakólimni at a similar altitude). Return to the refuge the way you came (**5hrs 30mins**).

*Looking up at Gamíla I (L) and Plóskos
(photo Michael Cullen)*

Stage 6 – *Astrákas refuge (1900m) – Tsepélovo (1100m) (or Kapésovo, 1100m) via Mt Gamíla pass (2000m)*

Walking time:	5hrs 30mins to Tsepélovo, 6hrs 15mins to Kapésovo
Distance:	13km to Tsepélovo, 15.5km to Kapésovo
Waymarks:	O3 (red-diamond-on-white) for first section, yellow-diamond-on-blue for last section and occasional red and blue dots throughout
Height gain:	350m to Tsepélovo, 400m to Kapésovo
Height loss:	1150m to Tsepélovo, 1200m to Kapésovo
Difficulty:	3

Follow the stony path down (east) from the refuge and at the junction of paths (**10mins**) turn right (G for Gamíla, painted on rock). This descends steeply to the southern end of the seasonal lake, crosses the grassy flats and starts climbing among the boulders. You may hear the springs of the Romióvrisi gurgling underneath the boulders R (faded 'Quele' – German – painted on rock). To your L is a curved rock wall where I have seen wall creepers.

Keeping your eyes peeled for O3 waymarks, thread southeast up through the boulders for 20mins until the path levels out on the west side of a gentle, grassy dip. Along here the O3 (Karterós pass) and red-dotted Gamíla trails branch L (southeast); for Tsepélovo stick on the R (true L) side of the dip, heading south–southeast (occasional blue dots). The path winds, like a notch in the limestone strata, up to an unexpectedly large dam at the northern end of the Rombózi reservoir (**1hr 5mins**). Here, on the saddle linking Astráka and Gamíla peaks, you are almost at the high point of your route (1970m). In late May and early June thousands of crocuses poke their purple and yellow heads through holes in the melting snow.

You can head around the pond, but a clearer option is to strike L (east) up the slope to the top of the mound (2000m). Here, between two cairns, pick up a clear path descending south, past a spring (*tapped in summer*), to a thistly meadow

The meadows at Stáni Mirioúli (photo Michael Cullen)

with a ruined hut L (**1hr 30mins**). This is Stáni Mirioúli, where the Astráka circuit path joins from the west. Continue southeast down a rocky hump with gullies developing on both sides. After 15mins it flattens off and bears R, contouring, then descending gently past the 1800m mark. After another 15mins you reach a lip with an easily missed sinkhole R (known as the Nifótripa – bride's hole – and apparently 113m deep).

Here the path drops L into the dry gully separating you from the lunar, indented slopes of Gamíla, Karterós and Meghála Lithária. On the way down you pass another grassy balcony below some spiny plum saplings, before reaching the gully floor at **2hrs 30mins**. The path climbs the far bank and straightens out in a southerly direction. Pass some scree and boulderfields dropping away to the deepening ravine now on your R. This is the head of the Méghas Lákos, which eventually joins the Víkos gorge at the Klíma springs.

Nearly **3hrs** from the refuge you pass an overhanging rock L, at the foot of which a weak but year-round spring fills a tiny, fern-fringed pool. Known as Kroúna, this is the only reliable water (and shade) en route.

There follows a long, stony ascent L-wards out of the ravine until, around 1750m, the path resumes R (south) and passes over a mini-saddle. At the first level ground below this (**3hrs 35mins**), there is an important and easily missed junction.

Méghas Lákos ravine near the Kroúna spring (photo Michael Cullen)

The main path continues straight on for Vradhéto/Kapésovo as follows: past a dry or murky *loótsa* (pond) and beneath a bump R where once a Turkish *kazárma* (prison-fort) stood. Here you can enjoy your first views over Tsepélovo and the wooded hills to its south. Do not descend towards Tsepélovo (despite what other guidebooks advise, this is a steep, rocky, pathless descent). Instead, follow the main path over some grassy humps to a shaly section, where you descend to a visible jeep track. This descends in an anticlockwise loop for just over 1km; then, where it straightens out, follow it down to the Kapésovo – Vradhéto road and turn R (or you can bear R onto the signed path which is shorter). Either way you should reach Vradhéto within 1hr of the junction, or in just over 5hrs' walking from the refuge. From there, follow Stage 1 to reach Kapésovo in a further hour.

For Tsepélovo, turn L, up a side gully, past your first yellow-on-blue waymarks. You soon amble through a grassy corridor bordered by limestone pavements, with violas, forget-me-not, cranesbill and *campanula glomerata* adding splashes of colour. About 20mins from the junction you leave the corridor and start the careful descent to Tsepélovo, which is waymarked with red dots and blue-on-yellow squares all the way.

226

After 10mins (**4hrs 5mins**) a path joins from the L and you descend to a bowl filled with thistles, mullein and hellebores. Bearing L (east), continue down the stony and grassy slope, then curl R-wards around the base of a meadow to a spur with square boulders R. Bearing L again, the path drops steeply down to the walled, dungy spring of Pétrino (**4hrs 30mins**). From its lowest trough, drop southeast into the dry gully, then branch R along a clearer, stone-built path. After zigzagging down past a lone walnut tree, it meets a jeep track on a spur known as Kángena (**4hrs 50mins**; more walnut trees just below).

Follow this track south for a minute, then turn R (southwest) down a faint but waymarked path. This descends just L of the valley-line, past shrubs and saplings, to meet the same jeep track at a bend near some more walnut trees (**5hrs 10mins**; red painted ΚΑΤΑΦΥΓΙΟ on a rock for those coming the other way). In the cliffs to the west you can see a narrow cleft, up which it is possible to clamber a short way. Follow the track straight/R (south), passing a dewpond (Láko Boúti) R. After about 500m the route drops R to shortcut a corner and rejoins the track. After a similar distance, with a wooden/wire fence L, keep L. About 100m later, by a concrete cabin, fork R down a small path which joins a cobbled lane by the first houses. This lane leads down past the walled spring and up, passing the church on your R, into the main square (**5hrs 30mins**).

Route 22
Zagóri Circuit Alternatives

Tsepélovo (1100m) – Khadzíou bridge (800m) – Kípi (800m)

Walking time:	2hrs 40mins
Distance:	7.5km
Height gain:	250m
Height loss:	550m
Difficulty:	1
Map:	See Route 21

A much easier – but also less interesting – route than the one via Vradhéto, convenient for those carrying heavy packs or wanting a recovery day.

> Follow the main road out of Tsepélovo towards Kapésovo and Yánina. After 500m pass the school boarding house L (next to a grove of tall evergreens), and the road bends R. Keep L/straight along a dirt road, with the basketball pitch R. This descends steadily through sparse oak woods, becoming impassable for cars, to reach the valley floor (830m) after **40mins**, where a driveable dirt road joins from the L. Ahead is the graceful Khadzíou bridge (1804) over the Skamneliótiko river.

Before crossing it is worth heading downstream – a tiny path threads down the R bank – to see the impressive but dilapidated stone span now known as Palioyéfiro, the old bridge. This links the sheer rock faces at the point where they converge dramatically, forcing the river into a 4m-deep channel. Swim through – if you dare – into the eerily enclosed gorge of the Vikákis. From here downstream to Kípi would be a 4km (2hr) wade over smooth boulders and through icy pools up to your waist.

> Retrace your steps to the Khadzíou bridge (**1hr**), cross over and follow the jeep track southwards up the side valley. After 800m it crosses the stream (flowing in spring), zigzags once and continues steadily southwest, climbing all the while. A further 30mins brings you to the top (**1hr 45mins**; 1030m) and a T-junction with a larger dirt track. Turn R and follow the road along the summit-line, enjoying intermittent views L over the densely wooded, interlocking spurs of the Víkos valley head. Keeping west, the track climbs to 1100m before starting its descent towards Kípi. At one point the track forks and rejoins; other than that, ignore minor turn-offs and, after 2km, pass below a large stone shrine R. At the junction of tracks just below keep R (or alternatively dive straight on down a small shortcut path which rejoins after 5mins or so). After rejoining, by a stand of firs, branch R down a narrow path past a smart walled house at the top of **Kípi** and follow your nose into the village centre (**2hrs 40mins**).

Kapésovo (1100m) – Víkos gorge (700m)

Walking time:	1hr+
Distance:	2.5km
Waymarks:	Red circle on white square
Height gain:	0m
Height loss:	400m
Difficulty:	1

A quick link between Kapésovo and the upper Vikos gorge. This would allow hardened walkers to complete a three-day Víkos – Gamíla circuit, with one night in Pápingo and one in the refuge.

Follow the main cobbled lane down through the centre of **Kapésovo** (sign to VICOS), past the huge plane tree. About 100m below the plane tree fork R down an unsigned cobbled lane (telegraph pole/streetlamp in front). At the bottom of the village, you pass the covered springs (dry) and the first red-on-white waymark. These and the occasional VIKOS sign guide you down the small, sometimes steep path to the gorge bed. Follow the gorge bed downstream for 10–15 mins (O3 waymarks) to join the route from Monodhéndri (Route 21, Stage 3) at the **45min** point.

Geranium subcaulescens

Route 23
Mt Gamíla and Aöós Gorge
Traverse (2–3 days)

This is a tough but exhilarating backpacking route over the limestone crest of Mt Gamíla via the 2200m Tsoúka Rósa pass and then down the wild, wooded flanks of the Aöós gorge to Kónitsa. You need a tent or bivvy bag even in summer, as the Goúra campsite is high; on the second night you might be able to sleep in the dormitory of Stomíou monastery (monks permitting). There is very little water on these northeastern slopes of Gamíla; the two campsites suggested here are the only reliable year-round springs on the whole route. An alternative, shorter descent – achievable in a long day – takes you to the remote village of Vrisokhóri.

Stage 1 – Skamnéli (1150m) – Goúra spring (2050m; camp)

Walking time:	3hrs
Distance:	8km
Waymarks:	Very sparse
Height gain:	900m
Height loss:	0m
Difficulty:	2
Map:	See Route 21

This is not the most beautiful ascent in the region, being largely treeless and laced with jeep tracks, but it is a relatively painless way of gaining 900m altitude, and you may be able to get a lift in a cowherd's pick-up. The old path has practically disappeared, so – apart from the first and last sections – the route described follows jeep tracks.

On a long summer's day you would just have time to arrive by afternoon bus and walk straight on up to Goúra. Otherwise catch the morning bus, take a taxi or stay overnight in the simple Hotel Pindos (tel: 26530 81280/81295). If you have time to kill, there is a short signposted walk (yellow Z22 signpost) heading west from the village to Áyia Paraskeví monastery and some Pelasgian wall fragments just above it.

From the asphalt road (1150m), go up the main cobbled lane passing the huge plane tree and Hotel Pindos on your R. After 100m keep R, passing the school on your L. Follow the main lane L (twin telegraph poles L) and then R again. The path leaves the village, climbing through stony walnut and cornelian cherry groves. Follow the most trodden path and the occasional ground-painted red arrow, aiming for a tree-speckled hill to the north–northeast, bisected by the faint diagonal line of a dirt road. Above this are cattle meadows, known as Vourtápa (Vourtápes on the map). If in doubt ask for directions to these.

At a disused concrete water channel (before the telephone wires, **10mins**), turn L (red arrow) and follow the channel uphill past a covered stone water reservoir. Ignore the L bend (water pipe) and continue straight up the dry gully (no waymark). This becomes a disused jeep track, bending R. At **20mins** it joins a larger track and almost immediately they debouch on to a wider gravel road at a hairpin bend 80m above a rusty shrine.

This is the main 'road' up to Vourtápa, and given your likely load and the difficulty of finding the old path from here, I suggest you follow it. Turn L (uphill). It bears R, zigzagging steadily uphill away from the gully and descending clifflets of Gomarórakhi on the L. At **50mins** pass on your R a shepherds' pen in the lee of a giant limestone pavement. After this it bears L across a rocky streambed – you can, before this, continue north–northeast straight up a giant-cairn-crested spur as a short-cut. Otherwise, stay on the track for a couple more switchbacks and it flattens out by the circular dewpond and the first crude huts of Vourtápa (**1hr 30mins**; 1550m).

At the junction (straight on leads over and down to Tsepélovo), turn R along a smaller track leading northeast into a jumbled cirque of rock castles and cliffs crumbling into scree, with verbascum-choked meadows R. This crosses the ridge south of Káto Tsoúka and joins a larger track (**1hr 55mins**); ahead you can see the cairn-crested spur mentioned earlier. Turn sharp L up the track back across the ridge, crossing the screefields at the southwest foot of Káto Tsoúka to pass beneath a cairn-topped triangular crag. You can see a tiny trail traversing the face of Káto Tsoúka – the only safe way up the main peak of Tsoúka. Finally the track descends slightly to end by some huts and a walled spring (**2hrs 15mins**; 1850m), both of which function only in summer when the cowherds overnight here.

Turn R (north) up a dung-spattered path, heading towards the western crags of Tsoúka and two silhouetted, nipple-like cairns on a closer hump. Underfoot you may see sections of the metal pipe feeding the spring, which follows the shortest (but not the easiest) route from Goúra spring. At a sea of jagged boulders (**2hrs 27mins**) the path veers R, away from the pipe, to a low ridge where it resumes north.

At a P-shaped boulder (**2hrs 45mins**) do not cross the grassy bowl ahead but bear R to another grassy dip. Lunar grey screes, scoured rock faces and twisted crags surround you. Pass below (R of) the twin cairns (pipe rejoins) and, a little higher, bear R into a grassy corridor. Tomorrow's pass is visible ahead (north), an open V which some cowherds erroneously call Karteroú. At the top of a string of puddles in a grassy meadow lies the covered ground-well of Goúra (**3hrs**; 2050m), below a knobbly, overhanging face to the east. ◀

Choughs wheel and whirr around these crags, and a muffled crash of stones spilling near the summit may signal an elusive Balkan chamois. There is plenty of soft, flat ground for camping, though it may be snow-covered until May.

Stage 2 – Goúra (2050m) – Tsoúka Rósa pass (2300m) – Stáni Katsánou (1650m) – Stomíou monastery (700m) or Vrisokhóri (1000m)

Walking time:	6hrs 30mins
Distance:	12km to Stomíou, 11.5km to Vrisokhóri
Waymarks:	Intermittent red paint splodges and red-on-cream plaques, with a short section of O3 red-on-white squares in the middle
Height gain:	500m to Stomíou, 300m to Vrisokhóri
Height loss:	1850m to Stomíou, 1350m to Vrisokhóri
Difficulty:	3

This is quite a long day, with some fairly punishing downhill towards the end. An early start will maximise your chances of cloud-free views from the pass.

Continue up the slight valley, now heading just west of north, and over the gentle saddle linking the rocky summit of Vlási to the west (also called Kourtétsi; easily climbed) with the more forbidding Tsoúka to the east (a steep scramble). Descend the cow-trodden path into and across a boulder-ridden cwm, passing a low stone corral L. The path dwindles, but make for the rocky summit L of the pass, known as Meghála Lithária (big boulders), and look out for occasional red-on-cream metal waymarks lying on the ground. At a small, flattish pasture, bear R (northeast), climbing more steeply towards the L-most needle of Tsoúka, before resuming L (northwest) to a spill of big boulders (which gave the area its name). A fading painted red arrow directs you R, zigzagging up a messy slope, until a visible trail straightens out to reach Tsoúka Rósa pass (**1hr**; 2320m).

The Tsoúka Rósa peak (2355m) juts up ahead R, at the end of a knife-edge ridge (for experienced scramblers only). Clouds broiling up the 1000m drop to its R (northeast) usually obscure the flanks of the more distant Mt Smólikas, but further L (northwest) the sheer cliffs and forests of Mt Trapezítsa are often visible and sometimes, in between, Mt Grámos and the Albanian hinterland. ▶

The descent starts R-wards from the pass, then cuts back L across loose scree – no fun to ascend. Pass below (R of) a cairned bluff, keeping near the gully floor to a thistle-filled meadow (**1hr 30mins**, excluding summits). On your L is a dramatic skyline of cliffs, gendarmes, couloirs and year-round snow patches – the dark side of Gamíla and Karterós peaks. From the far end of the meadow (old corral) continue northwest, climbing slightly (red splodges) and aiming for a large cairn atop a mound. Pass just to the R of this (**1hr 45mins**) and pick out, in the pathless rocky valley below, two red-on-cream squares. Beyond you can see the onward path climbing northwest of Stáni Katsánou.

Make your way as best you can down past the two square waymarks, then drop to the valley floor where more waymarks (in this direction only) guide you across the loose rocks. Looking back, your cairned mound is the L-most of three. At **2hrs 15mins** drop R to some low stone corrals and a crude hut, then turn L to regain the main valley. The waymarks are now the red-diamond-on-white of the O3 trail, which joined imperceptibly after crossing Gamíla via the steep and tricky Karterós pass. These guide you down the R flank and then into the valley floor, where a small circular dewpond and a makeshift boulderside hut mark the milking pasture of Kátsanos or Stáni

A steep 5mins up R is an exhilarating rocky summit overlooking the chasm above Vrisokhóri and Iliokhóri.

Katsánou (**2hrs 45mins**; 1670m). There is no spring, but the tallest of the firs and Balkan pines, some of them lightning-scarred, offer patchy shade. The wide V of Vasilítsa mountain and ski station is visible to the east, the long ridge of Smólikas to its L, with the village of Palioséli standing out.

Variant: descent to Vrisokhóri (3hrs)

From the far LH lip of the bowl – by a plaque on a rock commemorating the death of a young Greek rambler named Voúla – a path drops steeply northeast (red and orange arrows, mostly positioned for those coming up). After 45mins it crosses the still-dry gully, winds through mixed forest, rounds a spur and continues descending southeast to the spring of Neraïdhóvrisi (**4hrs 15mins**; 1275m), the first reliable water since Goúra. There follows 30mins of climbing and descending through beech woods, before hitting a logging road. Follow this for about 30mins (there are stretches of old trail L) until, after a RH bend (**5hrs 15mins**), the O3-signed trail continues L. It crosses an older dirt road, slips down shaly gully-sides before veering R to cross two bridges and climb to the chapel of Áyia Paraskeví, at the east end of Vrisokhóri (**6hrs 15mins**).

The total elapsed walking time from Skamnéli is thus a little over 9hrs, based on carrying a full pack, which makes it feasible only on a long summer's day. There is currently one bus a week serving Vrisokhóri, leaving Yánnina on Thursdays at 08.45 and turning straight round after its 2hr journey to return.

Link to Mt Smólikas

It is possible to cross the Aöós valley from here to Palioséli on the southern slopes of Smólikas by 12km of rough dirt road, whose construction unfortunately put paid to the beautiful old path. It is a frustratingly twisty route, particularly on the far side. The only consolation is the possibility of a swim in the Aöós by the bridge. I have not investigated this systematically but a cursory look suggests that worthwhile sections of the path are still traceable on the ascent to Palioséli where the road has taken a line well to the east. Work around the bridge has obscured the start, but it is still there. Clamber up the artificial steep earth 'cliff' to the left immediately after the bridge, drop down a few metres and you will find the path. The general line is up through the western extensions of the road's hairpins. It would be gratifying if some generous soul would check this out and report back; it would be wonderful to have a proper path connection again between the Zagóri hikes and Smólikas.

To continue on the main route to Stomíou monastery (3hrs)
From the far L of the bowl, a path climbs steeply back L (southwest) over loose rocks, towards the peak, Liméria Kleftón, which means 'the lairs of the brigands/*klephts*'. It looks suitably unassailable. In the shade of pines it bears R (north) to cross the spur below this peak (3hrs 10mins), offering final views back to Tsoúka Rósa and Karterós and down to the red roofs of Vrisokhóri. Descend to a boulder with a red-on-cream square – these have resumed – before bearing L and uphill again through beech woods to the next saddle (3hrs 30mins). Here the views extend northwest down the Aöós river gorge to its flood plains below Kónitsa.

Pass to the R of a large half-burned pine and find a path zigzagging nastily down the stony slope. After a few minutes a gentler option forks L into low woods (softer underfoot) before heading R across the gully to rejoin the main path. Pass under and around some monster pine trunks, before turning L (unsigned) across a dry gully to an open patch (3hrs 55mins) with fabulous glimpses up to the saw-toothed peaks of Gamíla and Plóskos. Ignore an old arrow pointing R and aim L of Gamíla, following red-on-cream squares in a big clockwise loop into the head of the meadows of the Siádhi Míghas (Vlach/Greek for 'pasture of the flies'). A clear path leads northwest through these meadows, past a dewpond and a house-sized boulder (**4hrs 20mins**). In the lee of this you stumble upon a shepherds' lean-to and, often, his fierce untended dogs.

From here, a path leads down the dip into enchanting beech woods, then climbs slightly to round a spur. Ignoring small paths which join R, continue west and level, in mixed forest now, hemmed in by the rocky flanks of Trapezítsa R and Plóskos L. Bright yellow arrows join in the waymarking, scratched with directions by Albanian immigrants using this path as an illegal entry into central Greece. At the next spur (**5hrs**; 1300m) a path joins from the L (very faded sign) and the descent begins in earnest: a steep but always clear and shady path zigzagging down the R banks of the Kerasiás gully for nearly an hour. Drawn on by the sweet sound of a gushing stream, cross the main gully (880m; *drinkable water all year; no possible camp-sites*) just shy of **6hrs**. A sign confirms that this is the *dhési* (pipe intake) for the monastery's water supply.

Consequently, the path widens and improves as it descends the L bank, past a sort of layby R just wide enough for a tent, after which a gap in the pines allows your first glimpse of the monastery, a large, modern-looking walled compound perched on an outcrop above the Aöós. The final descent is loose and stony, dropping to a walled spring and larger track outside the perimeter fence (**6hrs 30mins**). The main gate is straight ahead, but be warned that it closes shortly before sunset and may be locked up when you visit. You should wear long sleeves and trousers.

Stomíou monastery

Since the death of Fathers Païsios and Kosmás from Kónitsa, a lone but friendly novice monk called Pávlos holds fort here. He hoped to stay permanently from 2005, but it is not certain whether he has been able to. Founded in the 1770s, the monastery was burned by the Germans in 1944. The view over the Aöós from the far corner is breathtaking, and the whole setting is almost Tibetan in its wild grandeur.

The larger track leads R in 5mins to another walled spring set amidst tall pines, with ledges flattened out for pilgrim-campers, who gather here in droves for the 8 September festival. Camping here is the best option if the monastery is closed or you prefer privacy.

Stage 3 – *Stomíou monastery (700m) – Aöós gorge (450m) – Kónitsa (550m)*

Walking time:	1hr 50mins
Distance:	6km
Waymarks:	Red-on-cream squares
Height gain:	100m
Height loss:	250m
Difficulty:	1

From the spring outside the perimeter fence, follow the main track west and downhill. It was recently re-bulldozed (2005) to bring in building materials, but will soon revert to pedestrian use. Meantime, the old path offers agreeable shortcuts R, re-converging at the powerful stream of Ghrávos (**10mins**). A few minutes further, the old path forks L (red paint on rock to L) but, for once, I would advocate following the jeep track straight down to the Aöós river for a dip in its rather murky but surprisingly warm waters. At the water's edge, follow the cement wall on the LH side before resuming along the jeep track, initially uphill. You rejoin the river at **40mins**, with a (drinkable) side stream gurgling under the boulders; the sandy bank makes this perhaps the best swimming spot.

Within 10mins the jeep track brings you to a weir (built to offer a year-round canoeing course) and continues, now passable by car, down the plane-shaded L bank. Opposite, russet-barked arbutus trees poke out of the rock face at zany angles. Pass a sign listing the park by-laws, then a metal post where the old path rejoins. At **1hr 20mins**, just after the cable crossing for monastery goods, you reach the gracefully arching stone bridge of Kónitsa R. Cross it, looking upstream for tremendous views up to the pyramid of Gamíla I (2497m) and continue up the road. Just past a hotel/café a lane forks R and climbs quite steeply up past the minaret of a ruined mosque to join the main road at a hairpin bend opposite the vast plane tree of the Hotel Dendro; follow this road R to reach the centre of Kónitsa (**1hr 50mins**).

Campunula rupicola

PART 3 – ATHENS AND THE EAST COAST

CHAPTER 7
MT PÁRNITHA

Mt Párnitha (1413m) stands on the western rim of the Attic Basin, 50 years ago a fertile plain of olive groves, vines and wheat production, but filled now by the sprawling suburbs of Athens, which has grown to accommodate nearly half the population of Greece.

The mountain is the city's lung. What it lacks in height it makes up for in beauty; it is densely forested and big enough to provide a number of good walks. It catches enough snow in winter to turn the landscape into the proverbial fairyland and add an edge of excitement to walking. Its flowers are beautiful, especially in April and early May, and include mountain flora as well as the orchids, irises and ophrys of the *maquis*.

Although there is a tarmac road to the Mt Parnes Hotel and a dirt road encompassing the whole summit area (now largely closed to vehicles), it is little frequented and the few visitors are soon left behind. It is a real boon for the Athenian, whether resident or in transit, just an hour's bus ride from the city centre.

We have described two traverses and a circuit of the summit area. The Anávasi map will suggest many more routes.

Location:	Immediately northwest of Athens.
Maps:	Anávasi 1:25 000 Mt Parnitha.
Bases:	Báfi refuge (Athens EOS, tel: 210 3212355 & 3212429/refuge, 2102469050; open Fri–Sun evening); Flaboúri refuge, run by Akharnés EOS (tel: 210 2461528/refuge 210 2464666; open Fri–Sun evening).
Information:	Athens EOS (tel: 210 3212355 & 3212429) & Akharnés EOS (tel: 210 2461528).
Access:	To Thrakomakedhónes, bus no A8 from Odhós Stournára in downtown Athens to Néa Ionía post office, change to no 724 for Thrakomakedhónes – every 20mins. Get off at stop Serrón, on the corner of Odhós Thrákis. To Áyia Triádha, bus no 714 from Váthis square.

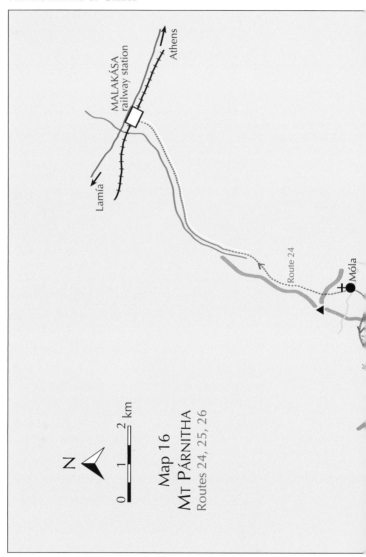

Map 16
Mt Párnitha
Routes 24, 25, 26

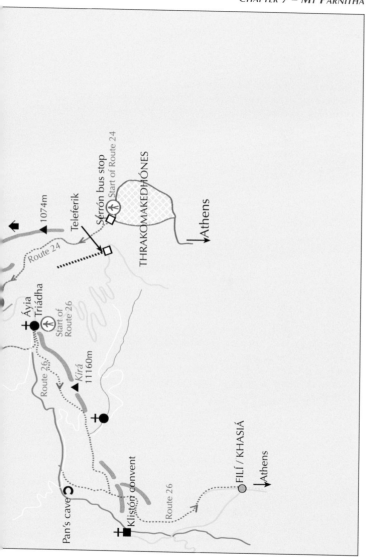

1074m

Teleferik

Sérrón bus stop
Start of Route 24

Route 24

THRAKOMAKEDHÓNES

Athens

Áyia
Triádha

Start of
Route 26

Route 26

Kirá
1160m

Pan's cave

Klistón convent

Route 26

FILÍ / KHASIÁ

Athens

241

Route 24
Malakása Traverse

The very best of Párnitha. This route takes you from the edge of the conurbation up into the montane region with its characteristically Greek mountain forest of *élata* or Greek fir, over the summit ridge and down the gradual gradients of the eastern outliers into the *maquis*.

Stage 1 – *Thrakomakedhónes (440m) –*
Báfi refuge (1160m)

Walking time:	2hrs
Distance:	5.5km
Waymarks:	Consistent; red squares and red diamonds with number 22
Height gain:	720m
Height loss:	0m
Difficulty:	2

The route follows the axis of the Khoúni (*khóonee*) ravine which cuts deeply into the mountain just east of the Mt Parnes Hotel (built on the edge of a crag and visible from all over the Attic basin) all the way from the last houses in the suburb of Thrakomakedhónes to the refuge. To get to the start of the route, take the bus as indicated above.

From the Serrón bus stop, continue for 20m in the same direction as the bus, then turn R up Odhós Thrákis past new villas. It is about **15mins** to where the road ends beneath some cliffs marking the beginning of the Khoúni ravine.

Go up the stony track at the end of the road. Almost at once it becomes a path which turns down L into a dry streambed. Cross over and continue on the opposite bank. The path is well trodden; there is no danger of losing it. The general direction of the route is in a slow leftward curve up the ravine.

Báfi refuge: morning over Athens

After a while the path crosses back to the true L bank of the stream, traverses obliquely up a steep slope through trees, comes out high above the stream, then drops down and crosses once more to the R bank, where it remains. There is a steep winding ascent immediately after this last crossing.

After about 45mins you come to a junction, with a signpost indicating Katára – Mesanó Neró – Móla to the R. Keep straight on, following the waymarks. After **1hr 35mins** you descend to the confluence of two small streams. A sign on a tree points L to Áyia Triádha. A second path branches R to Móla and Koromiliá. Take the third, middle, path up a scrubby spur. At the top (**1hr 50mins**) meet a wide path going off L, which leads to the Párnitha ring road, close to the turning to the Mt Parnes Hotel. Turn R and walk down into the head of a gully in thick fir forest. The path crosses the gully and doubles back R up to the refuge (**2hrs**).

A grassy hollow and picnic place behind the refuge makes a good campsite; spring water is available from a tap at the back corner of the building.

Stage 2 – Báfi refuge (1160m) – Áyios Konstantínos (1290m) – Móla spring (1060m)

Walking time:	1hr 5mins
Distance:	2.5km
Waymarks:	Red squares
Height gain:	130m
Height loss:	230m
Difficulty:	2

This section takes you over the summit ridge of Párnitha via the saddle between the military radar station on Karabóla peak and the TV tower on Órnio, and down the north side of the mountain.

Follow the track from the back of the refuge to the road and turn R. After about 200m there is a path on the L bank of the road which cuts back L through young fir trees and begins to climb steadily over stony ground in open forest, marked by red squares and ribbons of red and white plastic.

After **15mins** you come to the scar of a trench cut along the contour of the slope. The path crosses the trench, bears L and then follows the trench for a little way. A few minutes later bear R climbing away from the trench, meet up with a power line and come out on the road by the chapel of Áyios Konstantínos and the gate of the military radar station (**25mins**). Behind you the view extends south over the whole of Athens to the Saronic Gulf and beyond, and east and north to the island of Évia and the distinctive conical peak of Mt Dhírfis.

A few paces beyond the camp gate the path (signposted) descends L into the firs to Móla. The line has been obscured by fallen trees; basically, it runs down the gully. At **40mins** you reach the Móla – Skípiza path (see Route 25), with a signpost pointing L for Skípiza, R for **Móla**. Turn R. Soon you are descending steeply through thick firs. A few minutes later be careful to bear L and not continue straight ahead on a smaller path following the contour. In 15mins (**1hr 5mins**) you reach the road by a stand of mature poplars. Opposite is the chapel of

Áyios Pétros, with a paved picnic area and a copious spring on the R of the road.

Stage 3 – Móla (1060m) – Malakása/ Sfendháli railway station (280m)

Walking time:	3hrs 15mins
Distance:	10km
Waymarks:	Mauve squares and assorted paint
Height gain:	40m
Height loss:	800m
Difficulty:	2

Apart from some initial route-finding difficulties this section is an easy and relaxing descent, much of it along a wonderfully lush and shaded stream gully.

From the chapel of Áyios Pétros walk west, back along the road, to the stand of poplar trees. Turn R almost immediately on to a dirt track, and again immediately R on to a path that drops steeply down through fir trees to another track that you can see below. On reaching this track (*spring R*) go straight ahead for some 50m. There is an open meadow L, wooden railings and tables for picnicking. Just before the track turns R in a 90° bend, turn off L into the meadow. Immediately beside you is a large fir tree overhanging a picnic table, with a mauve square waymark. Head towards it and out into the open grassy ground beyond which rises gently towards some bushes.

There are no waymarks visible at first. Head up the slope in a general northerly direction – more or less straight ahead – until you pick up the first red paint marks on stones on the ground. Although the path is often not very clear, the paint marks, augmented by hanging ribbons of red plastic, are frequent. There is also the occasional mauve square (the official waymark for this route) either on trees or stones. You wind up through relatively young fir forest to the top of a broad ridge (**20mins**), with a view eastwards of the sea and the island of

On this section look out for a tiny colony of the very rare white peony *mascula* var. *hellenica*. It flowers in early May and is easily missed, although it grows right beside the path.

Attic tortoise

Évia. After 20mins of gentle descent you come out on a jeep track with a signpost pointing to Mílesi, the old name for Malakása, giving the distance as 4200m.

Cross straight over the track and continue down the path, following red paint marks. The path winds down through the scrub towards the valley below. At **50mins** pass an isolated stand of mature firs and drop down into a narrowing gully, increasingly dense with vegetation. Reach the bank of a stream in a plane-lined gully. Cross over into a patch of open meadow and turn L downhill. About 50m ahead red paint on an old pear tree shows the way ahead. Cross the stream again (**1hr 55mins**). Follow it down through grassy clearings and cross once more after a further 10 or so minutes. Soon after you debouch on to a rough track beside the stream. (A wooden signpost marked with red paint shows the start of the path for those coming up.)

Turn R on the track, uphill at first, along the R flank of the valley. After 30mins (**2hrs 46mins**) you pass a large concrete water tank on the R shaded by big plane trees. Another 25mins brings you to the first houses of **Malakása**, scattered among pine trees, and down to the railway line (**3hrs 15mins**).

Walk across the line to the station, now unmanned. Local trains from Khalkídha to Athens stop here, not infrequently; the timetable is a blackboard propped against the wall. You buy your ticket on the train.

Route 25
Summit Circuit – Báfi (1160) to
Áyios Konstantínos (1290m) to
Skípiza spring (1200m) to
Áyia Triádha (1000m)

Walking time:	2hrs 30mins
Distance:	7km
Height gain:	210m
Height loss:	370m
Difficulty:	2
Map:	See Route 24

This is a well-trodden path that allows an almost complete circuit of the summit area. It gives a taste of the 'Greek mountain experience', practicable even if you have little experience of mountain walking. If you added about 45mins to the overall time you could create a circular route from Áyia Triádha, which is perhaps more convenient for transport.

From the Báfi refuge to the junction with the Skípiza path (**40mins**), follow the route described under Route 24, Stage 2. Turn L for Skípiza. The path is soft and fairly level, contouring along under the fir trees; on a clear day you can see Mt Parnasós to the northwest. A surprising amount of snow collects here in winter and when it melts the ground is covered with crocuses, alpine squills, *corydalis solida* and *anemone blanda*. At just over **1hr** the path bears uphill to the L, crosses the western end of the summit ridge and begins to descend leftwards to reach the Skípiza (*skéepeeza*) spring 5mins later.

Three other paths start from Skípiza. One goes straight downhill to the Plátana spring and the ring road (20mins). To your L a second path (yellow squares) leads east back to the Báfi refuge in 40mins (cross a series of eroded gullies, turn L at the tarmac and down to the ring road close to the refuge car park). The third path, for Áyia Triádha (also marked with yellow squares), is at an angle of 10 o'clock (with your back to the spring). It is all downhill, heading southeast at first, then south.

Shortly after starting you cross a section of deeply eroded ground where the path turns into a stream after rain or snowmelt. On your L are the rocky bluffs along the top of which the Báfi route passes. Thereafter the path enters thick fir woods and crosses an eastward-rising slope into a well-defined valley that bends slowly right and south, bringing you down a stream gully to the ring road a few paces uphill from the Paliokhóri spring (**2hrs 5mins**).

For Áyia Triádha turn L up the ring road for 15mins. There is a tiny chapel, a spring, hotel and restaurant. The bus stops here.

Route 26
Khasiá Traverse – Áyia Triádha (1000m) to Tamílthi spring (780m) to Khasiá/Filí (320m)

Walking time:	3hrs
Distance:	10km
Waymarks:	Blue, then mauve squares
Height gain:	0m
Height loss:	680m
Difficulty:	2
Map:	See Route 24

This walk takes you from the centre of the Párnitha massif down to the village of Khasiá (*khasyá*) – now officially called Filí (*feelée*) – at its southwestern corner. The landscape is more Mediterranean *maquis* than mountain.

From the Áyia Triádha chapel go back to the west past the hotel/café, *Ta Kiklámina*, then turn R up the tarmac ring road. At the top of the rise, take the L fork. On your R the ground drops away into a tree-filled gully which eventually develops into the Goúra ravine. On your L there is a basketball pitch and various huts scattered about a grassy clearing. The tarmac soon gives way to a broad dirt road, which after a brief uphill stretch contours round the fir-clad north flank of a peak known as Kirá.

At about **45mins** you come to a junction. One track descends steeply R into the ravine. Straight ahead there is a wide space like a parking area with a blue sign on a post. The track is blocked by a barrier ahead, but go through this and on down the track. In a few minutes you cross a concrete culvert. Immediately after a path descends L (blue square on a tree) to the chapel of Áyios Yióryios visible below, and continues down the mountain to Amigdhaléza on the main Athens – Párnitha road. About 50m further on another blue square on a pine tree on the R bank of the track marks the continuation of this path. Turn up R here into the pines.

At the top of the rise (**1hr**), there is a wooden kiosk in the trees L. The path turns 90º to the R. About 50m later a blue curved line on a rock on the ground indicates a 90º turn to the L. Thereafter, follow the blue squares, descending slightly, through tall scrub and scattered pines. Pass through a stand of cypress trees and emerge on to a patch of open ground. Go straight across it (blue square visible on tree ahead). Bear R past the last blue square in the scrub and follow the blue paint marks on stones. A dirt track appears ahead. The path bears L before reaching it and you follow some stone cairns for a few moments before coming out on the edge of the track (**1hr 17mins**).

Do not cross the track; do not be tempted by the clear blue and mauve waymarks of the path that descends steeply on the other side (leading to the cave of Pan and on to the Klistón convent). Instead, keeping to your side of the track, turn sharply L and follow the mauve squares gently downhill, leaving the track behind you and heading almost due south. In a few moments (**1hr 20mins**) you hit the track again. Cross over; 10m on the other side the path forks. Follow the mauve square to the R; do not follow the blue diamonds. For the next few minutes the path is not very clear. Follow the small cairns of stones through the scrub. You emerge on to open ground by the remains of a thorn and corrugated iron goat pen on a kind of shallow col. Bear L-wards across what

Tamílthi spring

was once terraced ground for a couple of minutes and re-enter the trees, where the path becomes clearer.

After negotiating a couple of fallen pines climb steeply down beneath a rocky bluff to the lovely old spring of Tamílthi (780m) (**1hr 40mins**). The water, which is channelled into a hollowed pine trunk, runs all year round, creating a little oasis of freshness and greenery. ▶

Beyond the spring the path climbs over a rocky shoulder and begins to descend through woods of Aleppo pine, whose trunks are scarred by resin tapping. In 10mins you come to some old terracing with almond trees (E0470818/N4220194; **1hr 54mins**), followed by a level stretch which ends in a 90° turn downhill to the R (E0470892/N4220001; 733m; **2hrs**). The path, which has been worn down into a gully by the passage of men and mules, winds steeply down through the pines for about 20mins to another small clearing with remains of terracing. Some 5mins later you emerge from the woods to contour along an open rocky slope below crags, with a view of the Klistón convent on the opposite side of the valley. A tap and standpipe beside the path (**2hrs 25mins**) give you access to the spring water being piped down from the mountain. After a level stretch in young pines, the path turns into a dirt track and then tarmac by the garden wall of a new house (**2hrs 40mins**; E0470183/N4218828; 418m).

Follow the tarmac for about 1600m to a fork on the outskirts of the village of Filí/Khasiá. Turn R, and then L by the football academy playing field (Akadhimías Podhosféron; **3hrs**). Buses for Athens stop further up this main street. (Coming up, follow the signs to the monastery of SS Kiprianós and Ioustíni. At the second fork, ignore the R turn for the monastery and keep straight ahead.)

Just before you reach the spring a good path (cleared in 2004) leads back R to the cave of Pan (about 30mins).

CHAPTER 8

MT OLYMPUS AND THE PILION PENINSULA

These are two of the loveliest, most compact and accessible walking areas in the country. Not only are they adjacent to each other midway up the east coast of central Greece, they also complement each other. Mt Olympus (*óleembos*), at 2918m the highest mountain in the country, provides the alpine beauty and drama rising, as it does, more or less straight out of the sea. It is covered in dense forest of beech, black and Balkan pine. Its wild flower population is without parallel, even in Greece. Pílion is a more domesticated and densely inhabited montane region. Unusually green, many of the paths and *kaldereémya* that once connected its busy villages are still serviceable, some of them even cleared and waymarked – ideal for walkers.

A: MT OLYMPUS

Walking on Mt Olympus (2918m) requires no special expertise in favourable conditions. Its main paths are well signed and well maintained. Reaching Mítikas, the highest of the peaks, does, however, involve some modest scrambling. The approach via Kakí Skála, in particular, requires a head for heights.

The weather is fickle. It is easy to be seduced on a hot summer's day with the sea at your feet into thinking that nothing can possibly go wrong. Take no chances: I have seen lightning, snow and hail succeed each other in the space of minutes on a fine August day. Patches of frozen snow can block the path, especially in the Zonária area, until mid-June.

The classic starting point for walkers is Priónia (*preeyónya*) where the road ends, 18km up the north flank of the Enipéas ravine. There is a good chance of a lift in summer. A taxi from the square in Litókhoro currently costs 15–20 euros.

At km14, the spot known as Dhiakládhosi (*dheeyakládhosee* – Dhiastávrosi on the Anávasi map), there are two large signs on the R of the road displaying maps of the paths. An anti-clockwise circuit of Mt Olympus begins right here, leading up R to the Yiósos Apostolídhis hut in 5–6hrs' hard climb.

I am going to describe the clockwise route. The advantage of this direction is that – even after travelling all day to reach Olympus – you still have time to do the 3hr hike to the Spílios Agapitós hut before dark. The anticlockwise route also has its supporters. Firstly, having slept nearer to the summit, you can get up the Loúki couloir before other walkers appear and cause rock falls. Secondly it makes descent from Priónia by the old footpath (the well-marked route of the E4) a much more

Mt Olympus from the ancient city of Dion

logical end to your hike. This is a truly beautiful path along the Enipéas ravine to Litókhoro, which takes a good 3hrs going down; coming up puts even the Spílios Agapitós hut at around 8hrs from the village.

There are other interesting routes, notably the ridge walk on the south ridge of the Mavrólongos ravine via Áyios Antónios and Livadháki, and the ascent from Dion on the north flank of the massif.

Olympus refuge huts

Spílios Agapitós (Refuge A) 2100m; tel: +30 23520 81329/ 81800; manned mid-May–end Oct; 110 beds; night 10 euros, meal around 5 euros. Efficiently run by Kóstas Zolótas and his family (fluent German/English). Booking essential.

Yiósos Apostolídhis (Refuge B) 2700m, Plateau of the Muses (*pedhiádha ton moosón*); tel: +30 23520 81329/ 81800; manned mid-June–end Sept; 80 beds; food; belongs to Thessaloníki climbing club, SEO. Wise to book.

Kákalos (Refuge C) Also on the plateau; unmanned; keys from Zolótas.

Location:	Northeast coast, on the shore of the Thermaic Gulf 90km south of Thessaloníki.
Map:	Anávasi Topo 25 Central Olympus 1:25 000.
Information:	Tourist office in Litókhoro.
Base:	Litókhoro, 5km from the sea on the east side: hotels, tavernas, shops, seaside campsites.
Access:	Daily buses from Kateríni and Thessaloníki; trains from Athens (station 9km from village).

Route 27
Mt Olympus Circuit

Stage 1 – Priónia (1040m) – Mítikas (2918m)

Walking time:	5hrs 30mins
Distance:	9.5km via Kakí Skála, 8.5km via Lóuki
Height gain:	1878m
Height loss:	0m
Difficulty:	3

Priónia is a beautiful spot, enclosed by forest and dominated by towering crags. There is a small taverna-cum-snack bar. Do not be surprised to find a lot of people here in summer. Fill up with water; there is no more until Refuge A.

Monastery of Áyios Dhionísios
Just 1km short of Priónia a track descends L to the ruins of the heavily fortified monastery. Founded by the saint, Áyios Dhionísios in 1542, it was destroyed by the Germans in 1943 on suspicion of harbouring Resistance fighters. It is at last well on the way to restoration, and is definitely worth a visit. There is a copious spring within the walls. The E4 descent from Priónia to Litókhoro passes it (see Stage 4).

Stefáni and Mítikas peaks from the west (photo Michael Cullen)

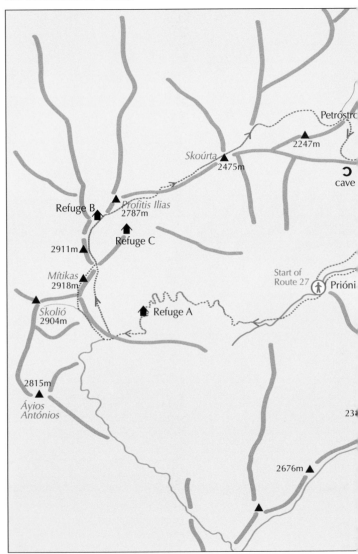

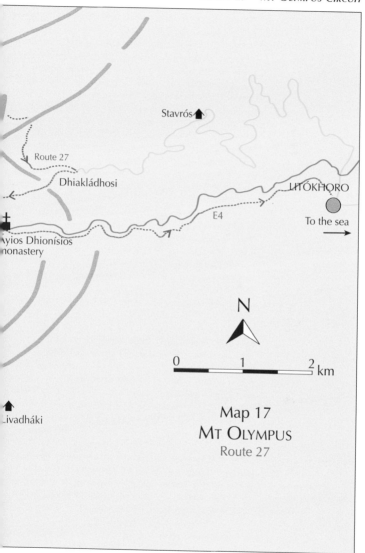

Stavrós

Route 27

Dhiakládhosi

LITÓKHORO

E4

To the sea →

✝
Áyios Dhionísios
monastery

Livadháki

N

0   1   2 km

Map 17
MT OLYMPUS
Route 27

257

The path begins just uphill from the taverna. An EOS signpost indicates the way, giving the time to the refuge as 2hrs 30mins. Cross a stream with a small waterfall R, and start to climb steeply up through woods of beech and black pine. The path is well trodden and there is no danger of losing the way. As you gain height there are superb views across the Mavrólongos ravine L and to the summits above your head.

Spílios Agapitós/Refuge A perches on the edge of an abrupt spur surrounded by huge, storm-beaten specimens of Balkan pine. Warden Kóstas Zolótas runs a tight ship, so get into his good books on entry by exchanging your boots for a pair of slippers (provided), and make yourself known to him. Let him know in good time if you want a meal and bed or are just passing through. This is the place to ask for information about the mountain.

It is best to make an early start for the summit if you want a clear view. Cloud often gathers on the peaks in the middle of the day. Fill up with water; the next source is at the Yiósos Apostolídhis hut/Refuge B (when open).

The path continues behind the refuge, climbing L-handed up a steep spur among the last of the trees. After 1hr (**3hrs 30mins**) you come to a signpost. From here there are two possible routes to Mítikas: via the Kakí Skála ridge or the Loúki couloir.

Kakí Skála (*kakeé skála*) ridge route (1hr 40mins)

The Kakí Skála route goes more or less straight ahead up the R flank of the featureless stony valley ahead, with the peak of Áyios Antónios L. You reach the summit ridge after about 1hr (**4hrs 30mins**) between the peaks of Skolió (*skolyó*) L and Skála R. You know when you've got there because there is a 500m sheer drop on the other side, into the chasm of Kazánia – the Cauldrons.

The *kakeé skála* itself begins in a narrow cleft on the R just short of the ridge. Paint splashes mark the way. The route starts with a slightly descending R-wards traverse to a narrow nick in the ridgeline revealing the drop to Kazánia, which is easily negotiated. In the main the route keeps just below the ridge, so you are protected from the drop. ◄

The drop R is steep, but not sheer. Although it can be alarming for someone unused to heights, there is no real danger.

Continue traversing R, skirting the base of the Skála peak, then climb L up a steepish gully made a little awkward by loose rock on sloping footholds. Bear R at the top over steep but reassuringly solid rock, and through a narrow neck. Step L round an awkward corner and there, scarcely 100m away, is Mítikas, a narrow boulder-strewn platform with a trig point, tin Greek flag and summit book (about 40mins from the beginning of Kakí Skála; **5hrs 15mins** total).

On a clear day you can see Mt Smólikas and all the peaks of the Píndhos range to the west, Parnasós in the south and Mt Áthos in the northeast. Just north of Mítikas is the Stefáni peak (2909m), known also as the Throne of Zeus. It is a precipitous hog's back closing off the north side of the Kazánia cirque. As you can see from Mítikas, it is not for hikers.

The Loúki (*loókee*) couloir route

To reach the foot of the Loúki couloir turn R at the signpost above Refuge A, up and over the rounded spur above, then all along the tilting striations of rock known as Zonária (*zonáreeya*), that lie directly beneath the tooth-like pinnacles guarding the summit area. The path here is cut by several gullies, which hold deep wedges of snow until mid- to late June. Crossing them requires care.

After about 40mins – just before the highest point on the path – a signpost indicates the Yiósos Apostolídhis (SEO) hut in 20mins. The start of the Loúki couloir is just up L, leading to Mítikas in about 45mins (**5hrs total**). It is a steep but straightforward scramble. A couple of moves at the top are airy, but not dangerous. I like this route, although Zólotas strongly

The tilting strata of Zonária (photo Michael Cullen)

counsels against it, for it is exposed to rock falls when there are other people on it. Descending this way saves a good 2hrs if you are going on to the Yiósos Apostolídhis hut.

Stage 2 – Mítikas (2918m) – Yiósos Apostolídhis hut (Refuge B; 2730m)

Walking time:	2hrs 30mins via Kakí Skála, 1hr via Loúki
Distance:	4km via Kakí Skála, 1.5km via Loúki
Height gain:	230m via Kakí Skála, 30m via Loúki
Height loss:	418m via Kakí Skála, 218m via Loúki
Difficulty:	3

Whichever route you pick you have to make your way to the signpost on the Zonária path below Loúki mentioned in Stage 1. If you have ascended Mítikas via Kakí Skála and want to come down Loúki, the mouth of the couloir is just a few metres north of the summit and, although it may appear that any move in that direction will lead to instant immortality, you are in fact quite safe.

Beyond the signpost turn downhill L below the northeast face of Stefáni. The Plateau of the Muses is on your R across

Stefáni: the throne of Zeus (photo Michael Cullen)

an intervening corrie, bounded to the west by the Toúmba and Profítis Ilías peaks, with the Yiósos Apostolídhis hut between them (from Priónia, **total 6hrs 15mins via Lóuki, 7hrs 45mins via Kakí Skála**). This section of path is very exposed to avalanching in winter. Toúmba and Profítis Ilías can be climbed in 20mins or so; the chief interest is the view. ▶

A small herd of chamois *(agreeyokátseeka)* still survives on Olympus and can often be seen in this area, especially towards evening.

Stage 3 – *Yiósos Apostolídhis hut (Refuge B; 2730m)* – *Dhiakládosi (dheeyastávrosee on the Anávasi map; 1100m)*

Walking time:	4hrs 30mins
Distance:	11km
Height gain:	0m
Height loss:	1630m
Difficulty:	3

Leaving the refuge, turn L/northeast and continue to the edge of the Plateau of the Muses, where the path bends R round the head of a precipitous drop. Thereafter it follows the Lemós ridge dividing the Enipéas ravine R from the Pápa Réma ravine to the north as far as a rounded bump with a survey point on top: Skoúrta (2475m). Here, the coarse turf slopes down to a flat-topped ridge just clear of the highest trees. The path winds down to this ridge, then traverses R into a broad shallow gully leading down into the trees. At around **2hrs 15mins** you come out on a rock-strewn shoulder among scattered Balkan pines, with an abandoned sheepfold among the boulders L. This is Petróstrounga (1900m).

This is a beautiful – but long and tiring – descent, which brings you out on the forest road to Priónia (see above).

From this shoulder drop down into an open grassy bowl and enter the trees again, where there is a signposted fork in the path. You are heading south at this point. The R branch leads to a spring in 15mins. Keep straight on. There is another junction a little further on, where again you keep straight. The R branch leads in 10mins to a rock overhang where an eccentric Greek landscape painter, Vassílis Ithakísios, once lived and painted.

The path now begins to descend steeply through mixed woods of beech and pine to a little patch of meadow known as Bárba, and thence first south, then east, to the road at *dheeyakládhosee* (**4hrs 30mins**).

Stage 4 – *Priónia (1040m) – Litókhoro (300m; E4)*

Walking time:	2hrs 45mins
Distance:	10km
Height gain:	520m
Height loss:	1320m
Difficulty:	3

The signposted path begins on the R just below the café. Cross a wooden bridge to the true R bank of the stream and descend through box and beech past mossy boulders to a second bridge. Cross to the L bank. After a few minutes turn R on to a section of track heading towards a riverside clearing with the remains of a goat pen and hut, where you turn sharp L. At **30mins** pass through a beautiful stretch of riverside meadow that would make a great campsite, and 10mins later find yourself directly underneath the Áyios Dhionísios monastery (*spring*).

There is a third bridge just below the monastery, where you cross back to the true R bank of the stream and climb up through cool beech woods to a tiny chapel built into a big rock over-hang, with a resurgent stream (**1hr**). A few minutes later there is a fourth bridge by a spring, this time crossing a tributary stream descending from the R. A 20min climb is followed by a steep descent. The gradient soon levels off, climbs steeply again to gain about 100m, levels off, then starts to climb again to reach the top of a jutting rocky pinnacle (**2hrs 10mins**) from which for the first time you can see Litókhoro and the coastal plain.

About 10mins later pass a bench beside the path; another 10mins takes you over a rocky spur and down – ignore a turn down to the L. Pass a last rocky shoulder with a bench and caves above the path and a view ahead to the sea. There follows a short stretch on a concrete-covered water channel beside a green railing until, at **2hrs 45mins**, you turn L on a path that leads down to the first buildings and on into the top of the village.

B: MT PÍLION

Pílion: the southern slopes

Pílion (1624m) is a long spine of high ground curling like a paw round the eastern side of the Bay of Vólos. What it lacks in height it makes up for with its spectacular beauty, both natural and manmade. The highest ground lies north and east of Vólos. The hillsides are scattered with frescoed churches and magnificent villages centred invariably on a paved square shaded by one or more centennial plane trees. Tourism has developed considerably, so restaurants and even quite luxurious accommodation are not hard to find.

We have confined ourselves – essentially – to five routes on the slopes just east of Vólos, which could easily be joined up to form a complete circuit. There are many other possibilities, on the higher ground and also lower down towards the southern end of the peninsula.

Location:	Midway up the east coast, north and east of the port of Vólos.
Maps:	Anávasi Topo 25 Mt Pilion 1:25 000; Road Editions Pilio 1:60 000.
Bases:	Vólos (large town with all amenities); good accommodation and food in Tsangarádha, Móuresi and many other villages.
Access:	Daily rail and bus service from Athens to Vólos (local buses). Charter flights from UK to neighbouring island of Skiáthos, with daily boat connections to Vólos.

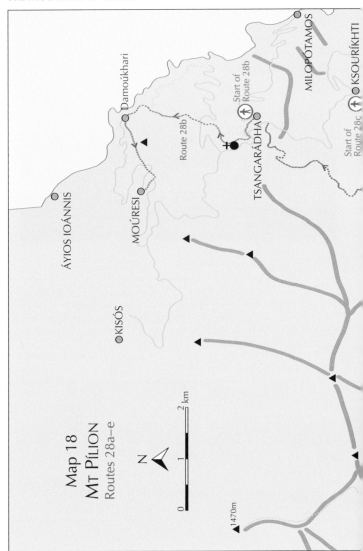

Map 18
Mt Pílion
Routes 28a–e

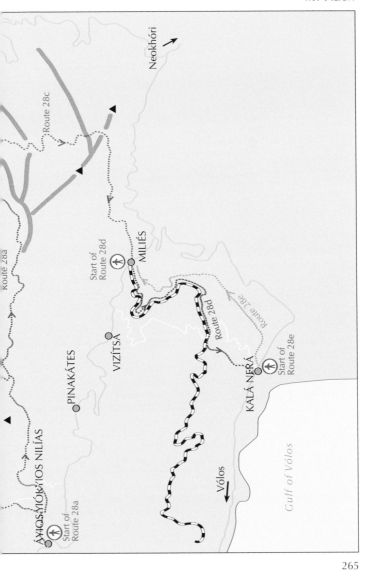

Neokhóri

Route 28c

Route 28a

Start of
Route 28d

MILIÉS

PINAKÁTES

VIZÍTSA

Route 28d

Route 28e

ÁYIOS NILÍAS
ÁNO SÝLYÓR

Start of
Route 28a

KALÁ NERÁ

Start of
Route 28e

Vólos

Gulf of Vólos

265

Route 28a
Áyios Yióryios Nilías (600m) to Kourvéndeli (1050) to Ítamos (1000m) to Tsangarádha/ Áyii Taxiárkhes (500m)

Walking time:	4hrs 30mins
Distance:	15km
Height gain:	450m
Height loss:	550m
Difficulty:	3

This route is a mix of little-used farm track and footpath. The first third is a steady climb through jungly vegetation overwhelming old cultivated areas, the middle third follows the 1000m contour on the edge of extensive beech forest, and the last third is a steady descent in the cool of the forest. The first – as far as Kourvéndeli – presents some navigation problems (see below).

Note This is not the same route as that marked on the Ánávasi map.

The path starts in the pretty central square of Áyios Yióryios, about 9km inland from Áno Lekhónia on the main coast road 10km east of Vólos (taxi rank by the turning).

From the top L corner of the square a fine old *kaldereémee* heads northeast uphill between the cottages and gardens. Bear L at a T-junction (**4mins**) with a red arrow on a telegraph pole and a walker sign by a white single-storey cottage and the water channel. A moment later you come to a second junction with a stone wall in front of you marked with a red arrow and the church of Áyios Thanásios. Turn R, then L and continue uphill, with a sign pointing to Agriólefkes. At the upper limit of the village, a red arrow points R (east) along the fence and orchard belonging to the last house. Shortly after (**15mins**) there is a sign fixed to an ancient plane tree, 'Tsangarádha 5hrs'. You are climbing a clear *kaldereémee*.

After a wet section – more path than *kaldereémee* – be careful to go L at a fork (sign and red paint). About 20m later

there is another fork (E0421892/N4355190); L is signed
Agriólefkes and Khánia, R Tsangarádha. You are beside a very
noisy water channel.

I turned R here, following the sign to Tsangarádha. I suspect that following the
Agriólefkes/Khánia route (the one highlighted on the Anávasi map) may be easier,
as it involves a few kilometres of dirt road whereas the Tsangarádha route – while
beautiful – involves some tortuous route-finding through very overgrown, though
regularly signposted, terrain. The two routes meet at the location known as Kourvéndeli.

Cross the water channel and follow the path east uphill over
open ground to meet a dirt road on a spur, signed Kremídhas
L, Tsangarádha R (E0421970/N4354936; 755m). (A left turn
here brings you back to the Agriólefkes/Khánia route, above.)
Turn R and follow the track through an apple orchard to a
crossroads (**30mins**) with signs: L to Evzónas and Skhitsoavlí,
straight across and bearing L to Tsangarádha, while going R
takes you down the main track past some substantial huts. Take
the Tsangarádha track which heads north and slightly downhill along the L flank of a gully with old apple orchards in the
bottom to your R. Above you to the north the ground rises to
a high, thickly wooded ridge.

At **34mins** a stream crosses your track in a concrete culvert on a RH bend beneath some plane trees. A sign on a tree
R of the track points to a path up the L bank (E0422144/N4355468).
Go up the path and up the RH edge of a cherry orchard, leaving a stone hut on your R. Look for a red arrow on a terrace
wall towards the top of the cherry orchard, pointing R on to
an old track, pretty much on the level, through young chestnut trees. You are heading east–southeast, then east into more
old orchards. There are frequent red paint marks.

At **45mins** an arrow on a terrace wall points R. About 40m
later cross a stream and pass a concrete water tank R. You come
out in an apple orchard on a track heading downhill
(E0422472/N4355464). Go down the track a short distance
to a fork and turn back L. Very soon the track starts to climb
through chestnut trees. At the first LH bend (**50mins**), on a
slope covered with scrub and broom, an overgrown path leaves
the outer edge of the bend to the R (red paint and signs). There
is a gully R of the path and the sound of running water. About

5mins later you come to a stream gully full of big boulders (sign to Tsangarádha and red paint). Climb gently up and L to a bigger stream (signs). Bracken obscures the path. At **1hr 8mins** cross another stream. The path becomes clearer in the chestnut wood; you are climbing L-wards uphill on the L side of a small dry gully (frequent signs and red paint). Some 5mins later, at the top of a small spur with a black water pipe on the ground, a faint track leads L. In 2mins you come to a LH hairpin; 30m beyond turn R on a higher track (red arrow; **1hr 16mins**). Continue up the track, traversing across a scrubby slope. After 5mins you reach a junction (E0423627/N4355357) with a blue signpost: Pinakátes R, Tsangarádha L. Branch L.

At **1hr 30mins** there is a fork (E0423885/N5355551), with long views south over the bay of Vólos. Do not go up to the L. A sign and red arrow point straight ahead; follow them. The track ends after 50m. There is a water storage cistern below R and a pink-roofed hut visible on a terrace in the trees up to the L. Do not go up to the L beside the water conduit. Take the path to the R/straight ahead, round the top side of the water tank; a sign on a plane tree says Trípia Pétra (Hollow Rock).

Head uphill and L-wards below the above-mentioned water conduit on the L side of a beech-filled gully, soon crossing the gully (**1hr 36mins**). A sign says Rematiá Vasilikís (Vasiliki's stream). Once out of the gully the path winds steeply up L to the pink-roofed hut on its chestnut-shaded terrace that was visible from the last fork in the track (**1hr 45mins**; E0424127/N4355644; 1000m). Turn R along a faint track and come very shortly to a fence round a stone cottage set in an orchard. Continue up the track L. Pass a sign to the spring of Kría Vrísi (somewhere in the woods below R). About 5mins later there is a junction; one sign points back L to Khánia (this is the highlighted route from the Anávasi map), while a red and blue one indicates Tsangarádha to the R/straight ahead in the direction of some beech trees.

Come to a stream flowing across the track – the Réma Galáni – shaded by beech (**2hrs**; E0424606/N4355903; 1080m). Keep along the track, over a ridge and slightly downhill. At a fork (E0425144/N4355911) bear L and 50m later you reach the Kourvéndeli ridge, where for the first time you can see out to the east. The ridge stretches R through open beech woods. The ground ahead drops into a gully. A silver water pipe runs along the ridge out of the woods to your L, from which a path signed Khánia also emerges. Go straight across the pipe (red paint and sign) and down to the L round the head of the gully, and bend back R out along the L flank of the gully, heading east. At **2hrs 11mins** the path crosses the Réma Kakiá Skála stream (blue and red paint), bends L or northeast and becomes a forest track. A better track arrives from the L soon after. A sign indicates Tsangarádha R. The track descends with a view ahead to the Sporádhes islands of Skiáthos, Skópelos and Alónisos and brings you to a wooden kiosk (**2hrs 20mins**; E0425928/N4355510) with a water cistern just below it and a stream gully L.

Continue down the track for about 130m to the signs: Vizítsa straight on, Áyios Yíoryios and Khánia behind, Tsangarádha and Ksouríkhti L. Turn L on a descending path. You pass the remains of drystone walls among the beeches and a section of old *kaldereémee*. At **2hrs 31mins** you cross the Miliótiko stream; 5mins later a sign indicates the Koromiliá spring below R. At **2hrs 40mins** you come to a ridge in beech woods (E0426634/N4355546; 1000m) with a sign to Miliés to the R along a forest track, Tsangarádha and Ksouríkhti straight on down a path-cum-track under the beeches. There is a bit of a rocky bump R along the track.

Take the track for Tsangarádha/Ksouríkhti. Around 5mins later there is another wooden kiosk under the trees by a dry stream gully with a water trough for goats. Past the kiosk, a track bends R and a path turns off to the L with a sticker of the Panellínio Dhíktio Íkoloyikón Organósion. Another 5mins and you pass the Ksourikhtianó stream and the path begins to bear gradually northeast to north–northeast. At **3hrs 7mins** you hit a forest track; Ksouríkhti is signed to the L. Across the track, on a little knoll in front of you, is another wooden picnic kiosk (E0427897/N4356226; 940m).

Turn L for Ksouríkhti. Very soon there is a fork (**3hrs 10mins**), with Vouloméni Pétra and Mégha Ísioma L. Keep R. After 5mins, on a RH bend in a locality known as Anáthema, take the track L signed Tsangarádha and Katsakári. Ksouríkhti is to the R. A couple of minutes later the path for Tsangarádha leaves the track, climbs out over the L bank (E0428203/N4356985; 900m) and heads west down into a gully where it turns sharp R and continues downhill, descending through tall beeches. The path is a bit overgrown here but there are frequent red paint marks. Cross a muddy stream with remains of terrace walls L.

At **3hrs 33mins**, after negotiating a fallen tree, you meet a very rough bulldozed track on the edge of a gully where you turn 90° R and after 40–50m come to a group of chestnut trees. At these trees turn more than 90° L so that you are doubling back on a path above the gully. Go round to the R and back L. There is a wall L of the path and a stream below R. Zigzag down R-wards towards the stream with the remains of a *kaldereémee* under your feet and you come to the Milopótamos stream with a dam and pipes to carry the water down to the villages (**3hrs 37mins**).

Cross the stream and turn R up the L flank of the gully. In a couple of minutes you come to a junction where you keep R, descending northeast and bearing L away from the Milopótamos stream. The beeches give way to sweet chestnut. In 20mins you reach a junction with a dirt road (**4hrs**). Turn down R following the sign for Tsangarádha. Pass a big concrete water cistern R and keep along the main track to a junction with a red-painted shrine by a ruin L and a water cistern R (E0428721/N4358815; 607m; **4hrs 13mins**). Go straight ahead, bearing L following a red arrow, past the first white house of Tsangarádha. The houses become more frequent. There are signs all the way until you come out on the main tarmac road (**4hrs 20mins**) by a sign pointing back the way you have come to the church of Profítis Ilías. ◀

Tsangarádha has four quarters spread out over a considerable area of hillside around the 400m mark. You have arrived in the southernmost quarter, Áyii Taxiárkhes.

Route 28b
Tsangarádha (500m) to Damoúkhari (0m) to Moúresi (400m)

Walking time:	3hrs
Distance:	7.5km
Height gain:	400m
Height loss:	500m
Difficulty:	2

Follow the road north from the Áyii Taxiárkhes quarter until you reach the junction with the Milopótamos road (**20mins**;

signposted 7km; *beautiful beach*). Turn R; 50m along, where the parapet wall ends, a sign points L to 'Eklisía Ayías Paraskevís 1914'. Turn down L on this path, which doubles back to cross the tree-filled stream gully below. Very shortly you come to the Xenia Hotel; bear L on a good *kaldereémee* and descend at a gentle gradient past the 1909 Nanopoúlios school. Bear L again at the sign to Ayía Paraskeví to come out by The Lost Unicorn Hotel on the edge of the *platéeya* with its cafés and immense plane tree.

Pass below the *platéeya* to the R, where there is a copious arcaded spring. Bear 90° R downhill; 100m down the path, above a bridge, keep straight/bearing L. At **35mins** cross a bridge and bear L beside a fence to come to a concrete road. Turn uphill L. The road is steep and curls L-wards. Pass a sort of walled and embanked platform R with two plane trees and a gate. Keep straight ahead up a grassy track for about 130m, then bear L on a path following a fence round an old house. Turn R at 90° up a cobbled stretch for 50m and L at the top. Another 50m brings you out on a tarmac road with a sign to Damoúkhari.

Turn down R on a path, now heading northeast on an old *kalderéemee*. At a sign saying 'Rákhi Apostolídhi' keep L down the *kaldereémee* to meet the tarmac by a chapel R (E0429219/N4360308; **56mins**). Turn L for 30m, then R at a

Áyios Ioánnis and the north coast

sign for Damoúkhari. In 5mins you come to a spring opposite a big solitary stone gatepost: a sort of *plateéya* with a very straight plane tree and a church. Past the church, turn down to the R.

Hit the tarmac at **1hr 5mins** and cross straight over, descending steeply to a stream and bridge with a spring. Climb uphill to a cement track and a house on a bend. A sign points R. After 80m, past some new houses and a gate L, a sign points L to Damoúkhari. Descend to a little clearing on a spur with a kiosk (**1hr 20mins**, E0429425/N4361182) – a natural belvedere with a view over the sea and up the coast to the north. To the L is a deep gully. The slopes all around are thickly covered with heather, kermes oak and other shrubs typical of the *garrigue*.

From here the *kaldereémee* continues steeply down to the shingle beach in about 15mins (R fork to the secluded little bay of Fakístra towards the bottom of the descent). Follow the path along the back of the beach and bear L through the hamlet of **Damoúkhari**, unfortunately now in the process of steady development. At the end of the hamlet bear L up a stretch of *kaldereémee* for 100m to the car park and end of the road, where you turn sharp L up a cement lane for 50m, then R and straight up the *kaldereémee* (signed). It winds steeply up to meet a track (**2hrs**). Turn R uphill for 150–200m until you overlook the resort of Áyios Ioánnis and the coast to the north.

At a sign on the L turn up the *kaldereémee* (**2hrs 7mins**). Hit another track and keep L. Soon after there is a remnant of *kaldereémee*, then a concrete lane. Ignore a sign indicating the minor bump of Tsoúka L. You come to the first houses of **Moúresi** and keep up to the R. Cross the tarmac road and keep uphill. Turn L on the tarmac for 40m, then L up a concrete lane. After 30m turn R up a *kaldereémee* to another concrete lane, where you turn L and pass a house L at the end of the lane. By this house bear R up a narrow path beside a water channel. Around 50–60m later rejoin the *kaldereémee*. Around **2hrs 30mins** you reach the tarmac where a sign points back to Damoúkhari. Another 5mins brings you to the junction with the main road; the village *plateéya* is 800m R. To the L the road zigzags up past The Old Silk Store (delightful guesthouse run by Jill Sleeman who also conducts walks; tel: +30 24260 49086; www.pelionet.gr; email: jill@pelionet.gr) to the main Zagorá – Tsangarádha road (just short of **3hrs**).

Descent to Damoúkhari

Route 28c

Ksouríkhti (480m)
to Miliés (350m)

Walking time:	2hrs 15mins
Distance:	12km
Height gain:	310m
Height loss:	440m
Difficulty:	2

The old road, now a mixture of path and track.

From the gas station on the main road at the Tsangarádha end of Ksouríkhti, head R up the concrete lane to the *plateéya*. Leaving the *plateéya* on your R, continue uphill/southwest on a road called Odhós Áyiou Dhimitríou past white cottages and apple orchards, until (after **20mins**) you come to the small white chapel of Áyios Dhimítrios. There is a deep gully L and a view over the sea to the islands of the Sporádhes. The concrete comes to an end.

The track bends R and forks. One branch leads to the chapel, the other continues on up. There is a signpost riddled with bullet holes.

Go down to the L on a path marked with red paint dots. At **25mins** cross a stream and climb up the other side. You are on a good *kaldereémee* here, burrowing through a tunnel of greenery with occasional openings under the sweet chestnut trees. In 20mins you come out on a bulldozed track. Pass a clearing with a hut and the remains of a stone bridge over a stream; paint splodges mark the route. Climbing the north flank of the stream under beech woods you come to a RH zigzag where a rock is marked Miliés with an arrow (**1hr**). Follow the arrow up a well-defined gully under beech woods. Descend to a stream and ascend again through beeches and over a spur (**1hr 15mins**). Descend through prickly oak scrub on a south-facing slope with your first view of the Gulf of Vólos and the mountains of Évia to the south and the islands of the Sporádhes strung out along the horizon.

At **1hr 30mins** the *kaldereémee* gives way to a broad dirt track through the *garrigue*. There is a heather-covered tump L with a fork in the road. Stay on the main track, downhill and bending R. At **1hr 40mins** you reach a crossroads by a cluster of ivy-covered plane trees and a ruined house. There are cherry and walnut trees, sure signs of former cultivation. Keep straight ahead between two cypress trees. After 100m ignore a side track to the R. The *kaldereémee* is still visible under the dirt track, but ends on a bend. The track begins to climb again; don't follow it. The continuation of the *kaldereémee* cuts down L by a blue arrow; it bends L-wards but is rather broken up. When you cannot go any further, zigzag back down R; there is a faint blue paint dot on a stone. The path passes under an overhang of prickly oak, but quickly becomes clear again, winding up R through the scrub.

By **1hr 45mins** the way is quite clear, leading through a lovely jungly stretch of chestnuts to a concrete bridge with iron railings. A few minutes later you reach the first apple orchard before coming out on the bend of a concrete road. Turn down L, then after a few metres go R, where you can see the *kaldereémee* start again. Follow a series of paths down into the village of **Miliés** (**2hrs 15mins**).

Route 28d
Miliés (350m) to Kalá Nerá (0m)

Walking time:	1hr 20mins
Distance:	6km
Height gain:	0m
Height loss:	350m
Difficulty:	2

There are two possibilities. One is to follow the single-track railway, now operational only for summertime tourists; the other – more interesting – is to follow the *kaldereémee*. For the start of both, make your way to the now restored railway station on the edge of the lush overgrown gully at the bottom of the village. For the *kaldereémee* reverse Route 28e.

The old railway

The railway route

Past a memorial to villagers executed by the Germans on 4 October 1943, you set off along the narrow-gauge track. The going is pretty level and smooth, round the head of the gorge and south along the further flank. In **45mins** come to a stone bridge carrying a *kaldereémee* over the track where it curves R round a spur. Leave the track and head L down the *kaldereémee*. You can see the village of Kalá Nerá on the shore below.

Stick to the *kaldereémee* as far as possible. Where you lose it follow the track, cutting off the loops and continuing downhill through beautiful, well-tended olive groves. After about 20mins the ground levels off and you come to **Kalá Nerá** and the main road to Vólos (**1hr 20mins**).

Route 28e
Kalá Nerá (0m) to Miliés (350m)

Walking time:	1hr 5mins
Distance:	4km
Height gain:	350m
Difficulty:	2

Heading east out of Kalá Nerá by the Miliés road you come to a petrol station. Turn L into the olive grove, and after 40m you encounter a track running parellel to the road. Turn R on the track, which begins to curve L-wards away from the road. You start to climb and arrive at a junction (**10mins**), where a sign indicates Áyia Marína and Ayías Triádhos to the R.

Directly in front of you a *kaldereémee* begins. Head straight up it (red paint arrows), along the R flank of a stream gully, in an olive grove all the way. At **30mins** you reach a shoulder where you look over into the main Miliés gully to the east. A farm track cuts back R. The *kaldereémee* keeps up to the L; it is very clear and marked with red arrows. (*For those coming down, there is a red arrow and a sign saying 'Kalá Nera'.*) There is a bit of bulldozer damage here, and then you come to another track. The *kaldereémee* cuts over the spur L (sign to Miliés) and contours along through more olive groves.

Continue to a T-junction (**50mins**). Ignore the track to the R; Miliés is in sight ahead. There is a red arrow on the ground; 5mins later you begin to lose height. At **1hr 5mins** the *kaldereémee* brings you out on the road to **Miliés** station – Odhós Garéfi – just a short distance R of the Old Station Hotel. (*For those going down, look out for an ivy-covered plane tree with a fountain at its foot on the L just before the hotel.*) Turn R and up for the centre of the village.

CHAPTER 9

MT ATHOS

View of Athos peak

Mt Athos (2033m) – known to the Greeks as *Áyion Óros*, or the Holy Mountain – is one of the most beautiful and fascinating places in Europe, both for its scenery and its monasteries. Administratively, it is a sort of 'monkish republic', consisting of 20 monasteries and their dependencies, in certain important aspects governed independently of the Greek State. The earliest surviving foundations date from the 10th century; Meghísti Lávra, the oldest, was founded in AD963.

Physically, the Holy Mountain is a narrow ridge, about 40km long and bounded by the sea, rising from 300m in the northwest to culminate in the peak of Mt Athos at over 2000m in the southeast. It forms the easternmost prong of the Khalkidhikí peninsula immediately east of Thessaloníki. Although its extensive forests are now logged, the land has not been cultivated or grazed since, according to legend, the Virgin Mary came ashore here and declared it her garden.

The walking is superb, although it is best not to emphasise that this is your principal interest, rather than some more spiritual purpose. For convenience we have divided our description into two circuits. In both, the routes mainly follow the old mule trails and footpaths that have served Athos for 1000 years. They are slightly harder to find in the northern part where the vegetation is mostly *maquis* and the logging roads are more intrusive. The southern part is stonier and more mountainous, and roads far fewer. The times given cover the walking only, and do not allow for stops.

Location:	The easternmost prong of the Khalkidhikí peninsula close to Greece's second city, Thessaloníki, in the northeast of the country.
Access:	Bus from Thessaloníki (terminus at Karakási St 68) to Ouranópolis (hotels) on the Athos 'frontier', where boats leave for Dháfni, the port of Athos, at 09.45 daily.
Map:	Athos: 1:50 000 by Reinhold Zwerger (available from Stanfords in London).

Obtaining a pilgrim's permit

You have to be male and over 18 to qualify for a permit (*dhiamonitirion*, pronounced *dheeyamoneeteérion*). Call the Pilgrims' Office (English spoken) in Thessaloníki, tel: +30 2310 252578, Mon–Fri 09.00–13.30, and tell them your dates. You are allowed three nights/four days. If demand is heavy, you may not get the dates you want. Once the dates are agreed, send or fax a photocopy of your passport, showing your occupation and religion, to Egnatias St 109, TT 54635 Thesssaloníki, Greece; fax: +30 2310 222424. The permit costs 35 euros and you pick it up at the Pilgrims' Office in Ouranopolis. It entitles you to free board and lodging in the monasteries, and should be presented to the monk/guestmaster – *arkhondárees* – on arrival. Many monasteries (listed on the *dhiamonitirion*) now require you to reserve your place by phone.

Some points to remember

Visitors to Mt Athos are pilgrims, not tourists, and it is important to keep that in mind. Keep any non-Orthodox– or indeed simply un-orthodox – beliefs to yourself. Tolerance of other faiths is not a notable feature of the Greek Orthodox monastic mindset, and the reception you receive (as an outsider) is not always very welcoming.

You will be expected to put in an appearance at church, both in the morning and the evening. In a sense you are singing for your supper, for you go straight from church to the refectory for breakfast and dinner (the food is invariably cold and not what you will be used to, especially breakfast, when you may well be served cold lentils, beans or baked aubergines). You may find unfamiliarity with Othodox practice daunting, but the services are very informal. The congregation does not play an active part, and you can come and go as you please without embarrassment. You are not expected to take part in the kissing of icons and other Orthodox practices. If you do not want to stay for very long, just go discreetly for the last 30mins of the service, take up a position in a pew, and watch and listen. Orthodox services are beautiful, and the singing often deeply moving, even if you cannot understand what is going on. This is also the only way to see the beautiful interiors of the churches and refectories which are nearly always locked at other times.

Be discreet at all times and dress modestly; no shorts, for example. Also, stock up with some snacks at least before you leave the workaday world; monastic fare is frugal,

279

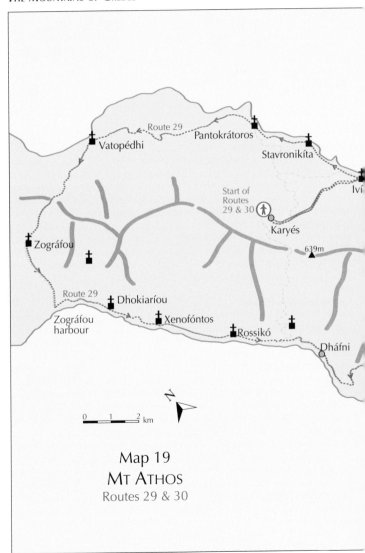

Map 19
MT ATHOS
Routes 29 & 30

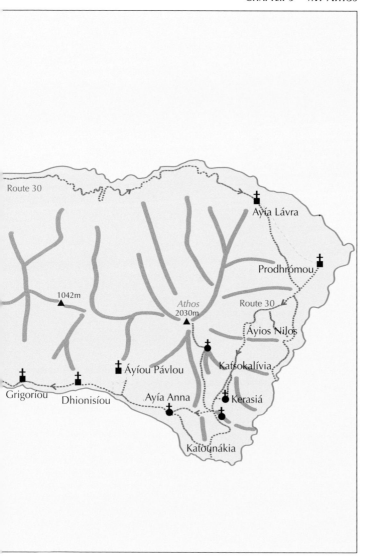

even when not fasting. Remember: monastery gates shut at sunset.

On arrival at Dháfni the boats are met by various monastery minibuses, as well as a proper bus which will take you up to Karyés, the monasteries' administrative capital. There is also a small launch for those who wish to go further on down the coast.

Route 29
Northern Circuit

None of the routes described in this circuit exceeds 350m in altitude, so be prepared for considerable heat.

Karyés to Ivíron to Stavronikíta to Pantokratoros to Vatopédhi to Zográfou to Dhokiaríou to Xenofóntos to Rossikó to Dháfni

Stage 1 – *Karyés (350m) – Ivíron (5m)*

Walking time:	1hr 25mins
Distance:	4.5km
Height gain:	0m
Height loss:	345m
Difficulty:	2

Leave **Karyés** by the Protáton square and the cobbled lane that leads south to Koutloumousíou monastery. Carry on past the monastery, following the now concrete road downhill. About 20m before a bridge over a re-entrant (**15mins**; the old stone bridge also survives), turn R on a path signed to I.M. Ivíron. A 15min descent on the old *kaldereémee* through a tunnel of greenery, mainly evergreen oak, brings you to a stream (**30mins**). A few minutes later cross a bridge and climb briefly uphill. At just under **1hr** you get your first glimpse of the conical peak of Mt Athos rising over the southern tip of the peninsula.

Cross a stone bridge arching high over the stream; soon after pass a pretty pathside chapel with a dedication by an abbot of Ivíron from the old Greek Black Sea town of Trebizond. At **1hr 12mins** cross a dirt track by an impressive stand of cypress, again with a view away to Mt Athos, and 10mins later

arrive at the edge of **Ivíron**'s kitchen gardens with a view over its massive walls (**1hr 22mins**).

Monastery of Ivíron

Stage 2 – *Ivíron (5m) – Stavronikíta (40m)*

Walking time:	1hr
Distance:	3km
Height gain:	50m
Height loss:	3m
Difficulty:	2

Go down to the shore to **Ivíron**'s harbour (*arsanás*) and follow the dirt road climbing up L. After 10mins take a small track heading down R, then after a few metres turn L on a signed path. You come out on the beach by the fortified tower protecting the *arsanás* of Koutloumousíou monastery. Head along the beach and pass behind the tower. Go along the next section of beach and at the end turn up L into the *maquis* on a fairly clear path.

At **42mins** in a brief patch of open ground some way above the sea, be careful to turn sharp L and then up, bearing L and

Monastery of Pantokrátoros

R over the headland ahead, reaching a wooden cross at the top of the climb. Descend to a dirt road, turn R and follow it uphill to the monastery of **Stavronikíta**, built like a castle on the cliffs above the sea (**1hr**).

Stage 3 – Stavronikíta (40m) – Pantokrátoros (15m)

Walking time:	50mins
Distance:	3km
Height gain:	60m
Height loss:	45m
Difficulty:	2

Keep along above the aqueduct and outbuildings of **Stavronikíta** and on to the path to **Pantokrátoros**, which runs through a tunnel of greenery above the shore. After **20mins**, past an old house on the L, keep L. About 20 mins later you emerge on top of a spur with the monastery in front of you; it is not one of the most welcoming.

Stage 4 – *Pantokrátoros (15m)* – *Vatopédhi (20m)*

Walking time:	2hrs
Distance:	7.5km
Height gain:	380m
Height loss:	385m
Difficulty:	3

From the front gate of **Pantokrátoros**, go down the *kaldereémeee* on the R to the bottom, then turn uphill R beside the arches of the ruined aqueduct. You come to a dirt road (**10mins**) and cross straight over on to a path signed to Vatopédhi. After about 20mins the gradient levels off and you follow the contour on a slightly overgrown section of path. At **40mins** pass a spring and cattle trough on a wide bulldozed section at around 330m altitude. After 5mins there is a ruined house just below R; almost immediately after you hit a dirt road.

Turn L up the road (sign to Vatopédhi). A 15min climb brings you to a junction with the main dirt road from Karyés (to the L) to Vatopédhi (**1hr**), barred by a white metal gate (E0519603/N4460889, 404m). Turn up L and then very shortly afterwards up a sort of ramp to the R (signed) on to a path. Cross the road again and continue downhill (sign to Vatopédhi). Cross the road again at **1hr 30mins** and start down a track opposite, bearing R. About 40m along, a path bears down R through the *maquis* to rejoin the main road after 15mins with a view ahead to the sea. Turn L down the road and in 15mins you reach the monastery of **Vatopédhi**, as big as a small town with its out-buildings, harbour and extensive kitchen gardens. (**2hrs**).

Stage 5 – *Vatopédhi (20m)* – *Zográfou (150m)*

Walking time:	2hrs
Distance:	6km
Height gain:	325m
Height loss:	175m
Difficulty:	3

Khera column: crossroads on the ancient ridgetop mule road

Go down L to the shore below the monastery and follow a walled enclosure along to the first lane that turns inland to the L. After 200–300m, past tall plane trees and a shed R, come to an old sign on the R pointing to Zográfou. You climb up R through abandoned terraces. The ground is wet in places, the water leaking from a reservoir, which you pass on your L.

At **27mins** you meet a dirt track at about 100m altitude and cross straight over, cross it again a few minutes later. Half an hour later (265m altitude) the path doubles back L from a superb viewpoint and levels off at around 350m, contouring along the reverse slope through oak woods for about 15mins, to reach the Khéra (hand) column (**1hr 20mins**).

This little brick monument sits on the old Athos ridgetop main road, indicating the times and directions to various monasteries. Karyés (the way is rather overgrown) lies back to the L/south. Khiliandári (a Serbian foundation of somewhat dubious reputation since the wars in Bosnia) and the very conservative Esfigménou lie straight ahead to the north (the path – after 35mins walk – was completely overgrown in 2005, but is due to be cleared by the Friends of Mt Athos English path-clearing teams in 2006).

For Zográfou, turn down L. The path leads to a grassy track and then to a junction with a dirt track (**1hr 33mins**). Keep straight ahead for a moment, then bear L uphill (large red arrow on a rock) on the main road to Zográfou. At **1hr 40mins** a signed path cuts down R. It is the old *kaldereémee* to Zográfou, in good condition underfoot but obstructed by fallen or over-hanging trees. After 15mins you pass a walled enclosure R with an enormous chestnut tree and shortly after meet the road, where you turn downhill R and come to the vast, dilapidated and poverty-stricken Bulgarian monastery of **Zográfou** (**2hrs**).

Stage 6 – *Zográfou (150m) – Dháfni (0m)*

Walking time:	3hrs 30mins
Distance:	13km
Height gain:	0m
Height loss:	150m
Difficulty:	3

From the gate of **Zográfou**, take the *kaldereémee* that turns down L just below the main buildings and above the kitchen gardens. Keep L at the only fork. You soon reach a dirt road, which you follow down a narrow ravine to the Zográfou *arsanás*. Bear L along the beach to the beginning of a rough track which bears up L and then R through an olive grove and down to the *arsanás* of Konstamonítou monastery (**25mins**; *spring water in a tap against the wall*).

The boat from Ouranópolis to Dháfni stops at all these monastery harbours on its return journey. Whenever you've had enough, just wait on the nearest jetty and you will be picked up.

For Dhokiaríou, climb up the path behind the building through the olives and on to the track that leads along or close to the shore all the way to **Dhokiaríou** (**1hr 15mins**), one of the prettiest of the monasteries on the Holy Mountain. Leave the monastery by the main *kaldereémee*. Continue uphill for about 10mins on a rough track. Turn downhill R on a signed path, which leads through neglected old terraces to the beach and you come to **Xenofóntos** (**1hr 45mins**). A track leads thence along the shore to the Russian monastery (**Rossikó**; 3km – about 45mins) and on to **Dháfni** (4km; 1hr). ◀

Route 30
Southern Circuit

Karyés to Ivíron to Lávra to Áyia Ánna to Áyiou Pávlou to Grigoríou to Dhionisíou to Simópetra to Dháfni

The principal difficulty in completing the full southern circuit is reaching Ayía Lávra. Its minibus meets the boat in Dháfni, but if you want to do the whole journey on foot you will need to spend the first night at Ivíron (see Route 30, Stage 1) then, since the path has long disappeared, face 17km of dirt road. The scenery is beautiful, but the road is tedious nonetheless. Allow a good 5hrs.

An alternative would be to take the boat on from Dháfni to the *skeétee* of Kafsokalívia and follow the routes described below. A *skeétee* is a sort of rural cell, dependent on a monastery, inhabited by monks who have chosen to live a more reclusive life than is possible in a main monastery.

Stage 1 – *Kafsokalívia (150m) – Ayía Lávra (100m) via Prodhrómou (250m)*

Walking time:	3hrs 30mins
Distance:	9km
Height gain:	475m
Height loss:	375m
Difficulty:	3
Map:	See Route 29

The climb from the little harbour of **Kafsokalívia** (*kafsokaleévya*) at the foot of the Athos peak to the stone houses of the *skeétee*, scattered like a small village either side of a steep gully, takes about 30mins.

From the church, cross to the R of the gully. The path heads east on the contour. After 25mins you pass a sign to Meghísti Lávra. Keep up; don't go down to the R. You come to a stream, and 20mins later – after a climb – pass some buildings on the L (**Áyios Nílos**) and a spring by a wall with stepping stones set into it (**1hr**). About 1hr later, after a long climb across scree, you reach the cross of Koukouzélis, where the path turns the spur and begins to descend. For **Lávra**, keep on (about 1hr going

Monastery of Ayía Lávra

289

down). For the Romanian monastery of **Prodhrómou**, turn down R. You can see it below, a 19th-century barrack-like building with a tall cypress in the central courtyard. You come out on a bulldozed track by the monastery gate (**2hrs 30mins**). **Lávra** is about 1hr from here along the track – unavoidable, except for the last stretch, where the old path joins from the L.

Stage 2 – Ayía Lávra (100m) – Kerasiá (600m)

Walking time:	3hrs 30mins
Distance:	9.5km
Height gain:	675m
Height loss:	175m
Difficulty:	3

Kerasiá (*kerasyá*) is a good base for climbing Mt Athos (see below). It is a *skeétee*, not a monastery.

Turn L out of **Lávra** gate – Kerasiá is signposted – along a good *kaldereémee* past the monastery kitchen gardens. A **15min** walk brings you to the dirt track to the Romanian monastery of Prodhrómou. Turn L, then R after 5mins. The path continues uphill in a southerly direction under the spurs of the mountain, with the road below L.

After about **1hr 30mins** you reach a point about 500m directly above Prodhrómou, where – by a chapel and the wooden cross of Koukouzélis – the path bends abruptly R round a spur, with fine views north and south. Round this corner, keep up to the R; do not take the path down L to Kafsokalívia and Áyios Nílos. Continue on the level as far as a fork, where what appears to be the main path bears downhill L. The uphill branch – the right way – looks uncertain for the first few paces, but soon improves. The scrub begins to give way to small trees, mostly oak, and the gradient increases.

At **2hrs** there is a stone bridge and the fir trees begin, mixed with chestnut and holly. About 10mins later at the top of the climb beside a steep stream gully in the firs there is a crossroads: L to Áyios Nílos, R to Ayia Ánna. Go R. At **2hrs 25mins** you pass the copious spring of Kría Nerá, spilling across the path in the middle of woods. At **3hrs**, by two wooden crosses and a large boulder L, ignore a small path L. The main path turns downhill; 5mins later you come to a fork with a

The path to Kerasiá

sign pointing L to Kerasiá. Keep straight ahead to reach another junction (**3hrs 18mins**): Kerasiá and Kafsokalívia back to the L.

For Kerasiá, turn L here. You quickly reach another fork by a spring and water trough – the beginning of **Kerasiá**. Down R is a gawdy church with a green dome. A couple of terraces below it a severe stone building houses the headquarters of the *skée-tee*. The site is spectacular, about 600m above the sea, enclosed between two arms of mountain, with the distinctive peak of Profítis Ilías to the west. The monks will put you up on request and feed you frugally; be as polite and discreet as possible.

For **Áyia Ánna** (*aeeyána*), keep on along the main path. At **3hrs 25mins**, in a small clearing under big oak trees, another signpost points L to Kerasiá; this is where you rejoin the path coming up from Kerasiá.

Stage 3 (optional) – Ascent of Mt Athos (2030m) from Kerasiá (600m)

Walking time:	3–4hrs
Distance:	5km
Height gain:	1430m
Height loss:	0m
Difficulty:	3

From **Kerasiá**, climb back to the main path and continue L for 5mins until you come to the saddle between Profítis Ilías and the ridge rising behind Kerasiá, where there is a cross and a spring (750m). A bronze signpost at the foot of a gnarled oak points the way (R) to Athos. A few metres up the path there is a clearing with a water trough. (*Hide the bulk of your gear in the undergrowth: you have to come back this way.*) The path continues up a well-worn channel through prickly scrub, before climbing steeply up an exposed spur. You look down on the roofs of Áyia Ánna and the monastery of Grigoríou (*gree-goreéyoo*) on the shore a little further north.

At the top of the spur the path levels out and enters a small oak wood. Keep R at the junction in the middle of the wood. Bearing R you come out into the open again above the ridge overlooking Kerasiá. The path bends L, following the contour, along the L side of a gully through a very open oak wood. Cross to the R of the gully into fir trees, out into sparse oak, then back to the L of the gully. The trees are thinning out; above L is a long grey slope rising to the skyline.

The path tends R-wards with a small rounded height above the gully R. Before long a grey squat building on a level platform of ground comes into view directly ahead – the chapel of the Panayía or Virgin Mary (about 2hrs from the signpost). You could camp here. (*There is a well inside the chapel – bucket provided.*)

To the L (north) above the chapel, a wide shallow gully leads to a ridge, rising R-wards to an apex of white-grey rock. Head up the gully to the ridge, then scramble up R to the summit (about **3hrs**). There is a tremendous drop on the far side and views all up the peninsula. They say you can see Istanbul on a clear day – that may be wishful thinking – but you can certainly see Mt Olympus across the sea to the southwest. The chapel of the Transfiguration sits right on the summit, with a great iron cross dated 1897 beside it. Spectacular.

Stage 4a – *Kerasiá (600m) – Áyia Ánna (200m; direct route)*

Walking time:	1hr 30mins–2hrs
Distance:	3km
Height gain:	150m
Height loss:	500m
Difficulty:	3

From the start of the Athos ascent path, keep straight on. Descend gently through the woods for about 1km until the path veers east and, abruptly, you find yourself at the brink of the huge limestone cliffs that tower over Áyia Ánna. There follows a ferociously steep descent of some 400m over loose stones – luckily, in the shade.

Áyia Ánna is a very pretty 'village' of whitewashed monkish cells scattered over the steep hillside above the sea. Hung with vines and wistaria, the houses stand among ancient ter-

You have a choice of two routes between Kerasiá and Áyia Ánna, direct or via Áyiou Vasilíou/Katounákia.

races of rich, black soil. There is water everywhere. The path brings you out by the church, where the guest quarters are also located.

Stage 4b – *Kerasiá (600m) – Áyia Ánna (200m) via Áyiou Vasilíou/Katounákia*

Walking time:	2hrs 15mins
Distance:	5.5km
Height gain:	0m
Height loss:	500m
Difficulty:	3

At the crossroads at the start of the Athos ascent path, turn L for the *skeétee* of Áyios Vasilíos (*for a direct route to Katounákia, turn L a moment later*). For 10mins the path contours along the western flank of the Profítis Ilías peak before dropping down to the three or four stone-roofed houses of the *skeétee* of Áyios Vasílios (**25mins**). There begins a long descent to the west to reach a crossroads (**1hr 15mins**), with houses below L and a church on a spur to the R (**Katounákia**).

Bear R and down towards the main coastal path, visible on the spur ahead. In 10mins you reach the spur below a makeshift building by the telephone line. About 15mins later (**1hr 40mins**) you reach the settlement of Dhaniléi, with a dramatic view up the west coast of the Holy Mountain from the little col above the site. Keep heading north up the coast to reach the main church in **Áyia Ánna** at **2hrs 15mins**.

Stage 5 – *Áyia Ánna (200m) – Dháfni (5m)*

Walking time:	7hrs
Distance:	17km
Height gain:	765m
Height loss:	1060m
Difficulty:	2

Turn L coming out of the church gate in **Áyia Ánna**. After the initial stretch the path contours along about 100m above the sea, passes through a kind of fortified gate and soon turns the corner into the valley of Ayíou Pávlou monastery (*aeéyoo pávloo*). Cross the dirt road connecting the monastery with the shore and continue up the old *kaldereémee* past the terraced gardens to reach the gate at about **1hr.**

To continue up the coast, turn down to the sea and follow a track to the R behind the beach until you come to the foot of a cliff, where there appears to be no way forward. Go down on to the beach, round a jutting cliff and there in front of you the path continues straight up the cliffside to about 100m before levelling off. You reach the monastery of **Dhionisíou** (*dheeyoneeseéyoo*), one of the most picturesque, in about 1hr (**2hrs**).

At the end of the beach below Dhionsíou climb steeply up a gully, then over headlands nearly 200m above the sea. At the highest point a finger of rock sticks up beside the path (**2hrs 45mins**). From there you drop down into the shade and damp of a deep gully (**3hrs**), then up and over into the next gully with a magnificent waterfall high up. Another 40mins brings you to the monastery of **Ayíou Grigoríou** (*greegoreéyoo*; **4hrs**).

Beyond the harbour of Grigoríou the path continues to a fork, where a good *kaldereémee* continues uphill to the R and a path marked 'Símonos Pétras (dhásos)' branches L. Go L down to the sea where there is a shingle beach. There begins a long and bruising climb of some 300m to reach the gate of the monastery of Símonos Pétras or **Simópetra**, perched at the top of a pinnacle of rock (**5hrs 10mins**).

Dháfni is another 2hrs (**7hrs**) to the north along a sandy track. Keep downhill to the L at the only junction.

PART 4 – THE PELOPONNESE

The path to Ayia-Irini

CHAPTER 10

Mt Khelmós

Khelmós (2338m) is the 'big' mountain experience most accessible from Athens, thanks to the Athens – Patras highway. It has been somewhat tamed in recent years by road building and development as a ski station, which has transformed Kalávrita, the little local town, from sleepy backwater to desirable property, with chalets springing up in the surrounding forest. Of the routes described here Route 31, a low-level traverse from west to east, from the Mégha Spílio monastery to Lake Tsivloú, escapes this modernity completely. Route 33, a high-level traverse through the beautiful valley of the River Styx, at least remains wild in its central core.

Location:	Overlooking the north shore of the Peloponnese, midway between Corinth and Patras.
Map:	Anávasi Topo 50 Chelmos 1:50 000.
Bases:	Kalávrita (hotels, banks, shops, tavernas); Tsivlós and Peristéra (rooms and food); EOS refuge above ski station, unmanned (no porch).
Access:	Daily buses from Athens to Kalávrita and Patras, stops at Akráta or Dhiakoftó. Train from Athens to Dhiakoftó and from Dhiakoftó to Kalávrita.

Route 31
Mégha Spílio monastery (900m) to
Lake Tsivlós (740m)

Walking time:	5hrs 30mins
Distance:	14.5km
Height gain:	640m
Height loss:	740m
Difficulty:	3

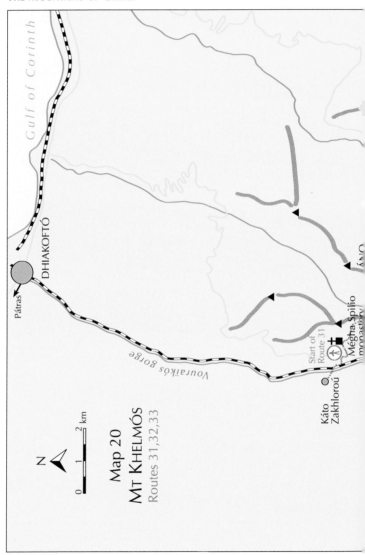

Gulf of Corinth

DHIAKOFTÓ

Pátras

Voraïkós Gorge

Start of
Route 31

Méga Spílio
monastery

Káto
Zakhloroú

N

0   1   2 km

Map 20
MT KHELMÓS
Routes 31,32,33

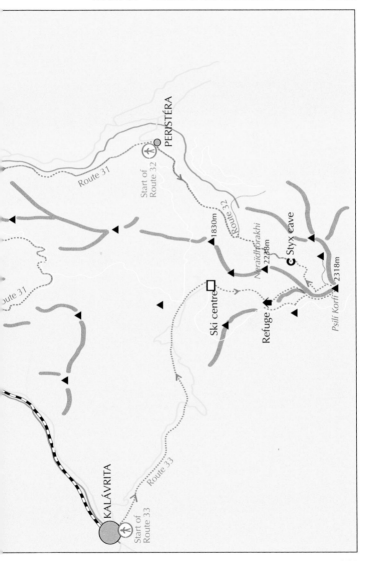

The monastery lies on the east flank of the gorge of the River Vouraïkós, at km25 on the road from the coast to Kalávrita. There is a train station on the rack-and-pinion railway from Dhiakoftó to Kalávrita at Káto Zakhloroú in the valley below (hotel and restaurant), about 50mins walk from the monastery. A clear path leads up to the main road, where you turn L for a short distance, then R into the monastery car park. A further possibility is to walk the whole distance from Dhiakoftó, following the railway up the gorge (14km/5hrs; another 2hrs on to Kalávrita). It is a beautiful and popular route. There are several short tunnels; although trains are infrequent and slow, it is as well to find out when they are due.

From the road, go up the drive to the front of the monastery (*fountain under the monastery arcade.*) A blue triangle shows the way: up R through a gate and out on to a path skirting the rocky crags that dominate the monastery. In 5mins you come to a jutting rock promontory from which the Nazis threw several monks to their deaths in a rampage of killing in December 1943 (which included butchering the entire male population of Kalávrita). Carry on round the cliffs to the L, where you begin a long, steady, winding climb through open firs on what was obviously once a well-used path until you come out on top of the ridge above (**45mins**; E0340627/N4216273; 1170m; *30mins to the monastery going down*) by some old wooden water troughs fed by a black pipe.

Turn R along the ridge following the black pipe, at first slightly to the R of the ridgetop and then (**1hr**) on the open top clear of the trees. A few minutes later, as you climb towards a wooded height ahead, the path bears L of the ridgeline (E0340558/N4215466) on to the R flank of the valley that opens below L. You reach a bare shoulder jutting over the valley (the sea is visible back to the north). Above towers a big conglomerate cliff; the rather leaky water pipe is carried across its flank on piles (**1hr 10mins**).

A clear path descends gradually towards the stream in the wooded gully below. Fallen trees obstruct the way and a disused concrete water channel acts as a guide. At **1hr 30mins** cross the stream beside a line of wobbly stilts carrying the water channel. There follows a long flattish stretch under the firs: you are on or beside the old water channel (*eedhragoyeéyo*) all the way. There is a short section of climbing up and over a bit of rocky terrain.

At **2hrs** (E0341503/N4213446; 1340m) cross back to the true L bank of the stream where it appears to emerge from the rocks. The path immediately climbs steeply up the further bank before veering sharply L and following the R flank (true L) of the probably now dry stream gully. In 10mins (E0341607/N4213222; 1412m) you come to a bit of a clearing and the beginning of a grassy track where trees have been felled. (*Coming the other way, look out for blue-and-yellow triangles L of the stream channel.*)

About 5mins later you come to a signpost at a junction with the main dirt track. Turn L. (Very soon you see a signpost indicating 'Tsivlós 3hrs 45mins' to the L through the trees. I tried a section of this indicated route a little further on and found it very unclear, so stick to the track for the moment.)

A little further along the track (**2hrs 20mins**; E0341877/N4212428) there is a blue triangle on a fir tree. Turn L on a secondary track 100m later. The track cuts back L uphill, passing a concrete water trough before veering R and up to join a higher track (**2hrs 25mins**). Turn sharp L and continue uphill for 10mins before the track levels out, in fir trees all the way now, leaving the valley of the Kaloyerávlako (the monks' ditch) back to your L. The track winds in and out of two or three shallow gullies. The map shows sections of the old path cutting off some of the loops, but they are overgrown and obstructed by fallen trees. It is very much easier to stick to the track.

At **3hrs** you pass a well-appointed sheepfold under trees in a clearing R. About 5mins later there is a yellow triangle on a tree L of the track. The track curves slightly R. Around 100m after the triangle, on the L below the track, is a large rock at the top of a shallow gully with a faint yellow-and-black blaze on it (E0343010/N4213863). (It is probably easier to stay on the track for another 10mins, but the path starts again at this rock, descends through the trees, bends R into a clearing, then L and down across open grass to join an almost extinguished track where you turn R and 40m later cross the upper end of a deepening stream gully.)

Alternatively, keep along the track which loops sharply R, then L round the head of a gully, and descends past a junction with a track coming in from the R. At **3hrs 15mins** (E0343084/N4214066) turn off on to a faint track sloping down L. It curves round to cross the deepening stream gully mentioned above (E0343041/N4214008; two yellow-and-

Approaching Áno Potamiá

white waymarks). Turn R here, before crossing the stream, and follow a level path above the deepening stream gully.

Route finding over this section requires vigilance.At **3hrs 20mins** the path soon descends slightly and bears L-wards across an open rocky clearing, passing below the remains of a drystone wall, with the main track about 30m above R (yellow-and-white waymarks). Bear northwest, first at 306°, then 340°. A few moments later bear L-ish at 358°, keeping your eyes skinned for the paint flashes; the alignment of the paint strokes sort of indicates the direction to the next one. At E0343020/N4214245, after about 5mins (**3hrs 30mins**), there is a yellow triangle and a curving paint flash. Follow the curve of the paint flash. The way is confused here by fallen trees, and there is scarcely any trace of a path. Zigzag L–R–L–R down the slope. There is paint on a rock at E0342979/N4212261. Bear 348° to the next mark 50–70m above the stream, where you make a sharp L turn down to the bank of the stream (E0342947/N4214303; 1224m; **3hrs 40mins**). There is a yellow triangle, a yellow-and-white paint flash as well as a red arrow on a rock. Turn R along the slope above the stream. There is another yellow triangle visible ahead.

You traverse the R flank of the valley about 100m above the bed of the stream, bearing just east of north at 12°. After a few minutes patches of open ground appear among the firs on the further flank and the valley begins to open out. After 10mins (**3hrs 54mins**) you come to a big conglomerate boulder with a sharp edge beside the path (E0343122/N4214801; 1145m), marked with yellow-and-white paint. There is a distinctive mesa-like hill across the valley at 340°. A few moments later the path loses height by zigzagging sharply down to the L, then straightens out again to the R.

At **4hrs 10mins** a black pipe appears running parallel below your path. A couple of minutes later you come to a dry gully and make a sharp L turn out of the forest and along the upper edge of a grassy open space (formerly fields), accompanied by the pipe. About 5mins later, approaching the village of Áno Potamiá, keep L at a fork, leaving the pipe above R, before zigzagging down through prickly oak scrub and over an awkward outcrop of conglomerate rock. Clamber down into a walnut grove and keep R under the cliff and round to join the concrete road by the first house of Zotiánika (yellow triangle; **4hrs 25mins**), the upper quarter of **Áno Potamiá**.

Turn R on the road and continue uphill to rejoin the dirt track that you left further back. Keep straight ahead. You come shortly after to a junction on the col (**4hrs 50mins**); turn down to the R. (Fifteen paces from the col, over the earth embankment on the R, a clear path heads off through the pines down to the lake. There are signs at the beginning, but I only went down this path for 5mins and could not find the beginning of it from the bottom; it is, however, marked on the map.) I went down by the dirt road, about 3km/40mins (**5hrs 30mins**) to the very nice taverna/guesthouse – To Pétrino (tel: 26960 34190, mob: 6973 620237) – on the road just south of the little round lake of **Tsivlós**. There are no more than a handful of houses in the hamlet.

Link: Tsivlós to Peristéra

Walking time:	2hrs
Distance:	6.5km
Height gain:	300m
Difficulty:	2

A 2hr combination of track and path following the west flank of the valley of the River Kráthis allows you to join Routes 31 and 32 and make a complete circuit of Khelmós.

Turn R just after To Pétrino. There is a modern cottage on the corner; just past it a small track marked with a yellow triangle heads L. For 1hr the route follows a water conduit, pretty much on the contour, between 700–800m. At E0345080/N4211750, at the end of the track, ignore the remains of the old cobbled path, cross the streambed and continue on the path opposite, climbing across a couple of stream gullies to meet the end of a track that joins up with the now tarmac road into **Peristéra**.

Route 32
Peristéra (1000m) to
Styx waterfall (1700m)

Walking time:	2hrs 40mins
Distance:	6.5km
Height gain:	650m
Height loss:	0m
Difficulty:	2 (except for a tricky passage just before the waterfall)
Map:	See Route 31

Start from the upper *plateéya* in **Peristéra** (café/taverna). Follow the paved road southwest, past scattered and fairly derelict cottages, keeping L at the junction with the new road up to Kserókambos. The road becomes a dirt track; after about 1km (**20mins**) you leave the last houses – new villas – behind. Ahead, blocking the view up the valley L, lie the peaks of Neraïdhálona (2252m) and Psilí Korfí (2318m) with the Styx ravine cutting down R at their feet. The waterfall (in Greek *ta eédhata too steegós* or sometimes simply *mavronéree*) is hidden from sight by the steep ramparts of the Neraïdhórakhi peak (2238m) to the R.

Continue up the track past still cultivated terraces. After 36mins pass a stream. A further 30mins steady climb brings you to a concrete water trough and a copious spring (**1hr**; E0343129/N4207045; 1331m).

The track comes to an end shortly afterwards in a deep stream gully, full of various waymarks. On the further side head steeply up on the old path to emerge on the top of an open grassy shoulder (**1hr 15mins**), where the path to Kastráki heads off L, down the nose of the spur to the river and on to a track that brings you eventually to the hamlet of Sólos on the other side of the valley.

Cross the shoulder and bear R back into the woods. At **1hr 30mins** you reach the edge of a deep cleft-like gully where the path zigzags up on embanked sections on the R flank in order to gain height and find a suitable crossing point. A few minutes later cross a further gully, climb to an open shoulder (**1hr 50mins**), and cross another gully on white, friable rock

Fill up with water from the fountain in Peristéra's upper *plateéya* before you set off.

The Styx ravine from the Hunter's Saddle

beneath the precipitous east face of Neraïdhórakhi. Zigzag steeply up a grassy slope to reach the Hunter's Saddle, *to dhiáselo too keeneegóo* (**2hrs**), a wonderful viewpoint among scattered firs overlooking the Styx ravine. ▶

It would make a spectacular bivouac, although there is no water.

From the saddle the path bears R, descending slightly along the R flank of the ravine, before turning a corner and practically disappearing on steep, slippery and rather dangerous slopes of gritty, white, friable ground. There are two or three tricky, albeit short, passages over a nasty drop with little in the way of footholds and no handholds. Someone has fixed a length of wire by way of a 'fixed rope,' though it serves little purpose. Beware of rock falls from the cliffs above early in the season when ice is melting.

At the end of this passage cross on to surer ground and climb steeply up R on the scree-covered nose of a spur between two gullies. The waterfall – which reduces from a wavering 200m column of spray to little more than a trickle by the end of summer – is right up ahead, with a low slit of a cave at its foot (**2hrs 40mins**). The path onward veers L out and round the rocky outcrop which borders the cave.

To continue towards Kalávrita, reverse Route 33 below.

Route 33
Kalávrita to Styx waterfall

Walking time:	6hrs 30mins
Distance:	18.5km
Height gain:	1530m
Height loss:	480m
Difficulty:	3
Map:	See Route 31

Much has changed over the last 30 years. Since the opening of the ski centre on the plateau of Kserókambos, a tarmac road leads 16km right into the heart of the mountain. As a result the old path has either been overlaid or is much less used. The Anávasi map marks an alternative route to the EOS refuge (4hrs) that branches R off the road just before the locality known as Valvoúsi (7km) and passes to the west of the Avghó peak overlooking the ski centre. It is part of the E4.

The Valvoúsi – Kserókambos section of the old path is still worth doing. Perhaps it is best to do it coming down, and to take a taxi as far as the ski centre if you are going up.

To walk the whole way, starting from **Kalávrita** railway station, head east up the street called Ayíou Alexíou towards the upper end of town. Follow the signs to Kalimanopoulío. When you come to a signpost to Lóusi, turn L. A few metres later – by a sign to Eftikhía Studios (E0334497/N4210605) – the E4 is indicated, heading off R uphill at 94° between two houses. You hit the main tarmac road in about 30mins (**50mins**).

Turn R and keep along the road as far as Valvoúsi (3km; **1hr 30mins**). The road crosses a stream on a RH bend. Trees have encroached on the open meadow L of the road and holiday houses are being constructed. Just past the bend, a track turns off L (E0337914/N4208555; 1273m). Follow it; you pick up the old path a little way in, still in good condition, climbing steadily through beautiful old fir woods, bearing slightly north of east, then east (green triangle waymarks). Cross the main road twice, once at E0339742/N4209016 (1524m) and again at E0340361/N4208953 (1564m). At E0340881/N4208740 (1613m) you come out on the road once more (**3hrs**) by a sign 'Refuge 2hrs 30mins, Styx 4hrs 30mins and Kalávrita 2hrs 30mins'. Follow the road southeast, straight and flat, for 1km to the ski installations (**3hrs 15mins**).

The old path climbed south up the treeless stream gully between the Neraïdhórakhi ridge to the east and the Avghó peak to the west. The ski installations have deformed the lower reaches of the gully completely. The general direction, however, remains the same.

Set off south, keeping R of the broad bulldozed piste behind the car park. When you reach the first level, where the lift machinery is installed (**3hrs 45mins**), continue south and up, again keeping to the R side. There are occasional green-and-white paint signs. Another 40mins bring you to the ugly 'new' refuge astride the col at the head of the gully. Due to some dispute it is never used, and there is no porch for emergency shelter. It looks out west, with wonderful views of the Erímanthos massif. Just below it, beside the rough shepherds' track that comes up from Kserókambos, is a spring, *too poolyóo ee vreésee* (the name often used to refer to the locality).

To continue to the Styx waterfall, there are two possibilities. One is to climb the stony nose of the spur which rises southeast of the refuge and leads to a track on the south ridge of Neraïdhórakhi (constructed to serve the new observatory visible on the ridge; about 40mins). Turn R on the ridge and go down the track as far as the Páno Lithári sheepfold (see below; about 50mins in all). The alternative is to drop down from the refuge on to the track below and follow it southward.

Turn L on the track and keep going for 25mins (**4hrs 50mins**) until you reach a fork signed 'Páno Lithári 1km'. Here turn sharp L and up, before traversing across a west-facing slope with views down over an old sheepfold and the long valley of Stronghilólaka. You reach another LH hairpin beneath a large overhanging rock on the watershed, Páno Lithári (**5hrs 7mins**).

Here, turn off the track and pass to the L behind the big rocks and down through a narrow rocky passage to come out by the sheepfold. There is a long concrete shed and a cottage tucked in under an outcrop. Below the fold the ground slopes away into the upper reaches of the Styx valley. A path, marked yellow and black, goes down the L flank of the gully from the L end of the shed, bearing 54°, past two or three seepages to the Lithári spring at E0341495/N4204620 (2182m; **5hrs 20mins**).

The path descends to the R across the spring-watered turf into a small gully, then bears away L on the R flank of this gully to come out on the top of a fairly short but distinct grassy spur, with the ground dropping sharply away to either side. Paint marks lead you down the top of the spur to the end, where the path bears sharply R and begins to zigzag down towards a stream and the Mavronéri tarn lying in a hollow at the foot of a nearly sheer crag. Cross the stream (**5hrs 35mins**, E0341791/N4204720; 2067m) by a waterfall running over an overhanging rock. Leave the tarn on your R, and pass to the L round behind the rocky hump on your L. Bear diagonally L downhill on the R flank of the Styx gully towards the stream in the bottom, aiming for a crossing just above the point where the stream dips into a narrow cleft (E0342062/N4204901; 1978m). Cross over (**5hrs 51mins**) and up the far bank, bearing 90° R along the rocky L flank of the rapidly developing ravine beneath the steep crags of Neraïdhórakhi. The Styx waterfall is about 30mins further on (**6hrs 30mins**). ▶

Going up, it is about 1hr 30mins to the Lithári spring and 1hr 45mins to the main track on the Neraïdhórakhi ridge.

CHAPTER 11

MT PARNON

Mt Párnon (Párnona) is a long narrow spine of mountain, running southeast from the Trípoli plateau in the middle of the Peloponnese. It is not a dramatic mountain, but there are beautiful woods and fine views from the summit. Access to the summit area is through the village of Áyios Pétros (*hotel, tavernas, provisions*), reached either from Ástros on the coast south of Árgos or from the Trípoli – Sparta road. Polídhroso, the starting point for Route 35, is more easily accessible from Sparta or from km45 on the Trípoli – Sparta road.

Location:	40km southeast of Trípoli.
Maps:	Road Editions Peloponnese 1:250 000; HAGS sheets Ástros and Goritsá 1:50,000.
Bases:	Áyios Pétros (hotel and rooms, tavernas); Polídhroso (hotel, taverna).
Access:	Daily buses from Athens to Trípoli and Spárta. Less frequent to Áyios Pétros.

Route 34
HAC/EOS refuge (1420m) to Profítis Ilías (1650m) to Krónio summit (1934m) to Malevís convent (920m)

Walking time:	4hrs 15mins (add 1hr for summit)
Distance:	17km
Waymarks:	Red squares and red diamonds with white 33
Height gain:	450m to Profítis Ilías, 730m to summit
Height loss:	730m (1000m via summit)
Difficulty:	3

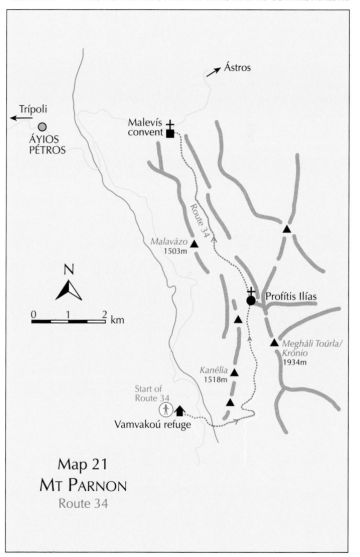

→ Ástros

← Trípoli

ÁYIOS
PÉTROS

Malevís
convent

Route 34

Malavázo
1503m

N

0   1   2 km

Profítis Ilías

*Megháli Toúrla/
Krónio*
1934m

Kanélia
1518m

Start of
Route 34

Vamvakoú refuge

Map 21
MT PARNON
Route 34

311

From Áyios Pétros an asphalt road now runs to the HAC refuge (1420m) halfway to Vamvakoú (*vamvakóo*). It is signposted from the turning outside the village: 14km. There is plenty of room for camping round the refuge, and a spring 5mins to the southeast. There are taxis in Áyios Pétros (on the square) which will deliver you to the refuge to start the walk and pick you up at a prearranged time from the Malevís convent at the end. It is a beautiful forest walk, presenting no real difficulty.

Remember that there are no reliable water sources until the end of this walk.

From the refuge there are splendid views southwards over the forest to the Taÿgetos massif. Just outside the building a wooden signpost points to Megháli Toúrla (the vernacular name for the Krónion peak) and Malevís convent. Turn your back on the refuge and set off back down the access road. Past a football pitch R you come to the first waymarks – a red square and red diamond with a white 33 in the middle – which will guide you all the way to Malevís. A sign indicates 'Krónion 3½hrs'. Turn L down the path, descending a spur through open pine forest. Cross a forest track and continue down in a southeasterly direction. At **15mins** you pass a small spring and a pool at the edge of old terraces planted with walnut trees and come out on the road.

Turn L along the road for 100m and then R (sign on the L: 'Krónion 3hrs'), down across another neglected walnut grove into the damp, pine-shaded valley bottom, where you bear R and cross the stream (*last water of the day*). Continue up the opposite bank to a forest track (**25mins**) which you cross, bearing slightly leftwards into the mouth of a dry stony streambed (red square visible on a pine on the L side). About 15mins later, at a fork in the streambed, take the L gully. You can't go wrong, even though the waymarks are infrequent here; the gully bottom funnels you upwards between steep fir- and pine-clad flanks.

At **1hr** you emerge on to a forest track, cutting across your line of march at 90°. A wooden arrow points L-wards up the track. Continue L up the track, rounding a spur after a few minutes, where you get a view southward to Taÿgetos. Keep on along the tree-clad northern slope, pretty much on the contour, until the track peters out in a stony gully at **1hr 25mins**, some 20m past a fir tree marked with two red squares and a red arrow.

Continue up the gully for a few moments before climbing out L, then turn R at a waymarked tree and immediately L

up a steep open slope, bearing gradually R-wards (waymarks). The path drops back into the gully (**1hr 35mins**), climbing gradually and bearing R-wards, to emerge at the top (**1hr 50mins**) in a beautiful little meadow with an old stone shepherds' hut and *mandreé* or sheep-pen shaded by firs beneath the summit ridge.

A rough track leads north to a shallow col marking the edge of a wide grassy plateau with a wooden signpost pointing to the bald rocky peak of Megháli Toúrla (1934m; *no path; allow 1hr*). Around 15mins later, at the far end of the plateau, you come to the little white chapel of **Profítis Ilías (2hrs 10mins)**, a good spot for a rest and picnic and shelter in an emergency. Above it, the Mikrí Toúrla peak makes for easier access to the eastward view than the summit itself and most of it can be seen anyway from the low saddle between the two peaks.

From behind the chapel follow the track downhill for about 100m and bear down L at the waymarked fork. Rejoin the track on a bend, follow it down for 80m and turn L over the bank on to a small path (signpost; **2hrs 10mins**). The path descends steeply through mixed forest of pine and fir, heading almost straight down the slope; do not be tempted by a path marked with red paint bearing off R. Keep a sharp look out here for the red squares. In about 20mins your path broadens into what was once a track created by Forestry tractors. Bear R and in a

Profítis Ilías and the summit plateau

few minutes you come to a dirt road (signpost; **2hrs 35mins**). Turn R and climb gently to a RH bend where a signpost points L. Follow the path down the L flank of the stony spur ahead. As you reach the bank of the dirt road (**2hrs 45mins**) veer off R into a broad hollow meadow with a shepherds' hut and pen and a sometimes cultivated field beneath the wooded height of Malavázo (1503m).

The path (red squares) bears R along the near edge of the meadow to a slight rise with a red square and a red arrow on a tree (**2hrs 50mins**), pointing L. Bear L along the edge of a dingle, R round its head, and slightly uphill to join a rough jeep track. Follow the track to the R among scattered juniper trees to the top of the rise (**2hrs 57mins**). Malavázo is on your L, Megháli Toúrla behind you.

Here a path bears L downhill into the trees, bears R across a slope scattered with juniper above a grassy hollow and continues, contouring round R until you reach a fir tree marked with a L-pointing arrow (**3hrs 7mins**). You can see the crumbling remains of some terrace walls just above R. The path veers L here and shortly after turns steeply L again down the stony slope of the gully bordering Malavázo. In a few minutes you reach the bottom of the gully (**3hrs 15mins**) and cross to the L bank, then back to the R, traverse a patch of open grass for 50m, and cross again. The gully bottom is shallow here, and the path meanders back and forth.

Soon cross once more to the R and begin to climb the flank of the gully. About 5mins later you find yourself climbing a RH side gully (**3hrs 30mins**). After a couple of minutes you zigzag back L along its opposite flank and soon begin a steep slippery descent. The angle eases, and shortly afterwards the path doubles back L and down through a collapsed stone wall (red arrow on a stone).

At **3hrs 50mins** you pass a very weak spring and some old wooden water troughs. There is a short sharp drop and you come out on a grassy slope with no waymarks and no clear path. Turn R and slightly uphill. There is a spring and concrete reservoir. The path continues through mature juniper trees to another cement spring under a large plane tree (**4hrs 2mins**). Around 5mins later you come out by a large whitewashed reservoir directly above the **Malevís convent**; make your way L down on to the road and R round to the front of the building (**4hrs 15mins**).

There is a card phone just to the R of the entrance from where you can call a taxi from Áyios Pétros.

Polídhroso (1000m) to Stamatíra (1361m) to Áyii Anáryiri monastery (900m) to Polídhroso (1000m)

Walking time:	5hrs including Stamatíra (2hrs 40mins without)
Distance:	13km with Stamatíra (8.7km without)
Waymarks:	Blue squares and blue triangles
Height gain:	461m including Stamatíra (220m without)
Height loss:	461m including Stamatíra (220m without)
Difficulty:	2/3
Map:	No map (in this guidebook)

This is a particularly beautiful walk, not too strenuous and with a much smaller height gain than usual. The return along the stream from the monastery is idyllic in spring when the flowers are out and there is plenty of water in the stream.

The path starts in the plane-shaded main square between the café and church. A signpost points downhill to 'Góghena, Stamatíra, Vasarás'. Follow the lane, waymarked with blue squares (for the Stamatíra peak) and blue triangles (for the monastery and the return journey), down to the stream at the bottom of the village. Cross the bridge and bear R on a clear uphill path into the forest of pine and fir.

Cross a small ridge, descend into a gully and climb again to a second ridge (within **20mins**), from where you can just make out the chapel on the wooded summit of Stamatíra far ahead. The path contours through beautiful open forest of fir and pine, carpeted in May with colonies of the carmine *cyclamen repandum*. At almost **30mins** you reach a third ridge. Cross open ground. At a bend in the path, bear L towards the two blue squares you can see below and L. Descend into the gully and climb back along the further flank, in the trees once more. Cross another gully and climb to a fourth ridge (**50mins**), where open grassy fields mark the site of Góghena, where the villagers once sowed their wheat and barley.

Head straight across these fields on the contour, keeping an eye open for the blue squares. At **1hr** you re-enter the trees, losing height now. In a few moments you come to a fir tree on the edge of a deep gully, marked with a blue triangle. Here the path forks. Straight on leads to Stamatíra, while the R fork descends sharply towards the pink roofs of the monastery, visible below.

Variant: Stamatíra

For Stamatíra keep straight on. The path climbs gently through open forest with glimpses of the monastery below. At **30mins** you turn unexpectedly L, then bear R over a fallen tree. Approaching the summit ridge fork R by a red arrow on a fir tree, go 50m downhill and fork L again uphill by a blue square and red '45' to regain the ridge. Follow the ridge northwest. The forest is patchier here and the ground rockier. At **1hr** pass to the R of a huge limestone slab. The village of Véria is visible R, with the barren hump of the Megháli Toúrla peak beyond and above it. After a short sharp climb you pass beneath the summit, cross the ridge, bear L and climb back up the south slope to the summit chapel of Análipsi (the Ascension; **1hrs 20mins**) with wonderful views south over the Taÿgetos range. Return the same way (1hr).

Those who remained on the main track take the R fork down towards the valley bottom. At **1hr 15mins** you reach a forest track. A moment later bear L at a junction, following a wire fence. This leads to a gate where a newly cleared path continues downhill, still following the fence, to reach another forest track and a second gate. The path continues down R and 5mins later comes out on a wide dirt road by a stream in the valley bottom (**1hr 26mins**). This is the stream that flows down from Polídhroso village that you crossed at the beginning of the route. The monastery entrance is to the L.

Turn R on the dirt road. Keep to the track that follows the stream bank. It comes to an end after a few minutes (**1hr 35mins**). There a path begins, going straight ahead along the R side of a plastic pipe. Turn L across the stream into a walnut orchard and almost immediately back R at a small dam. Keep straight along this – the true L – bank, negotiating the tangle of felled trees. A blue triangle appears to confirm you are on the right route.

At **1hr 41mins** cross the stream to the true R bank by a big hollow plane tree, then back and forth a few times before returning to the true R bank and following some old terrace walls beneath a red cliff. Around 5mins later cross to the true L bank and zigzag up to a higher path, drop back to the stream and cross once more (**2hrs**). Another 15mins bring you to a ruined mill and a streamside terrace of walnut trees. About 5mins later cross to the true L bank by a black gate and turn L, following that bank. Return to the true R bank and follow the path up into some terraces of apple trees. Bear R along a wall, cross the stream twice more and – on the true R bank for the last time – zigzag up a cobbled path. Past the ivy-covered remains of an aqueduct you come to the first house in **Polídhroso**, standing in its neat vegetable garden. At the bridge you crossed at the start of this walk, turn L up the lane to the square (**2hrs 40mins**). ▶

There is a *maghazeé* on the square and a hotel – the Skolarkhio in the old school building (though it may not be open). There are plenty of possibilities for camping round about.

The first house in Polídhroso

CHAPTER 12

MT TAÏGETOS (TAŸGETOS)

Profítis Ilías summit with its chapel and other ruins

Seen from the north and east, the long serrated ridge of Mt Taïgetos appears to have five knuckles, whence its nickname, *pendadhák-tilo* – five fingers. Some people say they are the dents left by the hand of God as he lifted the Prophet Elijah up to heaven, and point to the fact that its highest peak bears the name of Profítis Ilías. Certainly, the scale of the mountain, looming like a dark shadow over the orange groves of Sparta, with streaks of snow shimmering through the summer heat, lends it an otherworldly quality.

Its spectacular 2407m summit is the scene of one of the few remaining mountaintop celebrations in Greece, a fragile link with pagan rituals of the past. Every 19–20 July a hundred or so revellers make the ascent to spend the night playing guitars and eating soup (supplied by the army), while a priest intones early morning mass in the derelict summit chapel.

The mountain's beauty is not limited to its peaks. Its forested eastern flanks are riven by a series of short, deep gorges and criss-crossed with historic mulepaths. The more complex western foothills hide longer ravines and, near the Messinian coast, there are some lovely villages and chapels, also linked by old trails.

Location:	The mountainous central 'finger' of the southern Peloponnese, between the towns of Sparta and Kalamáta.
Maps:	Anavasi Topo 50 Taÿgetos 1:50 000 (with guidebook); Topo 25 sheets Sparta – Mystras, Xirokambi and Kardhamíli – Stoupa 1:25 000.
Bases:	Sparta, Kardhamíli (all amenities); Místras, Anavrití (hotel, basic shops).
Access:	Frequent buses daily from Athens to Sparta and Kalamáta (Sunday charters direct from UK); from Sparta regular buses to Místras, occasional to Anavrití; from Kalamáta daily buses to Kardhamíli.

Route 36
Taïgetos Traverse via the
Pendadháktilo ridge

Hiking the length of the ridge is a breathtaking 8–10hr affair, but not to be under-estimated; snowpack remains from November to May, compounded by localised clouds and storms, while a complete absence of water and shade make it hot work in summer. Given the scarcity of and the distance from villages and roads, it requires a self-sufficient backpacking trip of two full days (if you arrange transport into and out of the trailheads) or four days (if you walk in and out). Given the beauty of the lower routes, I recommend the latter alternative – described below – with overnights at Anavrití (hotel), the EOS refuge/bivouac on the summit, and either Áyios Dhimítrios or Áyios Pandeléïmonas in Vassilikí forest.

There is a choice of exit routes: down the long Virós gorge to Kardhamíli on the west (Messinian) coast, or down a little-used path to Spartiá village in the east-ern (Laconian) foothills, which allows for easier return transport to Místras. A third option – avoiding the rocky Virós gorge – is to follow the spectacular (but soon-to-be-asphalted) mountain road to Panayía Yiátrissa monastery and thence a path via Miliá village to Áyios Nikólaos, which lies on the west coast near the resort of Stoúpa.

Stage 1 – *Místras (280m) – Anavrití (800m) via the Langadhiótissa cave-chapel and gorge*

Walking time:	3hrs
Distance:	8km
Waymarks:	E4 (yellow and black) from Faneroménis monastery
Height gain:	520m
Height loss:	0m
Difficulty:	2

From the plane tree in the centre of modern **Místras** village (280m), follow the lane heading southeast, signed to Paróri. (After 250m there is a turn-off to the R signed 'Taïgéti/Varsinikó

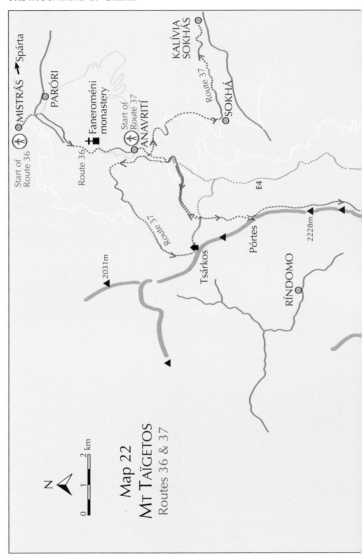

Map 22
MT TAïGETOS
Routes 36 & 37

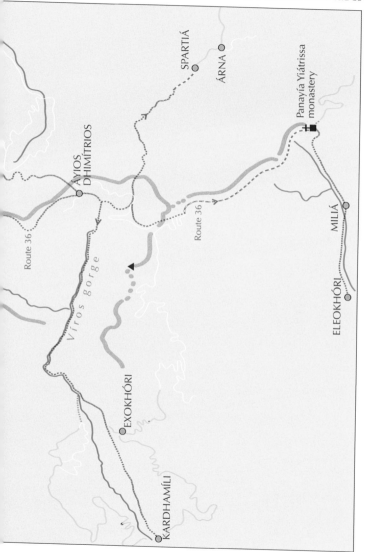

Langhadhiótissa chapel
(photo Michael Cullen)

E4', the official – but less interesting – E4 route to Anavrití: a lane which winds uphill and, keeping L after 3km, brings you to Sotíras chapel in about 1hr.) For our preferred (but slightly vertiginous) route, continue along the main road, keeping R, to the shady square of Paróri (1km from Místras) with its pair of tavernas and bank of gushing springs. Just beyond this, after the small railed bridge and by a sign and map, turn R up a small track. Where this ends at an old quarry (**20mins**), continue up the gravelly path ahead (southwest).

After another 5mins the path forks.

The R fork (signed) leads to Langadhiótissa chapel, a highly worthwhile 2min detour to a wonderfully peaceful spot: a tiny roofless chapel in the depths of a large cave, overhung with dripping stalactites and decorated with frescoes and fresh-picked flowers.

The Apothétes ravine is the most likely candidate for the site where the ancient Spartans left their unwanted babies to die.

The L fork is the onward route (red-and-white waymarks), winding generally uphill, with one brief, stone-laid descent, to reach a covered concrete water conduit. Follow the conduit R, walking on the slabs and admiring the almost sheer 50m drop R into the Apothétes ravine. ◀

It snakes around the curve of an orange-grey cliff, at one point cut into the face – this is the potentially vertigo-inducing

*The Apothétes ravine
(photo Michael Cullen)*

stretch, though the flat metre-wide surface should ensure that even the most fearful can get through. About 30mins above the cave-chapel (**1hr**) you enter plane woods and the conduit is lost under a path (red-on-white triangles), which climbs to meet the E4 track by the chapel of Sotíras (500m; **1hr 10mins**). Though rather drab inside, the shady benches and outside tap, built to supply the 6 August Feast of the Transfiguration, make it a lovely rest spot. Turn L, across the stream, and follow the jeep track zigzagging uphill, with views ahead to Neraïdhovoúna mountain and across to the crags of Xerovoúna.

After 1hr or so (**2hrs 10mins**) the track bears R by a cross-capped rock and joins a paved lane; L are the black gates of **Fanaroméni monastery** (780m), which is usually open to visitors.

From here the route to Anavrití is relatively easy, following either the lane heading south or the E4 path which runs alongside it. A few minutes along the lane you pass, on the R, the chapel of Áyios Stratigós; ignore the path for Pergandhéïka and Taïghéti hamlets. A few minustes later – if you dislike roadwalking – branch L by the E4 sign down a small path, bearing R by a stone wall and threshing floor, past a telephone pole (E4 sign) and up a paved section past Ayia Paraskeví chapel to a track, where you almost rejoin the road. E4 signs point you straight on past Ayios Yeóryios chapel, down a steep-stepped path and across a stream bridge by some ruined mills into the northerly quarter of **Anavrití** village. The main square, with its hotel, cafe and basic shops, is a few minutes down to your L, about 45mins from the monastery (whether by road or path; **3hrs** total).

Stage 2 – Anavrití (800m) – Pendadháktilo ridge (2300m) – Profítis Ilías (2400m) or EOS refuge (1550m)

Walking time:	8–9hrs
Distance:	15km
Waymarks:	E4, then red triangles to ridge; O3 red diamonds on white along ridge
Height gain:	1550m to refuge, 1750 to summit
Height loss:	800m to refuge, 150m to summit
Difficulty:	3

This stage is tough and also requires some organisation. At the end of it you must either be prepared to sleep out on or near the summit, or arrange to stay in the refuge at Ayia Varvára. The latter is more comfortable, but does involve losing 600m altitude (which you need to regain the following day). To book the refuge, contact EOS Spártis tel: 27310 22574 or at 97 Gortsologou St in central Sparta (evenings only). Bear in mind that the warden charges a fee. If there's low cloud or you simply prefer an easier route to the refuge, the E4 trail (not described) will take you there in 5hrs, on a path contouring from Lakómata through the forest around the 1500m mark all the way.

Take plenty of water with you; after the first couple of hours there is neither shade nor water until you reach the refuge

From just above the central square and hotel of **Anavrití** (800m), follow the concrete lane L (signed Odhós Taÿgétou) towards the houses of Kalamaréïka. Just after a four-spouted spring fork R up a track, which soon loses its concrete surface. Just before the last house on the L (**5mins**) fork R (E4 sign) up a path. Pass to the L of Ayios Stratigós chapel and reach a post marking

The Pendadháktilo ridge from Sokhá (photo Michael Cullen)

0.5km from Anavrití, alongside an E4 yellow-on-white way-mark and a red-on-white triangular waymark; the latter will accompany you all the way to the Pendadháktilo ridge.

Small paths thread south along disused terraces and threshing floors to three huge plane trees and the spring of Platanítsa, where a short descent brings you to a footbridge across the stream. The path, at times stepped, then climbs steeply through mixed woods to hit a dirt road (**1hr**). Turn R and, after 15m, fork L again to shortcut a bend (in doing so, you'll pass the 2km post and a L branch to the refuge via the E4 path). Regain the track and follow it up to the main Anavrití – Lakómata dirt road at a sharp bend (**1hr 10mins**).

Cross straight over, heading west-ish up a small path through scrubby bushes and low pines. Ignore a R fork to the fields and seasonal spring of Platanáki (**1hr 20mins**), and continue past the 3km post on a lovely, pine-needle-covered stretch. After crossing a gully and keeping L at the signpost, the gradient steepens and the woods thin out. Just over **2hrs** out of Anavrití, bear L (southwest) to recross the gully by the 4.5km post and soon reach the abandoned meadows and sparse firs of 'Livádhi Place', also known as Imerotópi (**2hrs 15mins**; 1370m).

Ahead the valley forks: the R gully leads up to the Botanical Station of Tsárkos in 50mins (yellow-on-white waymarks), the L gully is our onward route to the Pendadháktilo ridge (red triangles on white). In between looms the bulk of Spanakáki peak, northernmost of the five knuckles. A few minutes further up a signpost and path junction confirms this, giving 2hrs to Spanakáki and 7hrs 30mins to Profítis Ilías, with a further sign to 'Lakómata 50mins' on a sharp-L path. Continue south up the crumbling terraces, past intermittent firs, keeping the LH gully on your L, and looking out for red-on-white waymarks. Around 1600m altitude (**3hrs**), the firs peter out altogether and you head up the gullyline to crest the 1700m spur east of Spanakáki. ◀

You may see evidence of seasonal shepherds' camps just beyond the spur.

Continuing south, the now-faint trail traverses the southeast slopes of Spanakáki at a steady climb, with a final steeper pull up alongside a dry gully to crest the main Pendadháktilo watershed at a point about 1km south of the 2024m peak (**4hrs**; 1970m).

This col is known as **Pórtes**, being a 'gateway' between the two sides of the mountain, but should not be confused with other cols of the same name further south. The views to either side are magnificent in good weather: east to the long skyline of Mt Parnon, west over rocky gorges and forested foothills to the distant gulf of Messinia. Ahead (south) stretches the long, rocky edge of the Messinian – Laconian watershed. Behind (north) is the hump of Spanakáki, the first knuckle of the Pendadháktilo, which we bypass. At your feet the sharp bricks of limestone, shattered on their eastern faces, jut out at improbable angles. Overhead, choughs wheel in acrobatic dogfights, sometimes swooshing so close that you can hear – and almost feel – their passing wings.

From here to the foot of the Athánati Rákhi 2hrs away it is simply a question of following the ridgeline as closely you can. On your way you pass the second and third knuckles of Marmarókastro (2228m) and Sidhirókastro (2180m), with the watershed in places so sharp that you could almost point to it. The only tricky section is a steep scramble up the eastward slabs on the approach to Marmarókastro (45mins from Pórtes; **4hrs 45mins**), which requires a good head for heights (but no ropes – and, I gather, has now been waymarked). These waymarks belong to the National '32' footpath (red diamond on

Goats on the Pendadháktilo (photo Michael Cullen)

white square, sometimes inscribed with the number 32), which joins the ridge near here and which gives sporadic reassurance as you head south. If the clouds have descended, make absolutely sure that you are heading south, especially leaving Marmarókastro, where it is possible to start following a subsidiary ridge too far west (R).

Around 4km/2hrs from Pórtes (**6hrs** from Anavrití) you reach the base (2170m) of Athánati Rákhi, the penultimate knuckle, whose messy, near-vertical strata rear up ahead. If you want to make straight for Profítis Ilías and are not daunted by the crags ahead, climb the ridgeline, making use of jagged foot- and hand-holds, right up to the 2330m summit. From there it is a relatively easy descent to the next col, also called Pórtes (2250m), beyond which rises the pyramidal peak of Profítis Ilías, etched with a zigzagging ascent path. Allow at least 2hrs for the tortuous climb over Athánati Rákhi and the best part of another hour up to the 2407m peak of **Profítis Ilías** (**9hrs** from Anavrití – probably more if you are heavily loaded).

See Stage 3 below for more about the peak itself.

For a less challenging route, drop L off the watershed in a southeasterly direction, picking your way over large boulders and descending carefully. There is no trail, but you should use the Anavasi map to aim for the northernmost 'corner' of the marked path from the refuge to Profítis Ilías. As you descend, look back to see the summit of Vasilikó Vounó – an easterly offshoot from the main ridge – transform from a hump to a triangular peak, almost sheer on its R sides. It's impossible to say exactly where you will hit the path, but it is fairly clear and well marked with red '32' diamonds and orange paint spots; if in doubt, aim R so as to intercept it higher rather than miss it completely. You should locate it about 150 vertical metres (30–40 slow mins) below the watershed. You can then follow it down to the refuge in a further 1hr 30mins, aiming first for a ledge with boggy hollows (Goúves) around the 1800m mark, then winding down to another grassy level 100m lower, always in a southeasterly direction.

A final steep, rocky stretch takes you down to a gully and across into the first tall black pines around 1600m. The refuge and jeep track lie 5mins further down L, at the shoulder of a wooded 1550m spur pointing northeast. This completes **8hrs** hiking out of Anavrití. There should be running water in the refuge but, for reference, the weak spring of Ayia Varvára (sometimes dry by the end of the summer) lies 100m down the path (E4 and red waymarks) to the north of this shoulder.

Stage 3 – *Pendadháktilo ridge (Profítis Ilías, 2404m, or EOS refuge, 1550m) – Vassilikí forest (1500m)*

Walking time:	6hrs
Distance:	11km to Áyios Dhimítrios from refuge, 7km from summit
Waymarks:	Intermittent O3 (red diamonds on white)
Height gain:	From refuge, 850m
Height loss:	900m
Difficulty:	3

This is another tough day, with a similar degree of ascent and descent to Stage 2, but shorter in distance. If the weather has broken – or you need an easy stage – you can again follow the E4 path at lower altitude all the way to Vassilikí forest. Be warned that it's not plain contouring: you have to drop 350m to the fields and huts of Pendavlí (1200m) and climb back again on a little-trodden trail to the 1600m ridge just above Ayios Dhimítrios, making it barely 2hrs shorter than the high route described below. There is also a reasonably well-signed escape route from Pendavlí down to Koumoustá hamlet, 5km above Xirokámbi town, if the weather looks set foul.

Starting from the refuge, retrace your steps northeast back up the trail to **Profítis Ilías** summit. For those making this ascent for the first time – as a day hike from refuge to summit and back, for example – here are some pointers. From the far left (southwest) corner of the refuge, follow the path west, bending northwest past the last of the magnificent pines. At the gully the path climbs steeply for about 10mins – it is best to head R then L – before resuming a steadier gradient towards the outlying peak of Vassilikó Vounó.

Around the 1700m mark (**30mins**) there is a small grassy plateau, and at 1800m (**50mins**) a larger one with a hollow – sometimes water-filled – L. Shortly after this the path makes a marked LH bend and traverses southwest, with the occasional steeper zigzag (the trail-less 'escape route' from the Pendadháktilo ridge joins here). Around **1hr 30mins** walk up

The ridge between Profítis Ilías and Áyios Yióryis (photo Michael Cullen)

one of the slanting limestone *zonária* (strata) which point towards the summit. A last R turn brings you out on the 2250m saddle Pórtes, where you can shelter from the wind behind crude stone walls. (You might want to leave your pack here during the summit trip.)

From here, with the rounded bulk of Athánati Rákhi R (north), turn L (south) keeping just right of the ridgeline. At a natural sinkhole veer R, away from the ridge, and follow the clear lines etched in the loose slabby rubble of Profítis Ilías' north face. Around **2hrs 45mins** from the refuge, you crest the summit of **Profítis Ilías** (2404m), the highest point in the Peloponnese.

There are two tiny stone huts (dirty, but with watertight corrugated iron roofs at my last visit) and a roofless stone chapel dedicated to the Prophet Elijah just to the south. If you are bivvying here don't count on their shelter, as winter snows and gales may have destroyed them. There is a steep drop to the south before the knife-edge ridge of the Pendadháktilo resumes, dwindling into the forested bowl of Vassilikí, with the serrated peaks of the Deep Mani in the distance.

At sunset you may be treated to the 'Brocken' spectre effect from the summit. The setting sun may cast a multi-coloured band over the sea horizon behind the Messinian Gulf, or the peak may cast a triangular shadow onto a sea of clouds below, with your own shadow pricking the apex, haloed with an eerie rainbow.

This drop means that – unless you fancy scrambling down easily dislodged rocks – you have to retrace your steps to the Pórtes col. Here turn L (west) and descend the head of the valley for 5mins before leaving the obvious route and contouring L (southwest, then south) around the 2200m mark. There are a few traces of trail here and there, but it is basically pick-your-own route. After about 40mins (**3hrs 45mins**) you will be south of the peak, following the steep-sided watershed towards the 2019m summit of Aï-Yióryis, with a slightly lower hump of Patistó off to the R. Where the ground drops away ahead (**4hrs**), bear R (south–southwest). The clear path passes a distinctive triangular and vertical slab of rock to reach the grassy saddle between Aï-Yióryis and Patistó at about **4hrs 30mins** (1910m). To the north you can see where landslides have crushed swathes of fir forest at the head of the Stenó Langádhi valley. The route continues south, keeping R of the emerging gully (which soon starts to trickle with drinkable water). ►

About 100 vertical metres (15mins) below the col there is an improved spring and the faint trail crosses to the L bank, traversing the southern flanks of Aï-Yióryis in a gently descending southeast direction. If by any chance you miss this path it is possible to continue down through forest alongside the gully – steep but soft underfoot – all the way to a track at 1500m, which leads L to Ayios Dhimítrios in 1km. Otherwise you find yourself entering the pine forest on a small path which comes out on to Parighóri spur (**5hrs 45mins**; 1740m).

Follow the rocky spur (few waymarks) down to a shoulder at 1690m and bear R – almost south – to drop more steeply down past a large meadow to the dirt road and scattered summer huts of **Ayios Dhimítrios**, where they spill over a south-pointing spur (**6hrs 15mins**; 1510m). Most weekends there are a few Messinian shepherds lurking nearby with their flocks and beehives, but it is not out of the question to find the hamlet completely deserted on arrival. The most convenient campsites are near the stone church and spring, 5mins walk L (east) along the dirt road. This is also where the E4 trail arrives from Pendavlí and the EOS refuge. There are also lovely spots down in the cultivated valley floor, surrounded by endless fir and pine forest (see Stage 4b).

It is lovely, turfy ground with enough level space for a tent, should you feel like camping.

Stage 4a – *Vassilikí forest (1500m) – Kardhamíli (0m) or Exokhóri (450m) via the Virós gorge*

Walking time:	7hrs to Kardhamíli, 5hrs 30mins to Exokhóri
Distance:	17km to Kardhamíli, 12km to Exokhóri
Waymarks:	White cross on red, Exokhóri to Kardhamíli
Height gain:	100m
Height loss:	1600m to Khardhamíli, 1150m to Exokhóri
Difficulty:	3

The Virós gorge is deep and long, a snaking corridor linking the high routes of Taïgetos with the lovely coastal villages to its west. But do not be lulled into thinking it is easy; the greater part of the dry riverbed is trail-less and stony, with occasional patches of larger boulders to test your agility. By the time you reach the 'escape routes' to Exokhóri (L) or Tséria (R), you will have had enough. The Exokhóri route is the easier underfoot, and you can call for a taxi from one of the village cafés or catch the daily bus for Kardhamíli and Kalamáta (which currently leaves at 14.40). You can also, of course, walk the full length of the gorge all the way to the sea.

Between **Ayios Dhimítrios**' main group of huts and its church, the onward path – now waymarked in familiar E4 (yellow-on-white) and 32 (red-on-white) liveries – descends the south bank of the road. After 15mins you briefly intercept a new jeep track before bearing L off it, parallel to the gully on your L. At the valley floor and junction of paths (**30mins**, 1275m), a signpost indicates the onward path R (west) to Kardhamíli/Virós, marked henceforth with occasional 32 signs only. ◀

The E4 continues straight on/south up the tributary stream – see Stage 4c.

Follow the level path west over slippery pine needles. It switches to the L bank and back to the R, before settling on the L again, with a fine paved, walled section, the *kakí skála* (said to date back to Spartan times). To your R the valley is dropping away fast, and it is not until the **1hr** point (1060m) that you finally rejoin the riverbed after a knee-jarring descent. Pick your way along the dry boulder-strewn bed, passing occasional walnut trees and crumbling huts. You may spot a seasonal spring and a couple of side ravines entering from the south. Don't forget to stop periodically and look up at the fir-clad mountainsides hemming you in.

Around **2hrs** (slow hours) out of Ayios Dhimítrios, you reach an unmistakable *dilángadho* (junction of valleys), where the Stenó Langádhi (narrow ravine) joins from the R (north). A few minutes up this side valley lies a part-walled, part-cavernous sheep pen, and you may see their droppings hereabouts. Continuing down the main riverbed, you cross some green, bramble-lined terraces on the R bank around **3hrs 15mins**; above R you may spot the abandoned huts and chapel of Troskoná. About 30mins later the bed describes a fairly tight LH bend, the path sticking mainly to the L bank through one of the narrowest sections of the gorge.

Finally, after a RH bend (**4hrs,** 600m), stick to the shady L bank and the path starts to veer away from the watercourse over a mixture of gravel and fierce boulders. (It is also possible to remain in the riverbed and pick up a smaller path along the R bank, which then climbs to Tséria). Around 45mins later the blue-and-white marked path from Tséria joins from the riverbed below R; you can see it snaking down the steep slopes opposite. You soon emerge onto a water-service track (**5hrs**; 530m) and can make out the first roofs and cypress trees of Exokhóri ahead and of Tséria opposite. Continue straight (southwest) up the rough track, climbing steadily. After passing a shrine up to the L, it levels off briefly, then resumes up towards the houses of Exokhóri. Keep R, past the houses of Kolibetséïka, the first of the hamlets that make up Exokhóri. Where the now surfaced lane bends L, fork R past the new hotel and old church. Continue down a walled lane, past a broad cement parking area, and into the hamlet of Khóra, passing to the R of its church. At **5hrs 25mins** a concrete lane joins from the L.

For the central part of **Exokhóri**, follow this lane L past the school and across the asphalt road. Otherwise, keep straight on, down Odhós Vas. Trivouréa, which soon becomes a paved path in a dip. Up L is the chapel of Ayios Nikos where – after a late introduction to Orthodoxy and the mystic beauty of rural Greece – the travel writer Bruce Chatwin chose to be buried. With a mulberry tree and clearing ahead, fork L (red-and-white arrow); R leads back down to the Virós gorge. At **5hrs 35mins** you join an earthy track and keep straight (R), leaving the shady olive groves behind. Where the track bends R (**5hrs 40mins**) fork L, with a stone wall L, passing two white-cross-on-red waymarks .

Pass to the R of the small chapel of Ayia Paraskeví and cross straight over the same track twice. Follow the waymarks carefully down rocky slabs among scrub and sparse olive saplings. At **6hrs** rejoin the track and keep L (straight), passing the newly tiled chapel of Áyii Pántes (All Saints). After this, fork R down a smaller track (hidden waymark), which turns into a path, depositing you via some steep steps onto another dirt road. Turn L and, at the asphalt road (waymarks/small signpost pointing back to Moni Sotíra), turn R to the visible houses of Ayia Sofía (locally called Goúrnitsa, **6hrs 25mins**). ▶

The tall-domed chapel of Ayia Sofia is locked, but the key holder Eleni lives in the village and, if you speak some Greek, may agree to show you the carved iconostasis and early 18th-century frescoes.

By the white metal signpost near this chapel, turn sharp R (yellow-and-black arrow) down a wide paved path. At the bottom (**6hrs 30mins**), turn sharp L along a track and immediately fork R down a raised paved path (hidden waymark). You pass the squared-off base of a medieval tower L and the cliffs of the Mycenean acropolis of Kardhamíli R. Just after a LH bend give your pounding feet a rest and examine the twin vaulted niches cut into the rock L, gated with black grilles. ◀

Locals claim that these niches are the Mycenean tombs of Castor and Pollux, the heavenly twins whom we know as Gemini.

Continue down and through the arch ahead into the walled nucleus of medieval Kardhamíli (**6hrs 50mins**). On your R is the gracious 18th-century church of Áyios Spirídhon. Follow the path bearing L, past the small summer café, and turn R by two cypresses (black-and-yellow waymark). Cross the track and the stone bridge and follow the paved path into **Kardhamíli** (**7hrs**).

Stage 4b – Vassilikí forest (1500m) – Spartiá village (900m)

Walking time:	3hrs
Distance:	10km
Waymarks:	Sporadic orange blobs
Height gain:	50m
Height loss:	650m
Difficulty:	2

For those who need to return to their vehicles in Místras or Anavrití, this route offers a quick descent to Spartiá and Árna villages on the Laconian side of the mountain. **Note** Unless it has been cleared recently you are likely to be hampered by fallen trees and boulder-spills, so allow some extra time and patience.

From **Áyios Dhimítrios** follow the dirt road past the church, soon curving R to head south, descending gently. After 3km (**45mins**) you come to a RH bend with a fading orange arrow and Árna painted on a rock L (if you reach a hut and vegetable patch R you have overshot). Here turn L up a boulder-strewn gully, picking your way over huge black-pine trunks as best you can. After 15mins (**1hr**) you reach the 1440m saddle and crude stone chapel of Aï Yannákis. Cross the saddle and bear R (southeast) across sloping rock slabs towards the cliffs of Annína; descend and briefly climb on a path through a natural cutting.

After the next slabby spur (**1hr 20mins**) you enter the fir forest, descending steadily and stonily to a large boulder-spill, which you must cross with care. An open patch with bunches of cyclamen and (in spring) *anemone pavonina* is your reward. A cairn marks the best route across a second stone slope, after which a smaller path joins from the L. Follow the ledge-like path, descending all the while, round the base of a crag to some horizontally stratified slabs called *koménos vrákhos* (broken rock; **2hrs**), where you emerge from the woods to earn views east over the *vardhounokhória* villages.

Here the path bears R (southeast), with sporadic orange spots to guide you past fallen trees and gorse bushes (wear long trousers!). Below the trig point 1083m, the path bears L into denser firs and then R again out of the woods. Make for the chapel of Profítis Ilías, visible ahead and below; shortly before it, bear L and go through a metal gate onto a small track (**2hrs 45mins**). Follow this L, passing to the R of the chapel, and at the three-way junction of lanes keep R (downhill) to reach the village of **Spartiá** in a further 1km (**3hrs**). The village is fairly dead outside midsummer, so you may want to continue the 1.7km into **Árna**, which has several *psistariés* (grill houses) and a stylish little hotel.

Stage 4c – *Vassilikí forest (1500m) – Áyios Nikólaos (0m) via Panayía Yiátrissa monastery (1100m) and Miliá (500m)*

Walking time:	5hrs 30mins to Miliá, 8hrs to Áyios Nikólaos
Distance:	18km to Miliá, 26km Áyios Nikólaos
Waymarks:	E4 to Yiátrissa
Height gain:	300m
Height loss:	1300m to Miliá, 1800m to Áyios Nikólaos
Difficulty:	3

For the first **30mins** follow the directions for Stage 4a. At the junction of paths ignore the signpost R to Kardhamíli/Virós and continue straight on along the E4, heading south up the tributary stream.

You soon pick up the remnants of a bulldozed track on the L (true R) bank and the streambed gains a trickle of water (except perhaps in late summer). Opposite are a couple of pretty stone houses surrounded by vegetable patches.

About **1hr** into the walk the track joins the dirt road from Ayios Dhimítrios by a sign pointing back to Réma Vasilikís. Turn R, climbing past the wooden huts and stone building of the Dhasikós Stathmós (Forestry Station). Ignore minor turns and you will reach a 1500m saddle and road junction (**1hr 50mins**); R goes to Saïdhóna and Exokhóri above the Messinian coast, while L (our route) zigzags downhill rather frustratingly for 1km, before straightening out in a south–southeasterly direction. It is a pleasant enough roadwalk for 8km (**2hrs**), descending gently with lovely views ahead to the serrated peaks of Zizáli; but the road, now widened and gravelled, was due to be surfaced in 2004–5.

Crowning a rise ahead you can see the squat bulk of **Panayía Yiátrissa** (Our Lady the Healer) **monastery**, whose high, windowless perimeter walls make it look more like a prison than a place of sanctuary. About 2hrs from the road junction (**4hrs**), fork R up the track to its front gate.

Continue south along the rounded ridge behind it for 300m; then, just before the fir trees, turn R down a stony path (blue arrow/M). The going improves as you enter the firs and blue waymarks should help your route finding. A 15min steady descent brings you to a spring shaded by a fig tree L. The path descends another 30m, bears L and levels off briefly before descending again, now partly cobbled. At the valley floor (**4hrs 40mins**) the path starts switching from side to side, finally plumping for the R around the **5hr** mark. A few minutes later you pass to the R of a breezeblock goat pen and continue along a jeep track. A couple of minutes after this, at a RH bend, turn sharp L (easily missed) down a now overgrown bulldozed trail. Where this ends, cross the rubble and continue along a smaller, slightly overgrown path with a gully L. At the junction with a larger path (**5hrs 12mins**) keep L past a small chapel and across a lovely little stone bridge. The now-walled path is joined by another from the L and a third from the R. At the concrete lane turn R down to the asphalt road, which leads L into the square of central **Miliá** (**5hrs 30mins**).

To reach Káto Khóra (the lowest quarter of the village) continue along the concrete road heading west (towards Kivélia) and turn R down an overgrown path passing L of the disused school. In front of the telephone pole the path, almost invisible in spring beneath carpets of flowers, bends R, then L, then R again. Cross a stone bridge (**5hrs 45mins**) and bear L into Káto Khóra, following the concrete lane to the shady central square.

Just after the church, turn L along a concrete path (green sign and blue waymark). Follow the main path, level at first, then climbing briefly past a small whitewashed chapel. At a carob tree (**6hrs**) fork L, downhill (no signpost). The part-paved path soon resumes an intermittent climb until at its highpoint (**6hrs 20mins**) you can see the hamlet of Eleokhóri atop a cliff in the middle distance. On the highest hump of the nearer ridge, further R, you can distinguish the tiny chapel of Áyios Yiórghos. Follow the path zigzagging down, then straightening out with a small gorge L. Pass a ruined house R and soon afterwards (**6hrs 30mins**) you reach a shady flat shoulder. Go through the wooden gate R and follow the stone path as it winds down through intermittent oak woods. At the bottom cross the streambed; the path continues just R of opposite (blue waymark). At the jeep track turn R, uphill, and follow it L as it climbs through olive groves. At the first RH hairpin keep straight on along a paved path with a drop to your L. At just over **7hrs** you join a concrete road, with the tiny village of **Eleokhóri** a few minutes up R (*seasonal café*).

The easiest route back to civilisation is downhill (L) along the concrete road to Ríglia. It soon gains a new asphalt surface and zigzags R and L. At the first houses of Áno Ríglia you can shortcut R on to a cement path, passing the square and then the village church L. Rejoin the road by an Áno Ríglia signpost and continue downhill. After 200m turn sharp R down a concrete road, across a bridge and into (Káto) Ríglia.

At the square and cardphone, turn L past the café. At the main road (**7hrs 40mins**; you might pick up a bus or lift here), turn L and after 100m R, down an asphalt lane marked Paralía Pantazí. You pass several unfinished houses (ignore side turnings) and finally intersect the coast road between Áyios Nikólaos and Trakhíla (**7hrs 50mins**). Ahead is a sandy beach with

Áyios Nikólaos has a pretty fishing harbour with cafés, shops and several places to stay.

tamarisk trees and a summer café. After a well-earned swim, turn R along the coast road into the centre of **Áyios Nikólaos** (**8hrs**), locally still called by its Slavic name, Selínitsa. ◀

Route 37
Hikes around Anavrití

If the Pendadháktilo sounds too adventurous, it is possible – without the need for camping or backpacking – to combine the best of the eastern foothills with a taste of high mountain scenery by walking up from Místras (see Route 36, Stage 1) and basing yourself in Anavrití. From there you can follow the circuit up to the northern end of the Pendadháktilo ridge and finally leave Anavrití via Sokhá hamlet and the zigzagging path down to Kalívia Sokhás, which is just a short taxi ride back to Místras. The first and last stages have the advantage of being feasible all year round.

Circuit from Anavrití (800m) to the northern Pendadháktilo ridge (Tsárkos; 1750m) and back

Walking time:	6hrs 15mins
Distance:	17km
Waymarks:	Red, on descent
Height gain:	950m
Height loss:	950m
Difficulty:	3

This is a good option for those who want a taste of the remote, rocky grandeur of the northern Taïgetos watershed, without the exertions and logistical difficulties of backpacking. There are two routes up to the watershed: one follows the E4 trail south and then branches west up a smaller but still waymarked path to the Botanical Station (Votanikós Stathmós), which lies just below the ridge near Tsárkos summit. The other – much less trodden, especially in its higher reaches – approaches the same point from the more northerly Mavrólongos valley. This is wilder and requires a good sense of direction, but rewards you with glorious umbrella pines and impressive views of the sheer southern faces of Neraidhovoúna.

I suggest ascending via the latter to get the harder, steeper part out of the way first and then descending via the former (which, incidentally, overlaps with the suggested ascent route from Anavrití to the main Pendadháktilo ridge). This way you might also be able to arrange a lift up the first 5km of dirt road to the trailhead above Pergandéïka hamlet, though it requires a sturdy vehicle – and enough Greek to explain where you want to be dropped.

From Anavrití square (780m), follow the asphalt road R (northwest) **towards Fanaroméni monastery** and, at the road junction after 800m, turn L (signs to Sókhas 8, Anóyia 21). After another 800m turn sharp R along a rough dirt track (blue sign to Pergandéïka), which contours north then west, passing the headspring of Anavrití and some picnic tables. About 2km from the junction, ignore the sharp R turn down to Pergandéïka hamlet, whose handful of empty-windowed houses are visible across the deep valley. Continue to contour north along the ever-rougher jeep track until, about 1.5km beyond the Pergandéïka junction, you cross the gully and zigzag R, then L uphill.

About 5mins above the gully (about 5.4km/**1hr 15 mins** out of Anavrití) – where a smaller track forks L and the main track heads R through a large cutting (950m) – you need to find the best place to climb up the earthy bank in the angle between them. Once up, follow faint blue paint splodges southwest through low prickly bushes until you enter the fir forest on an old path in a slight dip. After 15mins the path bears L and climbs steadily. At a slight crest 15mins later, with an umbrella-shaped black pine ahead, bear L again. Follow a dry gully for 3mins before passing to the R of a boulder (**1hr 50mins**). A stretch of flat or gently descending path ensues. Pass to the L of a flat boulder (**2hrs**; blue arrow) and, after a short steep section, another path joins from the L and you climb over fallen rocks and trees. At **2hrs 30mins**, in open country, the route continues slightly R until, 10mins later, you emerge in a mint-filled clearing with a low stone wall (1400m).

From here up to the ridgeline due south, it is a steep and basically path-less 350m (1hr) climb, so take a breather. In my

Take plenty of water with you; there are no reliable springs en route.

experience it is best to head south up the R side of the clearing (occasional blue waymarks) and, at a 6m Christmas tree bear R through a small patch of forest to find yourself on the true R bank of a dry gully. Keep L (uphill), passing above a junction of gullies and staying always a stone's throw above (L of) the LH gully. Leave the forest and finally, around **3hrs 15mins**, cross this LH gully towards a stand of sparse pines on a rocky outcrop, climbing steadily among stones and fir saplings. Pass to the L of a thin isolated pine and bear R to gain the rocky spur, which you follow L (south), past a grassy patch (ignore contouring goat trails) and straight up to the main watershed (**3hrs 40mins**; 1750m). Ahead, the view is dominated by the south wall of the 2031m Neraïdhovoúna.

Just below (north of) the ridge, you intersect a clearer path with occasional red-on-white marks, which you should follow L (east). After 10mins you cross the open stony expanse where the spur-ridge of Tsárkos joins the main ridge. Here the red-on-white waymarks continue south up to Spanakáki peak, the northernmost of the five knuckles. To return to Anavrití, however, bear L down the grassly dip to the grandly named stone hut of **Tsárkos** Botanical Station (**4hrs**).

From here the descent path is much easier to find, though the loose stones do require some concentration. Yellow-on-white waymarks lead down the R bank, past a 3.5km post which indicates the distance from the head of this trail at Lakómata. It bears R to a junction of valleys and paths (**4hrs 30mins**). Here follow the signpost L to 'Livadhi place 10min, Anavrití 1h30min', looking out now for red waymarks (the yellow-on-white ones contour east to Lakómata in 50mins). After a 5km post (this being measured from Anavrití and therefore unrelated to the earlier posts), you pass the stony meadows of Livádhi (1370m; also known as Imerotópi) and cross to the L bank by the 4.5km post (**4hrs 40mins**) to re-enter the woods.

Around **5hrs 10mins**, ignore a path forking L and keep R, across a gully, on to a lovely flat stretch on pine needles. After the 3km post, a path joins from the fields and seasonal spring of Platanáki on your L. At **5hrs 30mins** cross straight over the Anavrití – Lakómata dirt road and down a small track opposite (wooden signpost 'Anavrití 40min'/red waymark). The village is clearly visible ahead. About 5mins later, at a slight L bend, fork R past an E4 signpost and keep L to 'Anavrití 45mins'. After the 2km post you rejoin the track for 15m, then turn L down a stepped path (waymarks) which winds steeply down through mixed woods and across a wooden footbridge over a stream (**5hrs 50mins**). A short uphill stretch ends by the spring of Platanítsa and three huge plane trees. Take the lower of two almost parallel paths, bear L in front of an old threshing floor and at the 0.5km post (**6hrs 10mins**) fork R to pass to the R of a chapel. By the first house, keep L/straight along a track, which joins a larger concrete track by a four-spouted spring and brings you to the central square of **Anavrití** (**6hrs 15mins**).

Anavrití (800m) – Kalívia Sokhás (300m) via Sokhá (800m)

Walking time:	3hrs 30mins
Distance:	10km
Height gain:	50m
Height loss:	550m
Difficulty:	2

From the top of the main square above the hotel, follow the lane marked Taïgétou to the L past a four-spouted spring and down, past the last, crumbling houses of the village to a stream (**12mins**). The track, now unsurfaced, passes beneath a pretty clutch of houses called Kalamaréïka, after the family who settled there. After a further 1km the track crosses another stream (**35 mins**) near some walnut-shaded meadows, with a makeshift bridge upstream. It then curves R into open scrub-covered hillsides and, after another 2km, Sokhá village appears ahead.

At a RH bend, look out for an iron cross on a rock L and 50m later (**1hr**) a tiny path scrambling down the stony bank. This is a shortcut to Sokhá church, visible on a spur opposite (the dirt track will also take you there if the path looks tricky). Follow the tiny path, keeping L, to a cement water reservoir. Here, slightly overgrown, it winds down steadily to the northernmost houses of **Sokhá**. Pass to the L of a well-maintained house (**1hr 10mins**), keep straight on down some wooden steps and fork R. The path crosses the stream which bisects the village (another plank bridge) and bears L to climb back to the

The path from Sokhá to Kalívia (photo Michael Cullen)

dirt road. Follow this L to the lovely church of the Presentation of the Virgin (**1hr 20mins**) which, though locked, has a covered arcade and a tap nearby.

From here the route is marked with blue squares. Start along the jeep track heading northeast, ignoring a small L fork. The track then descends gently; oak trees offer intermittent shade. In front of a gate and vineyard (**1hr 40mins**), fork R down a path (waymark) into fields of Jerusalem sage. The path divides and rejoins, bends R between two oak trees, then winds gently down – you can choose between the roughly paved route or the goats' shortcuts. At **1hr 55mins**, where the paved path gets overgrown, hop L onto a clear, marked path.

As you continue on the eastward trail, a shrine signals the start of a broad, flag-stoned mule path traversing across a steep rocky slope, with plunging views L over the Rétsa ravine, a spectacular feat of drystone engineering. A short climb brings you to Vígla (lookout) corner, with the olive- and citrus-studded Evrótas plain stretching out before you to the foothills of

Mt Parnon (**2hrs 30mins**). The path, still paved but less broad, now zigzags mercilessly downhill for 40mins, with one shrine to punctuate the descent.

At **3hrs 10mins** you reach a medieval watch tower overlooking the gorge to the south; bear L towards the red roofs of **Kalívia** and at the signpost (**3hrs 15mins**) turn R along a newly paved path to the chapel of Zöodhókhou Piyís. Go round to its R to reach the forecourt, with stone benches and a spring set beneath tall plane trees. The paved path winds down to the first house of the village, in front of which you can turn L for the centre and café (**3hrs 30mins**).

Kalívia, which means 'huts', was historically the winter quarters for the inhabitants of Sokhá. Although it's now a more permanent settlement, it's hardly worth lingering there.

Hikes around Kardhamíli

The foothills on the western side of Mt Taïgetos are wilder and more complex, with fewer marked paths in the montane zone (1000–2000m), but a wonderfully maintained network of short hikes in the coastal zone (0–1000m), centred on Kardhamíli. This ex-fishing village is now a minor tourist hub, but has kept its charm through careful development and, no doubt, the lack of a sandy beach. For some relatively undemanding day hikes among pretty villages and historic chapels it is unbeatable. A fuller account of these hikes can be found in Michael Cullen's *Landscapes of the Southern Peloponnese* (Sunflower Books, 2003); otherwise, you can probably manage with the 1:25 000 Anavasi map and some careful observation.

CHAPTER 13

CAPE MALÉAS

The rocky promontory of Cape Maléas, feared by coast-hugging seafarers for its treacherous winds and currents, is the easternmost of the three distinctive prongs at the southern end of the Peloponnese. There is an automated lighthouse on its north shore, and the beautiful and tiny abandoned monastery of Ayías Irínis at its southern tip. It is the hinterland of the port of Neápoli, known as the Vàtika, a wild and until recently extremely remote corner of Greece. There are – surprisingly, perhaps – a number of waymarked paths in the region, though I cannot vouch for their current condition. They are described in detail in Michael Cullen's *Landscapes of the Southern Peloponnese*. I have covered two short but magical routes that take you almost to the tip of the cape: one to the lighthouse, the other the monastery.

Location:	The southeasternmost prong of the Peloponnese, 128km from Sparta.
Maps:	Road Editions Peloponnese 1:250 000; NSSG sheet Lakonías 1:200 000; HAGS sheet Áyios Nikólaos 1:50 000.
Access:	Daily buses to Neápoli from Athens and Sparta and on to Velanídhia.
Base:	Neápoli (hotels, shops, bank, taxi).

Route 38
Velanídhia (200m) to lighthouse (20m)

Walking time:	2hrs 30mins
Distance:	7.5km
Height gain:	0m
Height loss:	180m
Difficulty:	2

From the café in the pretty hillside village of Velanídhia, there are two possibilities. The first is to follow the road round and out of the village, where it becomes a track signposted 'Fáros Maléa' (*faros* = lighthouse). Once past a windmill on a spur

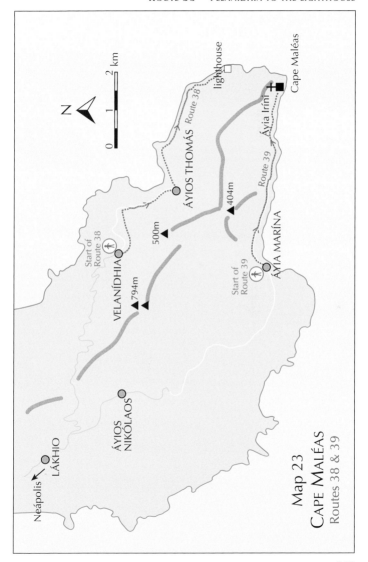

Map 23
CAPE MALÉAS
Routes 38 & 39

at about **25mins**, the track begins to descend with the scattered cottages of Áyios Thomás and the concrete shell of the new monastery of Áyios Míronas ahead. A track L is signposted to the lighthouse, 4.7km 2hrs. It leads down to and along the shore. It is easier to keep straight on down the track to the little white chapel and spring of **Áyios Thomás** (**1hr**; *last water*).

Variant to the windmill

The second option starts just below the village café, from where steps lead up R (signed 'Áyia Marína 6km/2hrs 30mins'). Keep on up to a spring and reservoir. Follow the path sharp R, then sharp L. Just clear of the village you come to a fork. Keep L; Áyia Marína is signed to the R. Cross a gully. There is a wonderful view back to Velanídhia until you fork L after about **30mins** down to a chapel dedicated to the Panayía Dhekapendístra (the Virgin of 15 August). Keep R up the dirt track to a bigger track and bear L (signpost to Lighthouse Malea 6.8km/2hrs 35mins). Come out on the dirt road (**35mins**) with the windmill in front of you, and turn R.

By the last house in Áyios Thomás a path turns down L across ancient fields to a dry gully and a little inlet (**1hr 15mins**), where you pick up the waymarks D10 and red squares and splodges. Turn R and follow the path along the barren scrubby shore. Shortly before reaching the lighthouse the path dips down and across a dry stream gully by ruined walls and a hut – a wonderful place to camp (if you are carrying enough water). The path ends at the lighthouse in about 15mins (**2hrs 30mins**).

Route 39
The monastery of Áyia Iríni
(Moní Ayías Iríni)

Walking time:	50mins (one way – from the signposted path)
Distance:	2.5km
Height gain/loss:	100m
Difficulty:	2

Cape Maléas:
the very tip

Take the road from Neápoli to Áyios Nikólaos (7km). From here a dirt track continues to the chapel and handful of primitive cottages at Áyia Marína close to the shore, and is passable for another 2–3km. Where it ends, a clear, signposted path sets off along steep rocky slopes above the sea. Within 1hr you reach the monastery, a chapel with a cistern on the terrace, a row of white cells and a cypress tree. It is a magical place, airy and silent. The path continues for another 10mins to the chapel of Áyios Yióryios and the remains of a Byzantine church on the furthest nose of rock rising sheer above the sea. You can see the island of Kíthira not far off to the southwest and an unceasing procession of shipping heading for Piraeus, Constantinople and the harbours of the Black Sea.

CHAPTER 14

THE MANI

Ruined towers of Mianés

The Mani is the middle of the Peloponnese's southernmost extensions, its tip – Cape Ténaro – the southernmost point of continental Europe after Tarifa in Spain, practically on the same latitude as Tangiers. The name applies to the promontory as well as the narrow strip of coastal foothills on the western flank of Mt Taïgetos all the way up to Kalamáta.

We have described two routes. They are not mountain routes – though one is hilly – but they give a flavour of a rather different kind of Greek wilderness. One takes you to the cape itself, the other leads through villages, long-derelict farmland, and past a remote and undeveloped minor classical site.

Location:	Areópolis, the 'capital', is 60km south of Sparta.
Maps:	Anávasi Topo 25 Mani Tenaro 1:25 000; Road Editions Peloponnese 1:250 000.
Bases:	Areópolis (shops, banks, hotels, tavernas); Yeroliména (hotels, shops, tavernas). Pórto Káyio, Marmári (rooms, tavernas).
Access:	Daily buses from Athens to Sparta/Yíthio to Areópolis and on to Yeroliména. Occasional buses to Váthia/Marmári.

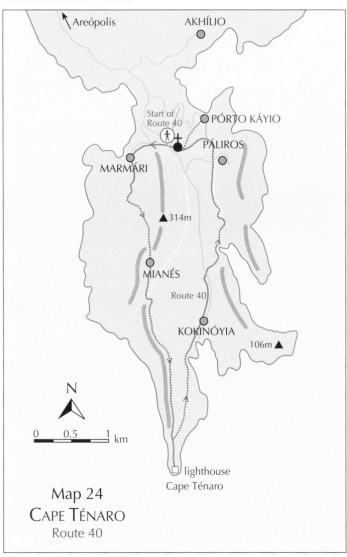

Areópolis

AKHÍLIO

Start of
Route 40

PÓRTO KÁYIO

PÁLIROS

MARMÁRI

▲314m

MIANÉS

Route 40

KOKINÓYIA

106m ▲

N

0   0.5   1 km

lighthouse
Cape Ténaro

Map 24
CAPE TÉNARO
Route 40

Route 40
Cape Ténaro

*Áyia Triádha (80m) to Marmári (40m) to
Mianés col (370m) to lighthouse (30m) to
Kokinóyia (0m) to Páliros (120m) to
Áyia Triádha (80m)*

Walking time:	4hrs 10mins
Map:	Anávasi Topo 25 Mani Tenaro
	1:25 000
Distance:	11.5km
Height gain:	530m
Height loss:	530m
Difficulty:	2

The walk begins by the chapel of Áyia Triádha on the L of the road between Váthia and its end at Kokinóyia, just past the turnings to Pórto Káyio and Marmári and before the village of Páliros. There is room to leave a car off the road.

It is a fairly easy walk except for the stretch between Marmári and Mianés where the path has disappeared and you have to strike out cross-country wading through very prickly scrub. You need to be well covered. However, this stretch can easily be avoided by following the road south over the low saddle below Páliros and then the track (300m) on the R leading up to Mianés (1.75km).

From Áyia Triádha walk a few metres back down the hill and turn L at the first telegraph pole on to an old but clear path descending gently along the thorny hillside to the village of **Marmári**, its dilapidated and partly restored towers perching prettily between two sandy coves (**10mins**). Turn L for a short distance when you reach the road in the village and then fork L uphill past the last stone house.

Continue straight downhill on a prickly old path between drystone walls, and round to the R across a gully. The path disappears under thickets of thorny scrub. You can see the walls of some old stone huts on the slope above. Keep to the wall on your R where it is possible to push your way up without getting too badly scratched. As you gain a bit of altitude the

351

scrub shrinks to knee height. Leave the wall and make your way as best you can more or less directly up the crest of the gently rounded spur that borders the gully you left behind after the last house in Marmári. Keep climbing, bearing gradually R towards the crest of the long hump above (Skoúrka), until you reach an altitude of around 200m. Then aim more directly R towards the dip in the skyline between Skoúrka and a smaller bump to the R. When you reach it (after 50–60mins patient labouring through the thorns; **1hr 15mins**) you find a shallow col with the remains of old walled fields, crossed by a faint path. ◄

*In front of you are the ruins of the abandoned hamlet of **Mianés**, its gaunt old towers ringed by thickets of prickly pear cactus.*

As you head past the first towers the path becomes concrete and ends at a junction with the track from Páliros (**1hr 30mins**; see above). Turn R, and where the track ends turn L between red dots towards the isolated tower on the low knoll L. Go round the tower, leaving it on your R and head down the rounded grassy and stony ridge stretching in front towards the cape. Red paint dots mark the route – mostly slightly east of the ridgeline – although there is no particular path until you reach the last section where you will see a clear line of path running along the westward flank. The sea is on both sides. ◄

The ancients believed that one of the entrances to Hades lay under the cliffs somewhere along this stretch of coast.

After about 45mins of descent you join the main, well-trodden path, with just 5mins more to reach the lighthouse (**2hrs 25mins**).

When the original research for the first edition of this book was carried out 30 years ago, the lighthouse was still manned. It was a lonely spot, accessible only after a 2hr walk, and you were greeted by a lighthouse keeper thirsty for company and only too eager to offer you food and drink. It is still a wonderful place to sit and picnic, surrounded by nothing but air and sea.

To continue to **Kokinóyia** return along the main path, keeping to the east flank of the promontory. In about 30mins the path descends to a small cove – passing traces of ancient cisterns, a piece of mosaic floor and other vestiges of the ancient settlement of Tainaron – to join the end of the tarmac road at **2hrs 55mins**. Continue up the road to the top of the first rise; 3–4mins further, just before a LH bend, a path leaves the road R to descend along the side of a stone wall (fairly frequent blue

Marmári and the route to Mianés

dots). It winds L and down to a gully, where it crosses to the R flank and descends towards the deeply enclosed little bay of Vathí (**3hrs 25mins**).

From the further end of the beach a path leads back into a gully beside a walled enclosure and a clump of umbrella pines before climbing steeply up the slope R. It follows round a wall before turning up R to a cottage with blue shutters by an electricity pole. Turn L on a path between the houses, following the direction of the power lines to reach the end of the concrete road by a small chapel (**3hrs 40mins**). Go up the road to the L, and in 15mins you reach the village of **Páliros**. Continue along the road below the village for 5mins to a junction (**4hrs**). To return to Áyia Triádha – which lies just in front of you – carry straight on down the road for 10mins. For Pórto Káyio, which lies on the sea just out of sight below, turn R at the junction and continue for 60m, under the power lines, to where a blue mark on a rock L indicates the start of a path descending across an 'amphitheatre' of abandoned terraces. Alternately you can carry on past Áyia Triádha on a good path that leads to the cemetery and then to the main road down to Pórto Káyio, named after the flocks of migrating quails that in more abundant times used to fly this way.

Route 41
Kiónia: the fallen columns

*Polemítas (300m) to Lákki (650m) to Kiónia
(410m) to Nímfi (50m)*

Walking time:	4hrs 20mins
Distance:	11km
Height gain:	350m
Height loss:	600m
Difficulty:	3

The walk starts in the village of Polemítas about 2km east of the main north–south road from Areópoli to Yeroliména. Take the turn-off for Mína. Polemítas lies at the foot of the apparently barren hills. The walk takes you up the old mule trail to Lákki, the surprisingly lush but long-abandoned fields of the Polemítas villagers, over the main watershed and down past the unticketed and unfenced ruins of two Doric temples at Aigila (known locally as the columns, *kyónya*) and the abandoned rustic monastery of Panayía Kroúnou. The route ends in the village of Nímfi on the east coast, where you can plunge straight into the sea on a hot day.

From the point where the road ends in **Polemítas**, continue straight uphill on a concrete track (ignoring a L fork), with olive groves R and a deep dry gully L. In a few minutes the track comes to an end and you pass some new farm buildings in an enclosure R. The old cobbled path – overgrown but clear – continues the track, following the drystone wall on your R. With the occasional zigzag it climbs steadily up the R flank of the deepening valley L, on the other side of which a new jeep track leads to some livestock installations in some caves. There are sporadic blue spot waymarks.

At just under **50mins** go through a metal gate and cross some ruined and overgrown terraces where the path is unclear. Cows graze on the damp green vegetation that has overtaken the old cultivated areas. As you climb higher, pushing your way past bracken and bushes, the path becomes clearer. Ignore a L turn downhill at just under **1hr** and a few moments later

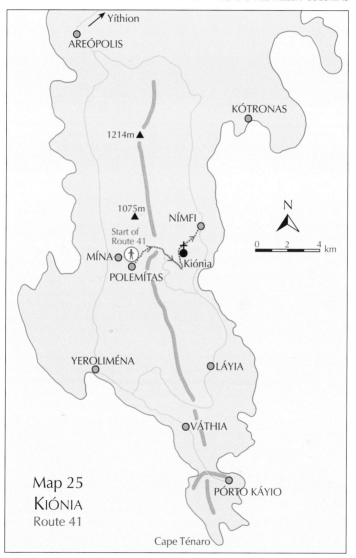

Yíthion

AREÓPOLIS

KÓTRONAS

1214m ▲

1075m ▲

NÍMFI

Start of
Route 41

MÍNA

Kiónia

POLEMÍTAS

N

0   2   4 km

YEROLIMÉNA

LÁYIA

VÁTHIA

PÓRTO KÁYIO

Map 25
KIÓNIA
Route 41

Cape Ténaro

355

be careful to bear up R and immediately L round a patch of boulders, marked with a curving blue line. About 10mins later you debouch on to a patch of level grassy ground by an almost subterranean stone water cistern overlooked on the R by a sharp little knoll shaded by an ancient spreading poplar (E0362232/N4044731).

Go over to the cistern and pass it, leaving it to your R (blue paint). The path, well trodden by cows, leads straight ahead, with a bracken-filled hollow that must have once been cultivated below R. It curves R round the head of this depression to a wall enclosing a large hornbeam and several walnut trees, where it bears L under a fallen tree trunk and comes out by the little group of huts at Lákki on the edge of an arid scrubby valley that drops away to the east (**1hr 20mins**).

A jeep track winds up here from the east side. Start down it; after about 10mins, on the crown of a sharp RH bend, an earthy path heads off L into some very overgrown terraces. Bear uphill a little to gain two terraces in height (it is not clear what might be a path and what merely the passage of cows) and pass below (R of) the first isolated oak tree that you see about 150m ahead. A moment later you pass a wild pear tree. Stay on this terrace and pass just above a third tree; you should see a blue paint spot before you reach it. Once past it a small but reasonably clear path bends back L through the prickly *maquis*, drops a little to cross a dry gully and continues to traverse (R-wards to your line of march) across a long thorny slope, pretty much on the contour, towards the near skyline.

Keep well above the cluster of ruined huts. Keep your eyes skinned for blue paint spots and, towards the end, small cairns of stones (be careful if adding to the cairns yourself; scorpions lurk under many of the flat stones). The path hits the skyline to the R and below the higher rounded height and L (uphill) of the lower rockier height. A solid-looking stone wall blocks the way ahead (**2hrs**). (**Note** *If returning this way, aim slightly uphill for 200m from the end of the wall towards the area of slabby-looking rock projecting through the scrub until you spot the cairns or the first blue paint at E0362000/N4044968, and be sure to keep well above the huts when you get to them.*)

At its RH end the wall abuts a big boulder with a blue K painted on it. Climb over here and head downhill towards the rocky peak with a trig point right in front. Before you get to it, you stumble over the fallen columns and dressed stones of the

temple of Demeter lying scattered in the grass (E0362232/ N404473, **2hrs 5mins**).

Fallen columns at the temple at Kiónia

To continue down to the village of Nímfi, return to the stone wall (**2hrs 15mins**) and climb over it. Turn R (northeast) and walk parallel to the wall along an improving path. The wall drops off R. Stay on the level and pass between two ruined huts. The path descends a rocky spur and, just L of an outcrop, crosses behind it. Continue north, moving over to a clearer stone-slabbed path R, to reach a fig tree below the whitewashed rustic buildings of Panayía Kroúnou (**2hrs 30mins**). Here a path forks L and divides again. The LH branch leads through a walled enclosure to a water tap. Cattle sometimes shelter here in the shade; be careful in case there is an aggressive bull among them (as I once discovered). The other branch leads through vaulted storerooms into the monastery courtyard. The remainder of the building is usually locked.

Monastery of Panayía Kroúnou

From the fig tree (**2hrs 40mins**) continue along the clear path which descends northwards beside a metal water pipe, crosses a dry gully, passes through a gate and descends to a small oak tree, where it promptly climbs again. After another stony descent the path crosses a narrow saddle below a rocky outcrop into the next valley and zigzags down into Atsoúpi (**3hrs 30mins**), the upper quarter of Nímfi. Pass L of the first tower house, go past a pallet gate and follow the concrete lane downhill, passing a shrine and concrete reservoir L. After a few zigzags you reach a junction (**3hrs 40mins**), with a shrine R. Turn L, and where the lane ends continue straight on along a path into the main part of **Nímfi**. Past crumbling towers and a church on the L, the path bends L to join a road at a hairpin bend. Follow this straight downhill to a junction; turn sharp R.

Where this road bends R (**4hrs**), turn L through a gate on a dirt track into an olive grove. Pass near a dozen cypress trees, go through two arched gateways next to a house and down a steep walled path. At the bottom turn R along an overgrown path, to reach the main road by a mirror on a pole (**4hrs 10mins**). For the beach, cross straight over towards the basketball pitch and, after 200m, turn R and immediately L down a concrete lane which takes you to the pebbly beach (**4hrs 20mins**; *taverna*).

Crucus sieberi

APPENDIX 1
GLOSSARY

Language is going to be a bit of a problem for most users of this book, and obviously we cannot teach you Greek here. (The alphabet, incidentally, will probably be less of a problem than you might fear.)

Listed below are a number of Greek terms commonly encountered when you walk in the mountains. You are most likely to hear people using these to address you, so I have arranged them in simple categories with the Greek word first. If the spelling looks strange it is because I have tried to find combinations of English letters which, if pronounced in the normal 'English' way, will produce sounds as near as possible to the Greek. The accents show which syllables should be stressed. Stress is vital in Greek; if you get everything else in a word right, but put the stress on the wrong syllable, people will not understand you.

A few tips:
- a is pronounced as in hat, e as in get, o as in hot, ee as in feet, oo as in food.
- The hard g (g before a or o) is slightly breathy – gh.
- kh sounds like the ch in Scottish loch.
- dh sounds like th in then.
- r is rolled in the front of the mouth
- s is always as in soft.

Terrain/landmarks

aneefóra	ascent
apótomos	steep, precipitous
dhásos	wood, forest
dheemósyo	public road or track
dhéndro	tree
dheeyakládhosee	fork, junction in road or path
dheeyáselo	saddle, col
dheeyastávrosee	crossroads
dhrómos	road (sometimes means 'the way')
eedhragoyeéo	water channel, pipeline
eépsoma	height, knoll, bump
eésyoma	level ground
ekleeseéya	church, chapel
élata	fir trees
faránghee	ravine, gorge
gremós	cliff, precipice
kaldereémee	cobbled mule path
kaleéva	hut
katafeéyo	mountain refuge
kateefóra	descent
keeládha	valley
kharádhra	ravine, gorge
khomatódhromos	dirt road
khoráfee	field, cultivated patch
khoryó	village
kolónes	telegraph or electricity poles
kordhéles	zigzags, in path or road
koreefogrameé	summit ridge, peak line
korfeé	summit, peak
láka	grassy clearing or hollow, cwm
langádhee	gully, especially wooded
leémnee	lake, tarn

leevádhee	meadow, pasture
lófos	hill
loókee	couloir
loótsa	pond, tarn
maghazeé	village shop, café
maghazeés	keeper of above
mandreé	sheepfold
meélos	mill
monasteéree	monastery
monopátee	footpath
oksyá	beech tree
orthoplayá	vertical cliff
paraleéya	seashore
peeghádhee	well
peenakeédha	signpost
peeyeé	spring (of water)
péfka	pine trees
pétra	stone
platánee	plane tree
playá	slope, hillside
poornárya	prickly oak scrub
potámee	river
potamyá	riverbed
rákhee	ridge
reéza	foot of slope or cliff
réma	stream
rematyá	streambed, gully
sára	scree
skoleéyo	school
smeéksee	confluence of streams
speelyá	cave
speétee	house
stánee	sheepfold
stroónga	sheepfold
tabéla	signpost
teékhos	wall
thálasa	sea
tsombánees	shepherd
velaneedyá	oak tree
vlákhos	Vlach (also, generically, for shepherd)
voonó	mountain
voskós	shepherd
vrákhos/vrákhya	rock(s)
vreésee	spring (of water)
yeemnós	bare, treeless
yéfeera	bridge

Directions

apénandee	opposite
ap'afteé tee meryá	on this side
apó teen álee meryá	on the other side
aristerá	on the left
dheépla	next to, alongside
dheksyá	on the right
edhó	here
eésya	straight ahead
eésya káto	straight down
eésya páno	straight up
ekeé	there
kat'eftheéya	straight ahead
káto	down
khameelá	low down
kondá	near
makreeyá	far
mékhree	up to, as far as, until
páno	up
péra	over there, beyond
pros	towards
pseelá	high up
anevénees...	you go up...
katevénees...	you go down...
pas...	you go...
pernás...	you cross/pass...
móles perásees...	as soon as you have crossed/passed
parakaló, o dhrómos ya...?	can you tell me the way to...?
parakaló, to monopátee ya...?	can you show me the path to..?
póses óres eéne?	how many hours is it?

Weather

aéras	wind
andára	mist
astrapeé	lightning
booboonitá	thunder claps
eélyos	sun
feesávee	it's windy
kateyeédha	storm
khyónee	snow
kreéyo	cold
omeékhlee	mist
seénefa	clouds

361

THE MOUNTAINS OF GREECE

vrokheé	rain
zéstee	hot

Transport

aftokéeneeto	car, vehicle
forteeghó	lorry
leoforeéyo	bus
tee óra févyee	what time does it leave?
tee óra ftánee	what time does it arrive?
boreétee na me párete?	can you take me?

Eating and shopping

avghá	eggs
batereéya	battery
brizóla	large chop, usually pork or beef
elyés	olives
fayeé	food
ghála	milk
gházee	gas
kebábya	spit-roasted chunks of lamb
kheelópeeta	local pasta
kokorétsi	spit-roasted offal
konsérves	tinned food
kréas	meat
neró	water
omeléta	omelette
psomeé	bread
saláta	salad
speérta	matches
teereé	cheese
venzeénee	petrol

Sleeping and camping

dheékleeno	double room
dhomátyo	room
kameenéto	camping stove
krevátee	bed
ksenodhokheéyo	hotel
ksenónas	guesthouse
skeeneé	tent
boró na steéso tee skeeneé?	can I put my tent up?

Numbers

éna/meéya	1 (masc/fem)
dheéyo	2
treés/treéya	3
téseres/tésera	4
pénde	5
éksee	6
eftá	7
októ	8
enyá	9
dhéka	10
éndheka	11
dhódheka	12
dhekatreés	13
dhekatéseres	14
dhekapénde	15
eékosee	20
treeyánda	30
saránda	40
peneénda	50
ekseénda	60
evdhomeénda	70
oghdhónda	80
eneneénda	90
ekató	100
dheeyakósya	200
pendakósya	500
kheélya	1000
dheéyo kheelyádhes	2000

Time

pénde leftá	5mins
éna tétarto	quarter of an hour
meeseé óra	half an hour
méeya óra	1hr
meeyámeesee óres	one and a half hours
dheéyo óres	2hrs
stees méeya	at 1 o'clock
stees trées ke tétarto	at quarter past three
stees téseres pará pénde	at five to four
apóyevma	afternoon (generally means 17.00 or 18.00 in Greece); early after noon is covered by *meseeméree*/noon
ávreeyo	tomorrow
khthés	yesterday

méra	day, daytime
neékhta	night, night-time
proeé	morning
seémera	today
vrádhee	evening (after 19.00 or 20.00)

Animals

agrioghoóroono	wild boar
agriokátsiko	wild goat
alepoódha	fox
álogho	horse
arkoódha	bear
asvós	badger
ayeládha	cow
ayetós	eagle
feédhee	snake
gháta	cat
ghayeedhoóree	donkey
katseékya	goats
khelóna	tortoise
koonávee	marten
laghós	hare
leékos	wolf
órnyo	vulture
pondeékee	mouse/rat
pooleé	bird
próvata	sheep
skeeleé/skeelyá	dog/s
yerákee	hawk

yeédhya	goats
zarkádhee	deer
zóa	mules

Miscellaneous

ne	yes
ókhee	no
leégho	a little
poleé	a lot, very
parakaló	please
efkhareestó	thank you
meekró	small
meghálo	big
kaleé andámosee	till we meet again
kaló	good
kakó	bad
kaleeméra	good day
na pas sto kaló	'may you go to the good' (a common way of saying goodbye to the person leaving)
óra kaleé	an old-fashioned salutation on parting, meaning literally 'good hour'
yásoo/yásas	'good health to you' (singular/plural): the commonest way of saying hello
tee kánees	how are you?
póso kánee	how much is it?

APPENDIX 2
SELECTED BIBLIOGRAPHY

Kevin Andrews *The Flight of Ikaros* (Penguin, 1984). A well-written and readable account of the author's experiences wandering about southern Greece during the Civil War in the late 1940s.

Juliet du Boulay *Portrait of a Greek Mountain Village* (Oxford, 1974). A detailed study based on the author's personal experience. Again, very interesting, though indigestibly academic in parts.

J.K. Campbell *Honour, Family and Patronage* (Oxford, 1964). A very interesting anthropological study of the Sarakatsani shepherds in the Mt Gamíla region in northwest Greece.

Patrick Leigh Fermor *Mani* (John Murray, 1958) and *Roumeli* (John Murray, 1966). The two best travel books about remote rural and mountain Greece.

Arthur Foss *Epirus* (Faber, 1978). A readable, if unexciting, account of the history, traditions and people of Epirus.

Tim Salmon *The Unwritten Places* (Lycabettus Press, 1995). An account of travels in the Píndhos mountains and especially of life among the Vlachs. Obtainable in the UK from: Edward Stanford, 12–14 Long Acre, London WC2E 9LP (www.stanfords.co.uk); Daunt Books, 83 Marylebone High St, London W1U 4QW; The Hellenic Book Service, 91 Fortess Rd, London NW5 1AG (www.hellenic-bookservice.com).

John Anthony Huxley and William Taylor *Flowers of Greece and the Aegean* (Chatto and Windus, 1977). The best field guide by far.

Oleg Polunin *Flowers of Greece and the Balkans* (Oxford, 1980). Expensive and bulky. Its big attraction is that it describes in detail particularly good flower-hunting areas of the mountains.

A.J.B. Wace and M.S. Thompson *The Nomads of the Balkans* (Methuen, 1914). A fascinating account of living among the Vlachs, when Vlachs were truly Vlachs.

C.M. Woodhouse *The Struggle for Greece 1941–49* (Hart-Davis, McGibbon, 1976). The best and most balanced account of the Resistance, with whom the author fought, and the ensuing Civil War.

Michael Cullen *Landscapes of the Southern Peleponnese* (Sunflower Books, 2003) for more details of walks in this area.

Of the numerous general guidebooks, *The Rough Guide to Greece* remains the most readable and useful.

APPENDIX 3
CONTACT INFORMATION

1 UK

National Tourist Organisation of Greece (EOT), 4 Conduit St, London W1S 2DJ (tel: 020 7495 9300)
   Free handout, detailing mountain refuges and ski facilities.

2 Greece

Hellenic Federation of Mountaineering Clubs (EOOA), 5 Milióni St, Kolonáki, 106 73 Athens (tel: +30 210 3645904)

   No real benefits of membership – unless you live in Greece – but you would be made very welcome, especially if you were a member of a foreign club. It could be worth checking their programme of guided walks, even if you are only visiting. This is also true of the EOS branch of Akharnón (a rather inaccessible suburb of Athens) which is particularly active and publishes the journal *Korfés* (5 euros), with an English-language account and 1:50 000 map of a particular Greek hike in every issue:
   Filadelfías St 126, 13671 Akharnés (tel: +30 210 2461528; www.eosacharnon.gr; email: eosa@otenet.gr).

Local EOS Clubs

The following are those most likely to be of any use; the name of any mountain mentioned in this guidebook, with a refuge controlled by the club, is indicated in brackets.

- Amfíklia (Mt Parnasós) tel: 22340 22640
- Ámfissa (Mt Vardhoúsia), 8 Staloú St tel: 22650 28577 & 29201
- Athens (Mt Párnitha), 64 Ermoú St tel: 210 3212355 & 3212429
- Karpenísi (Mt Veloúkhi), 2 G Tsitsára St tel: 0237 23051
- Kalávrita (Mt Khelmós) tel: 26920 22611
- Khalkídha (Mt Dhírfis), 22 Angéli Goviou St tel: 22210 25230
- Lamía (Mt Íti), 4 Papakiriazí St tel: 22310 26786
- Lárisa, 11 Skarlátou Soútsou St tel: 24105 35097
- Litókhoro (Mt Olympus) tel: 23520 84544
- Pápingo (Mt Gamíla) tel: 26530 41138
- Pátras tel: 26102 73912
- Sparta (Mts Párnon and Taygetos), 97 Gortsologou St tel: 27310 22574
- Thessaloníki, 19 Karólou Díl St tel: 23102 78288
- Tríkala tel: 24320 28943
- Vólos (Mt Pílion), Dimitriádos 92 tel: 0421 25696
- Yánina, 2 Dhespotátou Ipírou St tel: 26510 22138

LISTING OF CICERONE GUIDES

NORTHERN ENGLAND
LONG-DISTANCE TRAILS
The Dales Way
The Reiver's Way
The Alternative Coast to Coast
A Northern Coast to Coast Walk
The Pennine Way
Hadrian's Wall Path
The Teesdale Way

FOR COLLECTORS OF SUMMITS
The Relative Hills of Britain
Mts England & Wales Vol 2 – England
Mts England & Wales Vol 1 – Wales

BRITISH CYCLE GUIDES
The Cumbria Cycle Way
Lands End to John O'Groats – Cycle
 Guide
Rural Rides No.1 – West Surrey
Rural Rides No.2 – East Surrey
South Lakeland Cycle Rides
Border Country Cycle Routes
Lancashire Cycle Way

CANOE GUIDES
Canoeist's Guide to the North-East

LAKE DISTRICT AND
MORECAMBE BAY
Coniston Copper Mines
Scrambles in the Lake District (North)
Scrambles in the Lake District (South)
Walks in Silverdale and
 Arnside AONB
Short Walks in Lakeland 1 – South
Short Walks in Lakeland 2 – North
Short Walks in Lakeland 3 – West
The Tarns of Lakeland Vol 1 – West
The Tarns of Lakeland Vol 2 – East
The Cumbria Way &
 Allerdale Ramble
Winter Climbs in the Lake District
Roads and Tracks of the Lake District
The Lake District Angler's Guide
Rain or Shine – Walking in the
 Lake District
Rocky Rambler's Wild Walks
An Atlas of the English Lakes

NORTH-WEST ENGLAND
Walker's Guide to the
 Lancaster Canal
Walking in Cheshire
Family Walks in the
 Forest Of Bowland
Walks in Ribble Country
Historic Walks in Cheshire
Walking in Lancashire
Walks in Lancashire Witch Country
The Ribble Way

THE ISLE OF MAN
Walking on the Isle of Man
The Isle of Man Coastal Path

PENNINES AND
NORTH-EAST ENGLAND
Walking in the Yorkshire Dales

Walking in the South Pennines
Walking in the North Pennines
The Yorkshire Dales
Walking in the Wolds
Waterfall Walks – Teesdale and High
 Pennines
Walking in County Durham
Yorkshire Dales Angler's Guide
Backpacker's Britain – Northern
 England
Walks in Dales Country
Historic Walks in North Yorkshire
South Pennine Walks
Walking in Northumberland
Cleveland Way and Yorkshire Wolds
 Way
The North York Moors

DERBYSHIRE, PEAK DISTRICT,
EAST MIDLANDS
High Peak Walks
White Peak Walks Northern Dales
White Peak Walks Southern Dales
White Peak Way
The Viking Way
Star Family Walks Peak District &
 South Yorkshire
Walking In Peakland
Historic Walks in Derbyshire

WALES AND WELSH BORDERS
Ascent of Snowdon
Welsh Winter Climbs
Hillwalking in Wales – Vol 1
Hillwalking in Wales – Vol 2
Scrambles in Snowdonia
Hillwalking in Snowdonia
The Ridges of Snowdonia
Hereford & the Wye Valley
Walking Offa's Dyke Path
Lleyn Peninsula Coastal Path
Anglesey Coast Walks
The Shropshire Way
Spirit Paths of Wales
Glyndwr's Way
The Pembrokeshire Coastal Path
Walking in Pembrokeshire
The Shropshire Hills – A Walker's
 Guide
Backpacker's Britain Vol 2 – Wales

MIDLANDS
The Cotswold Way
The Grand Union Canal Walk
Walking in Oxfordshire
Walking in Warwickshire
Walking in Worcestershire
Walking in Staffordshire
Heart of England Walks

SOUTHERN ENGLAND
Exmoor & the Quantocks
Walking in the Chilterns
Walks in Kent Book 2
Two Moors Way
Walking in Dorset
Walking in Cornwall

A Walker's Guide to the Isle of Wight
Walking in Devon
Walking in Somerset
The Thames Path
Channel Island Walks
Walking in Buckinghamshire
The Isles of Scilly
Walking in Hampshire
Walking in Bedfordshire
The Lea Valley Walk
Walking in Berkshire
The Definitive Guide to
 Walking in London
The Greater Ridgeway
Walking on Dartmoor
The South West Coast Path
Walking in Sussex
The North Downs Way
The South Downs Way

SCOTLAND
Scottish Glens 1 – Cairngorm Glens
Scottish Glens 2 – Atholl Glens
Scottish Glens 3 – Glens of Rannoch
Scottish Glens 4 – Glens of Trossach
Scottish Glens 5 – Glens of Argyll
Scottish Glens 6 – The Great Glen
Scottish Glens 7 – The Angus Glens
Scottish Glens 8 – Knoydart
 to Morvern
Scottish Glens 9 – The Glens
 of Ross-shire
Scrambles in Skye
The Island of Rhum
Torridon – A Walker's Guide
Ski Touring in Scotland
Walking the Galloway Hills
Border Pubs & Inns –
 A Walkers' Guide
Walks in the Lammermuirs
Scrambles in Lochaber
Walking in the Hebrides
Central Highlands: 6 Long
 Distance Walks
Walking in the Isle of Arran
Walking in the Lowther Hills
North to the Cape
The Border Country –
 A Walker's Guide
Winter Climbs – Cairngorms
The Speyside Way
Winter Climbs – Ben Nevis &
 Glencoe
The Isle of Skye, A Walker's Guide
The West Highland Way
Scotland's Far North
Walking the Munros Vol 1 –
 Southern, Central
Walking the Munros Vol 2 –
 Northern & Cairngorms
Scotland's Far West
Walking in the Cairngorms
Walking in the Ochils, Campsie Fells
 and Lomond Hills
Scotland's Mountain Ridges

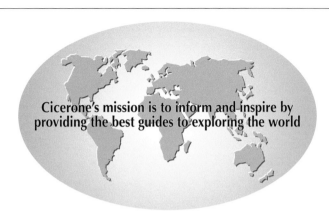

Cicerone's mission is to inform and inspire by providing the best guides to exploring the world

Since its foundation over 30 years ago, Cicerone has specialised in publishing guidebooks and has built a reputation for quality and reliability. It now publishes nearly 300 guides to the major destinations for outdoor enthusiasts, including Europe, UK and the rest of the world.

Written by leading and committed specialists, Cicerone guides are recognised as the most authoritative. They are full of information, maps and illustrations so that the user can plan and complete a successful and safe trip or expedition – be it a long face climb, a walk over Lakeland fells, an alpine traverse, a Himalayan trek or a ramble in the countryside.

With a thorough introduction to assist planning, clear diagrams, maps and colour photographs to illustrate the terrain and route, and accurate and detailed text, Cicerone guides are designed for ease of use and access to the information.

If the facts on the ground change, or there is any aspect of a guide that you think we can improve, we are always delighted to hear from you.

Cicerone Press
2 Police Square Milnthorpe Cumbria LA7 7PY
Tel:01539 562 069   Fax:01539 563 417
e-mail:info@cicerone.co.uk   web:www.cicerone.co.uk